Drive Around
Tuscany
& Umbria

The best of Tuscany and Umbria,
including the artistic heritage of
Florence, Siena, Perugia and Assisi,
the hill-towns and landscapes of
the Italian heartland and the beaches
and seaside resorts, with suggested
driving tours

Brent Gregston

Thomas Cook
Publishing

www.thomascookpublishing.com

Written and updated by Brent Gregston
Original photography by John Heseltine

Published by Thomas Cook Publishing
A division of Thomas Cook Tour Operations Limit
Company registration no. 1450464 England
The Thomas Cook Business Park, Unit 9, Coningsb
Peterborough PE3 8SB, United Kingdom
E-mail: books@thomascook.com, Tel: + 44 (0) 173:
www.thomascookpublishing.com

Produced by Cambridge Publishing Managemer
Burr Elm Court, Main Street, Caldecote CB23 7NU

ISBN: 978-1-84848-055-1

© 2005, 2007 Thomas Cook Publishing
This third edition © 2009
Text © Thomas Cook Publishing
Road maps supplied by Lovell Johns Ltd, OX8 8LH
Road maps generated from Bartholomew Digital Database © Bartholomew Ltd, 2000
City maps prepared by Polly Senior Cartography

Series Editor: Adam Royal
Production/DTP: Steven Collins

Printed and bound in India by Replika Press Pvt Ltd

Cover photography: Front: © Ripani Massimo/4Corners Images. Back: © Thomas Cook

Buckinghamshire County Council	
2371274	
Askews	Apr-2009
914.550493	£15.99

Drive Around

Thomas Cook

T &

YOUR GUIDE TO GREAT DRIVES

Titles in this series include:

- Andalucía and the Costa del Sol
- Australia
- Bavaria and the Austrian Tyrol
- Brittany and Normandy
- Burgundy and the Rhône Valley
- California
- Canadian Rockies
- Catalonia and the Spanish Pyrenees
- Dordogne and Western France
- England and Wales
- Florida
- Ireland
- Languedoc and Southwest France
- Loire Valley
- New England
- New Zealand
- Northern Italy & Italian Lakes
- Portugal
- Provence and the Côte d'Azur
- Scotland
- Tuscany and Umbria
- Vancouver and British Columbia
- Washington DC, Virginia, Maryland and Delaware

For further information about these and other Thomas Cook publications, write to Thomas Cook Publishing, PO Box 227, The Thomas Cook Business Park, 9 Coningsby Road, Peterborough PE3 8SB, United Kingdom.

About the author

Brent Gregston studied International Relations at Pomona College in California and read for a degree in Modern European Languages in Germany and Italy. After a stint working for a charity in the Middle East, he turned to writing. He has written several guidebooks and contributes to *Wanderlust*, the travel section of the online magazine *Salon*. His *Signpost: Bavaria and the Austrian Tyrol* was nominated by Thomas Cook for the British Travelex 'Best Guidebook of the Year' award. On assignment or for pleasure, Brent has been down almost every back road in Tuscany and Umbria, and still spends part of each year in the region.

Acknowledgements

I would like to say *mille grazie* to Alda and Claudio for firewood, wild mushrooms and other forms of hospitality, to former series editor Christopher Catling for sharing his passion for Umbria with me, and to Laurie for our 10,000 kilometres together.

Contents

About Drive Around Guides

Thomas Cook's Drive Around Guides are designed to provide you with a comprehensive but flexible reference source to guide you as you tour a country or region by car. This guide divides Tuscany and Umbria into touring areas – one per chapter. Major cultural centres or cities form chapters in their own right. Each chapter contains enough attractions to provide at least a day's worth of activities – often more.

Ratings
To make it easier for you to plan your time and decide what to see, every area is rated according to its attractions in categories such as Architecture, Entertainment and Children.

Chapter contents
Every chapter has an introduction summing up the main attractions of the area or town, and a ratings box, which will highlight its appeal – some places may be more attractive to families travelling with children, others to wine-lovers visiting vineyards, and others to people interested in finding castles, churches, nature reserves or good beaches.

Each chapter is then divided into an alphabetical gazetteer, and a suggested tour or walk. You can select whether you just want to visit a particular sight or attraction, choosing from those described in the gazetteer, or whether you want to tour the area comprehensively. If the latter, you can construct your own itinerary, or follow the author's suggested tour, which comes at the end of every area chapter.

The gazetteer
The gazetteer section describes all the major attractions in the area – the villages, towns, historic sites, nature reserves, parks or museums that you are most likely to want to see. Maps of the area highlight all the places mentioned in the text. Using this comprehensive overview of the area, you may choose just to visit one or two sights.

One way to use the guide is to find individual sights that interest you, using the index or overview map, and read what our author has to say about them. This will help you decide whether to visit the sight. If you do, you will find practical information, such as the address, telephone number for enquiries, website and opening times.

Alternatively, you can choose a hotel, with the help of the accommodation recommendations contained in this guide. You can

Symbol key
- ❶ Tourist Information Centre
- Ⓦ Website
- ✉ Advice on arriving or departing
- Ⓟ Parking locations
- Ⓠ Advice on getting around
- ⤵ Directions
- ❶ Sights and attractions
- ◖ Accommodation
- ❶ Eating
- ⬤ Shopping
- ❾ Sport
- ◗ Entertainment

Practical information

The practical information in the page margins, or sidebars, will help you locate the services you need as an independent traveller – including the tourist information centre, car parks and public transport facilities. You will also find the opening times of sights, museums, churches and other attractions, as well as useful tips on shopping, market days, cultural events, entertainment, festivals and sports facilities.

then turn to the overall map on pages 10–11 to help you work out which chapters in the book describe the cities and regions closest to your touring base.

Driving tours
The suggested tour is just that – a suggestion, with plenty of optional detours and one or two ideas for making your own discoveries, under the heading *Also worth exploring*. The routes are designed to link the attractions described in the gazetteer section, and to cover outstandingly scenic coastal, mountain and rural landscapes. The total distance is given for each tour, and the time it will take you to drive the complete route, but bear in mind that this indication is just for driving time: you will need to add on extra time for visiting attractions along the way.

Many of the routes are circular, so that you can join them at any point. Where the nature of the terrain dictates that the route has to be linear, the route can either be followed out and back, or you can use it as a link route, to get from one area in the book to another.

As you follow the route descriptions, you will find names picked out in bold capital letters – this means that the place is described fully in the gazetteer. Other names picked out in bold indicate additional villages or attractions worth a brief stop along the route.

Accommodation and food
In every chapter you will find lodging and eating recommendations for individual towns, or for the area as a whole. These are designed to cover a range of price brackets and concentrate on more characterful small or individualistic hotels and restaurants. In addition, you will find information in the *Travel facts* chapter on chain hotels, with an address to which you can write for a guide, map or directory.

The price indications used in the guide have the following meanings:

€   budget level
€€   typical/average prices
€€€ de luxe

Above
Badia Fiorentina, Florence

Introduction

Tuscany is paradise on earth in the minds of many northern Europeans: a region of hill-towns bristling with medieval towers, of lush vineyards and olive groves, rolling hills, Renaissance art and a Mediterranean coastline. Tuscany is also a theme park in Las Vegas, USA, and a line of American furniture. 'Tuscany' is in the title of best-selling cookbooks and the staple headline of lifestyle magazines. The British have put an imaginary county on the map – *Chiantishire* – inhabited, at least part of the year, by Tony Blair and Sting. The Germans have gone further and christened their left-wing politicos the 'Tuscan Faction' since they eschew beer and sauerkraut for Chianti and pasta. American New Agers are now seizing territory here – at least in their nous – because writer Frances Mayes bought a Tuscan villa, hired Polish workers to remodel it and wrote best-sellers about her 'life-transforming experience'.

There is, miraculously, a powerful antidote to all the hype: go there yourself. Outside of the coast, Florence and a couple of cities, Tuscany is not crowded with tourists. The region is, however, packed with medieval villages, monasteries, villas, castles, extinct volcanoes, hot springs, nature reserves and the crests of countless hills that reveal seemingly infinite vistas. Nature laps at the edge of most towns and even in the dreariest suburbs of Florence you sense that it is still within reach. Chianti, for all the good living, is full of dark woods, impenetrable bush and rutting wild boar. D H Lawrence, not an easy man to impress, observed: 'It is queer that a country so perfectly cultivated as Tuscany … still has so much room for wild flowers'. In spring, the land is covered with entire fields of sunflowers, and poppies, Spanish broom, cornflowers and marigolds.

Tuscans founded modern city states – such as Pisa, Siena, Lucca and Florence – that recalled the achievements of Athens in the 5th century BC and anticipated those of New York in the 20th century. They experimented with Republican ideals when most of Europe lived under feudalism. They founded the first banks (with cheques and a prime rate) and suffered the first bankruptcies; built the largest cathedral and cathedral dome; and wrote the first Italian novel (Boccaccio), biography (Vasari) and autobiography (Cellini). They re-discovered linear perspective in painting and sculpted the first modern freestanding figures. Tuscans gave us love as broken-hearted bliss (Dante and Petrarch) and made the case for cynicism (Machiavelli). Florentines performed the first opera and a Pisan (Galileo) invented the telescope. Chianti wine producers created the first market label (Gallo Nero) and an explorer born in one of Chianti's hill-towns – Amerigo Vespucci – gave America its name. Anyone will feel tempted

Opposite
View over Florence

to assert a claim to a land so rich in experience and beauty, at least temporarily, as home.

Although Umbria seems to offer many of the same things as Tuscany, it is distinctly different. It has a deeply rural atmosphere, stretches of solitary wildernesses, and more medieval architecture. The green heart of Italy, as a poet once rightly called Umbria, is an area of small-scale agriculture, steep-sided hills cut by deep ravines, of farmsteads, monasteries and ancient cities separated from the countryside only by stone walls. If ever there was a region in Europe with deep mystic roots, it is here. The mountaintops were sacred places to pagan stargazers and later to St Benedict, the founder of Western monasticism. The ancient Umbrian seers codified the flight of birds to interpret the will of the gods. In the same land, 2,000 years later, St Francis of Assisi taught Christians to see them as a manifestation of divinity.

Travel facts

Accommodation

The charm of hotels in Tuscany and Umbria is that, with a few exceptions, they were built as anything but: Gothic townhouses, Renaissance palaces, monasteries, convents, 19th-century villas, barns and stables have all become hotels. Italian state authorities inspect these establishments regularly, apply all sorts of criteria, and give them stars (max 5).

Prices, based on these ratings, are regulated but may vary a lot depending on location and season; also many perfectly charming places such as *affitacamere* (rooms in private homes) are not rated at all. Two-star hotel rooms usually have a private bathroom, three-star rooms telephones and television. Four-star hotels, if they are not in the middle of the city, will probably have a swimming pool as well as extras like satellite or cable television. Other forms of accommodation include campsites, youth hostels, holiday houses and apartments.

People on a driving holiday in Tuscany and Umbria have a well-known, and cheaper, alternative to hotels. Originally intended as a stimulus to the rural economy, *agriturismo* (agricultural tourism) has succeeded beyond anyone's wildest dreams and paying guests have become the leading 'cash crop' in areas like Chianti; almost half of Tuscany's farmers participate in the programme. The consequences have not all been positive though, and it is important to choose an *agriturismo* situation carefully. During high season, most places have a minimum stay of one week; however, some allow for a minimum of two or three nights, particularly in the off-season. It is always advisable to book any form of accommodation beforehand and to get confirmation by email or fax, especially for the month of August and during the Easter holidays.

Children

Travelling with a baby or young child is the easiest way to get attention in Italy, to say nothing of first-class service. Shopkeepers will spontaneously compare notes about parenthood; even jaded waiters will crack a smile. Discreet breastfeeding in public is no problem. Hotels and pensions are normally equipped to accommodate families. However, consider bringing safety seats for children with you as many car hire companies impose an extra daily charge for these, if they have them. Supermarkets in Tuscany/Umbria cater for the usual infant needs, but make a mental note of the opening times or they might be

Airports

Pisa's airport is easier to get in and out of and more convenient for reaching Tuscany than Rome's. It is also the destination of frequent charter flights. Both Pisa and Rome are about two hours' drive on the *autostrada* from Perugia, Umbria's capital. Florence's airport is used mostly by businesspeople. Tiny Sant'Egidio, 18km east of Perugia, receives regularly scheduled flights from the UK as well as domestic flights from Milan and Bologna. Its facilities will be expanded at some point in the future. There are some international flights to Bologna, next to the *autostrada*, and charter flights to Rimini airport (Rimini to Perugia 223km), which is located between the toll-free Adriatic highway (S16) and A14 *autostrada*.

Above
Medieval ironwork

closed just when you need them most. Ironically, a passion for children has not stopped Italy's dramatic falling birth rate, which is now one of the lowest in Europe.

Climate

The presence of the mountains and sea creates a wide range of climatic zones in Tuscany and Umbria. Spring begins early but is subject to bitter, cold winds called *tramontana*. May is the single most beautiful month of the year to visit when the wild flowers and vines are blooming and the green wheat is sprouting. Summers, particularly July and August, are invariably hot and dry. September is only slightly cooler and still high season on the coast. The end of September to late October is also a fine time of year to visit. The hillsides are changing colour and there are fewer tourists, but be prepared for some rain and mist. The Tuscan coast remains mild even in winter, while inland the cold can be intermittently harsh in the hill-towns and severe in the Apennines.

Currency and plastic

The unit of currency in Italy is the euro (€). Bank notes are available in seven denominations of different sizes and colours ranging from 500, 200, 100, 50, 20, 10 and 5 euro notes. Eight denominations of coins include 1, 2, 5, 10, 20 and 50 cent, 1 and 2 euro. There are 100 cents to the euro (for further information visit the website *http://europa.eu*).

Below
Romanesque lions in Assisi

The best way to get cash in Italy is by using a cashcard at an ATM (*bancomat*). Tell your bank about your travel plans and make sure that your PIN can be used abroad. A distant second – because of fees and potential interest charges – is to use your credit card for cash advances (again, check on the PIN). Use a VISA or MasterCard as a backup, at petrol stations, chain hotels and expensive restaurants. A few traveller's cheques are good for an emergency, though you will probably have to pay a small commission, about 1 per cent, when you buy them, and again when you cash them (in any bank). In an emergency, your bank or a friend can wire money through Western Union. American Express holders can take advantage of its Global Assist programme and arrange to have money wired within a couple of hours.

Customs regulations

There are no restrictions, taxes or duty on articles for personal use that you take into Italy (within reason: a truckload of whisky invites a few questions). Italy allows EU citizens to import or export duty-free: 800 cigarettes, 400 cigarillos, 200 cigars, or 1kg of tobacco, ten litres of spirits or 90 litres of wine (not more than 60 can be sparkling wine) or

110 litres of beer. Goods carried by travellers coming from outside the EU may not exceed 200 cigarettes, 100 cigarillos or 250g of tobacco, one litre of spirits or 2 litres of wine, 50g of perfume and 250ml of toilet water with the global value not exceeding €175. All nationalities must declare, upon arrival or departure, sums of cash exceeding €12,500. There are no restrictions on gifts purchased in Italy except for those set by destination countries, and antiques exceeding 100 years of age and works of art exceeding 50 years of age or made by an artist no longer living. These require the authorisation of the Ministero dei Beni Culturali e Ambientali (Ministry of National Heritage). For more information visit the Agenzia delle Dogane website (Italian Customs Agency) at *www.agenziadogane.it*

Eating and drinking

Most hotels serve a meagre breakfast – Nescafé and yesterday's bread. It is better to go to a corner bar where you are sure of first-rate coffee and, probably, fresh pastries. Coffee with hot milk – *cappuccino* and *caffè latte* – is a breakfast drink in Italy. If you order a cup of coffee at any other time of day and don't insist on milk, you will automatically get an espresso. Tea is served as a cup of hot water with a tea bag on the side.

Once there were clear distinctions, and a gradation in prices and service, between a *pizzeria*, *osteria*, *trattoria* and a *ristorante*. Now many a *pizzeria* serves a wide range of dishes, while an *osteria* or *trattoria* may be as elegant as a *ristorante*. The elegance costs money, of course, and as a rough rule of thumb you can assume that the smarter the décor, the higher the prices are likely to be – without the food necessarily being any better. Tuscans and Umbrians traditionally eat three (or more) courses for the main meal (usually at lunch). However, if you decide to eat in a formal restaurant but only want to eat one course,

Below
Montepulciano

Electricity

The supply in Italy is 220 volts, 50 cycles AC. All UK appliances will work but will require an adaptor; plugs are of the European type with two round prongs. American appliances need a transformer and an adaptor.

this is perfectly acceptable: just say so before you take a table. In a simple *trattoria*, it is not at all unusual for two people to each eat a *primo* (first course) and then split a main course; or order one dessert and ask for two spoons. Many expensive restaurants (in Florence, for example), add a separate charge to the bill for *pane e coperto* (bread and tableware), usually about €2, sometimes more.

Tip: Italians usually arrive for the evening meal (*cena*) at about 2000, so show up before then if you don't have a reservation. If a *trattoria* or *ristorante* is good, their *vino della casa* should be good, too, and perfectly adequate to accompany a meal. Wine lists usually focus on local vintages and you should, too. Italians almost always order bottled water to go along with a meal. Occasionally, dessert wine or grappa is drunk after a meal.

Entry formalities

Citizens of the EU only have to show a valid passport to enter Italy for an unlimited stay. Citizens of the US, Australia, Canada and New Zealand can also enter Italy with a passport (valid for at least three months from the date of entry). No visa is required for a period of up to 90 days.

Food

To quote a proverb, Tuscan and Umbrian cooking is 'peasant food fit for a king'. The recipes have been passed down through many generations and depend on freshness and simplicity of local ingredients and the careful way they are combined.

Tuscans eat beef from the Chiana valley as well as lamb, pork and goat. Umbrians eat more pork and pork sausages in all sorts of variations. Game, when in season, is popular everywhere except on the coast: wild boar, hare and pheasant are common themes. All kinds of wild mushrooms find their way into pasta sauces but the king of the *funghi* is the meaty *porcini*, best enjoyed on its own, fried in butter and garlic.

The main cheese is *pecorino*, made from sheep's milk and eaten fresh and aged. Vegetable and bean soups often take the place of pasta as a first course. Indeed, the Tuscans relish beans to the point of acquiring the nickname *mangiafagiole* (bean eaters). The Umbrians, for their part, grow lentils on a high mountain plain around the village of Castelluccio. Umbria is one of only two Italian provinces (the other is Piedmont) where the *tartufo* (truffle) is abundant, particularly in late autumn and late winter. You will find them on the menu at all times of year in the main market centres, around Spoleto, the Valnerina, Norcia and Scheggio.

Health

In general, standards of health care in Tuscany and Umbria are high and health risks few. There are scorpions and jellyfish that sting but they are not poisonous. *Vipere* (vipers), on the other hand, are very poisonous. They have a triangular head that inflicts a triangular bite. The chances of this happening are slight but if you are bitten, go to the nearest doctor. If you see a pharmacy (*farmacia*) on the way, stop there – the pharmacist might very well stock a serum antidote. *Zanzare* (mosquitoes) are common in low-lying coastal areas in spring and summer (don't worry, there is no more malaria). Tap water is safe everywhere; sadly, the same cannot be said of the river water. Boil the water ten minutes before drinking it, or use iodine tablets like Potable Aqua. Ticks can be a problem in some forests and brush. If you find one buried in your skin, coat it with oil or salt and it should dislodge itself. The pharmacies (*farmacie*) take turns in staying open for emergencies; the normal hours are *Mon–Fri 0830–1230 and 1630–1900.*

Information

Tuscany and Umbria have tourist offices in almost every town and in some villages. They are usually located at or near the main railway station and/or on the market square. APT (*Azienda di Promozione Turistica*) offices are found in the main tourist areas; look also for EPT (*Ente Provinciale per il Turismo*) and IAT (*Ufficio di Informazione e Accoglienza Turistica*). In smaller places, there may only be a humble little office with humble hours called a *Pro Loco*. Tourist offices are particularly useful for finding rooms in smaller pensions or private homes (sometimes charging a small fee). Usual hours are *Mon–Sat 0900–1300 and 1600–1900; in winter the hours are shorter.*

Insurance

No one should leave his or her home country without travel insurance. Citizens of EU countries are entitled to free emergency medical care in a public hospital. Showing a passport might be enough but, ideally, you should carry an EHIC card (European Health Insurance Card) – these are available free from *www.ehic.org.uk*, by phoning *0845 606 2030* or from post offices. Non-EU citizens are covered only if they have travel insurance. For further information for US citizens visit the *Bureau of Consular Affairs* website at *www.travel.state.gov*

Italian Government tourist offices abroad

UK *1 Princes St, London W1R 8AY; tel: 020 7408 1254; fax: 020 7399 3567; e-mail: italy@italiantouristboard.co.uk; www.italiantouristboard.co.uk*

Maps

The Italian Touring Club
and Kümmerly & Frey
publish the best road maps.

USA *630 Fifth Avenue, Suite 1565, New York, NY 10111; tel: 212 245 5618; fax: 212 586 9249; e-mail: enitny@italiantourism.com; www. italiantourism.com*

500 North Michigan Avenue, Suite 2240, Chicago, IL 60611; tel: 312 644 0996; fax: 312 644 3019; e-mail: enitch@italiantourism.com; www.italiantourism.com

12400 Wilshire Boulevard, Suite 550, Los Angeles, CA 90025; tel: 310 820 7898; fax: 310 820 6357; e-mail: enitla@italiantourism.com; www. italiantourism.com

Canada *175 Bloor Street, Suite 907, South Tower, M4W3R8 Toronto (Ontario); tel: 416 925 4882; fax: 416 925 4799; e-mail: enitto@italiantourism.com; www.italiantourism.com*

Australia *Level 4, 46 Market Street, Sydney, NSW 2000; tel: 02 9262 1666; fax: 02 9262 1677; e-mail: italia@italiantourism.com.au*

New Zealand *Italian Embassy, 34–38 Grant Rd, Thorndon, Wellington; tel: 04 473 5339; fax: 04 472 9302; e-mail: ambasciata.wellington.esteri.it; www.ambwellington.esteri.it*

Museums

Not only are Tuscan and Umbrian museums and art collections world-class but often they are housed in ancient palaces, churches, villas and monasteries. Most museums are usually open Tue–Sun 0900–1400/1700; small town museums close for a long lunch, with shorter (or nonexistent) winter hours; larger city museums stay open until 2000 or 2100 at least one night a week (Tue, Wed or Thu).

Online services

There is a vast array of websites related to travel and tourism for Tuscany and Umbria. Here are a few of the more useful ones:
www.enit.it Italian Government tourist office
www.museionline.it Italian museums online
www.camping.it Guide to Italian camping sites
www.provincia.fi.it The official website for the province of Florence
www.regione.toscana.it The official website for the Tuscan region
www.provincia.perugia.it The official website for the province of Perugia
www.regione.umbria.it Umbria's regional tourist office
www.umbria-turismo.it Umbrian Tourist Promotion Agency
www.autostrade.it Information on motorways throughout Italy
www.chiantimusei.it Museums in Chianti
www.terresienainbici.it Biking through Siena's countryside, with
    itineraries and suggestions
www.terresienabambini.it On holiday in Tuscany with children
www.paginegialle.it Italian yellow pages
www.trenitalia.com Italian State Railways network

Postal services

Post offices are normally open Mon–Fri 0800–1330/1400 and Sat 0800–1145. The main post offices in larger towns are open until 1930. They have many services so make sure you go to the right counter for *francobolli* (stamps). You can also buy stamps sold in a *tabacchino* (tobacco shop). Letters arrive much faster than postcards. You can receive mail via general delivery c/o the post office by adding 'FERMO POSTA' after the name of the town. Mail can be claimed by the addressee at the Central Post Office upon presenting identification. For more information visit the website *www.poste.it*

Public holidays

1 Jan	New Year's Day
6 Jan	Epiphany
Mar/Apr	Easter Monday
25 Apr	Liberation Day
1 May	Labour Day
May/Jun	Whit Monday
Jun	Corpus Christi
2 Jun	Anniversary of the Republic
24 Jun	St John's Day
15 Aug	Assumption of the Blessed Virgin
1 Nov	All Saints' Day
7 Nov	WWI Victory Anniversary Day
8 Dec	Immaculate Conception
25 Dec	Christmas Day
26 Dec	St Stephen's Day
31 Dec	New Year's Eve

www.quattroroute.it Autoroute traffic information service
www.ecs.net/cafe Directory of Italian Internet cafés
www.italiadiscovery.it Guide to tourism throughout Italy

Opening times

In general, opening times are confusing and 'lunch break' can mean anything from two to five hours beginning at 1200 or 1300. Larger shops are normally open Mon–Sat 0900–1300 and 1600–2000. Most other shops are closed on Monday mornings. Food stores are usually closed on Wednesday afternoons. Only major supermarkets near large cities, and petrol stations on the *autostrade* stay open during the middle of the day. In tourist places or during the summer, shops may remain open longer in the evenings and on Sundays. However, many businesses, even restaurants, take a holiday in August. Weekly markets (selling fresh produce, meat and often shoes and clothing) are generally held in the mornings between 0800 and 1200. Banks are generally open Mon–Fri 0830–1330 and 1500–1600 (later on Thursday); in many tourist areas they remain open all day. Restaurants will normally open at 1130 and close around 2300; almost all of them close in the afternoon.

Church hours vary from place to place. In general, a church will be open daily, beginning at 0700 or 0800 and closing at 1900 or later in summer; in winter the hours are shorter. Churches are usually closed in the middle of the day from noon, 1300 or 1330 until 1530 or 1600. There are plenty of exceptions and some village churches are open only on Sundays and holidays. A visitor should have the sensitivity not to enter during church services, or – God forbid – weddings and funerals.

Packing

Take light clothes but also a raincoat and umbrella. Warm clothes and waterproofs are essential for the mountains – regardless of the time of year. Definitely bring suntan lotion or block and something presentable to wear. Italians dress up a little more often than in Anglo-Saxon countries with an emphasis on quality rather than flashiness. Also recommended are: adaptor plugs and/or transformers for electrical devices; English-language books; aspirin, which you can buy only in a pharmacy; mosquito repellent; a torch, most useful in Etruscan tombs or the recesses of a dimly lit church; and binoculars or good-quality opera glasses to appreciate fully the details on Renaissance frescos and stained-glass windows.

Reading

(Most titles are available in Penguin editions)

Barzini, Luigi, *The Italians*: worldly-wise musings on the Italian psyche by one of Italy's most respected journalists.

Safety and security

Italy has high rates of car theft and break-ins. Although the risks are considerably lower in rural Tuscany and Umbria than in urban Italy, remember that anything left in a car could be stolen (and 97 per cent of thefts in Italy go unsolved). Florence has a real drug and crime problem so watch your wallet or handbag. If a robbery or break-in does occur, report it immediately to the police, if for no other reason than to back up insurance claims. By law, a person is always required to carry identification such as a passport. Africans hawking fake designer goods have become very much part of the tourist scene in Tuscany. Their persistence can be irritating but they are, for the most part, just poor illegal immigrants desperately trying to make a living. Needless to say, their 'Prada' and 'Gucci' handbags are not the Real Thing.

Boccaccio, Giovanni, *The Decameron*: the first and never surpassed Italian novel.

Cellini, Benvenuto, *Autobiography*: blow-by-blow (literally) life of a querulous, egomaniacal, hypochondriac, sexually omnivorous – and perhaps typical? – Renaissance artist.

Forster, E M, *A Room with a View*, and *Where Angels Fear to Tread*: blissfully predictable.

Lawrence, D H, *Etruscan Places*: communing at the end of his life with a mysterious people.

McCarthy, Mary, *The Stones of Florence*: the perfect literary antidote to all the nonsense written about this amazing and 'terrible' city.

Origo, Iris, *The Merchant of Prato*: life of a medieval merchant as told in his letters.

Romer, Elisabeth, *The Tuscan Year: Life and Food in an Italian Valley*: reverent peek into grandma's kitchen on a farm near the Tuscan-Umbrian border.

Unsworth, Barry, *After Hannibal*: a must-read for would-be expats.

Vasari, Giorgio, *Lives of the Artists*: utterly fascinating, sometimes spiteful and at least partly true.

Shopping

Popular souvenirs that you can take away from Tuscany and Umbria include shoes, leather goods, linen and clothes. The local markets, held outdoors, offer local colour as well as handicrafts and the makings of a picnic. Flea markets are a good bet to visit on Saturdays to find some unusual gifts. Other items to consider are *pecorino* (mountain cheese) and smoked ham (note: you are not allowed to import cheese to the USA unless it is 'commercially sealed'). Italy has a Value Added Tax (IVA) added to most goods and services. In theory, visitors from outside the European Union are entitled to a refund of this tax on purchases exceeding €175 from any one store. In practice, it is a hassle to obtain the refund. Look for the Tax Free Shopping sign in the shop window and ask the clerk for the necessary paperwork. The papers must be stamped by a customs official upon leaving Italy. For further information contact the Agenzia delle Dogane or companies specialising in refunding sales tax like Cashback at Premier Tax Free at *www.premiertaxfree.com* or Global Refund at *www.globalrefund.com*

Sports

The Apennines and Apuan Alps, and Monte Amiata have hundreds of kilometres of well-marked trails and vast cave systems for spelunking. Extended hikes often involve staying overnight in mountain huts.

Time

Italy is one hour ahead of GMT in winter and two hours ahead in summer (from the end of March to the end of October).

Tipping

Service is normally included in the price (*servizio compreso*) with the exception of some fancy restaurants, where it is added separately (the practice should be written clearly on the menu).

Toilets

There are toilets in any petrol station on the *autostrade* and in bus and train stations (*Uomini* for men and *Donne* for women). Otherwise, public toilets are rare. It is usually acceptable to duck into a café simply to use the facilities.

Direct dial numbers:

UK: BT 800 172 0044

Ireland: 800 172 0353

US: AT&T 800 172 444; MCI 800 90 5825

Canada: 800 172 1001

Australia: Telstra 800 172 1061; Optus 800 172 1611

New Zealand: 800 172 1064

Abetone, Monte Amiata and Norcia are the most popular skiing regions. Most lakes in Tuscany and Umbria are clean enough to swim in. There are spectacular routes for mountain bikers but trails are not always clearly designated. There is rafting in the mountain rapids in the Apennines. Cycling is popular as a sport rather than a means of getting around and Day-Glo cyclists are a fixture on many roads during the weekend; local drivers seem more considerate towards cyclists than pedestrians. If cycling, it helps to be truly fit because Tuscany and Umbria are full of steep hills. It is possible to hire bicycles locally, but serious cyclists will want to bring their own. Both Alitalia and British Airways will check bicycles on board as luggage on Gatwick–Pisa flights.

Telephones

Telephone kiosks are found on most main streets and squares and in some bars or public places. Some kiosks accept coins and others prepaid telephone cards. Prepaid telephone cards (*carta telefonica*) can be purchased from tobacco shops (*tabacchino*), post offices, service stations and some newsagents. The perforated corner of the card must be torn off before you insert it into the machine. In big cities and railway stations you may find telephone centres where you can make a call and pay afterwards, using a credit card if you prefer. Another option for lower rates when calling abroad from Italy is prepaid international calling cards. Additionally, rates vary throughout the day; it's cheaper to call during non-working hours (before 0900 and after 2000). Hotel telephone rates range from exorbitant to outrageous. Mobile phones in Italy use the GSM European standard.

To make an international call (*interurbana*) dial the access code 00, then the country code (UK = 44, Ireland = 353, US and Canada = 1, Australia = 61, New Zealand = 64) followed by the local number, omitting the first digit. Calling from the UK or any other country, the code for Italy is 00 39. For international inquiries dial 176 and for directory assistance dial 12.

Travellers with disabilities

Italy still has far to go when it comes to addressing the needs of people with disabilities. Most museums, theatres, cinemas and public buildings do not yet have access ramps for wheelchairs. Major hotel chains are marginally

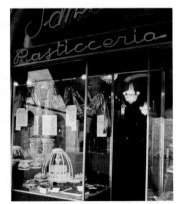

Right
Perugian pastry shop

more likely to offer special facilities to travellers with a disability. Parking is free for persons with a disability in the blue zones of cities and towns if you have an international disabled sticker for the car. In Britain, the Royal Society for Disability and Rehabilitation (RADAR) publishes a booklet called **European Holidays and Travel: A Guide for Disabled People** (*12 City Forum, 250 City Road, London EC1V 8AF; tel: 020 7250 3222; www.radar.org.uk*). In the US there is the Society for Accessible Travel and Hospitality (SATH), a non-profit organisation representing travellers with disabilities (*347 Fifth Avenue, Suite 610, New York; tel: 212 447 7284; www.sath.org*). Also contact Accessible Italy, tourism services for those with disabilities, at *www.accessibleitaly.com*

Wine

Tuscany has the greatest winemaking tradition in Italy; however, it is now busy turning tradition on its head and becoming one of Europe's most innovative wine regions. Producers are experimenting with French grape varieties and ageing reds and whites in oak. The very boundaries of DOC regions (*Denominazione di origine controllata*) are being revised to make the designation more meaningful. In addition to Chianti, hill-towns Montalcino and Montepulciano produce two of Italy's headiest reds, Brunello and Vino Nobile respectively, as well as some of the most interesting new blends. There are amazing wine bargains to be had, as well as some wildly overhyped and overpriced vintages sold mostly to foreigners. Although Umbria is not in the same wine league as Tuscany there are still some excellent wines that are good value for money. There are richer, traditional versions – called *Orvieto Abbocato* – of neutral-tasting, dry white Orvieto. Grecchetto is a breezy white wine that competes locally with Orvieto. The best and most expensive reds are produced by winemakers like Lungarotti and Adanti. However, they are now being challenged by Sagrantino, a wine made in Montefalco from an unusual grape supposedly imported by a medieval Saracen. Vin Santo, Tuscany's delectable dessert wine, tastes like Madeira or medium-dry sherry (named 'holy wine' because of its popularity with priests). Sagrantino Passito is made with late-harvested and semi-dried grapes. It is a naturally sweet red wine that tastes something like port.

Right
Umbrian wines

Driver's guide

Accidents

You must stop after any accident. Summon the police, carabinieri (*tel: 112*, the EU universal emergency number) or pronto soccorso (*tel: 113*) for medical assistance. Place emergency triangles in the road to alert approaching vehicles. Exchange insurance details with other drivers and complete a European Accident Statement form, which you should obtain from your own insurers before leaving home. Remain at the scene until police arrive, stay calm and request an English-speaking interpreter to assist you in making a statement. Notify the police of any injury, however slight. One of the advantages of the popularity of mobile telephones in Italy is that accidents are reported and help summoned almost immediately.

Automobile clubs

Members of UK automobile clubs can extend their services to Italy, which gives them access to the Automobile Club d'Italia (ACI) (*see sidebar*). The ACI also has a central multilingual service centre (*tel: 06 491 716*) to provide updated information on weather and road conditions, tolls, ferries, mileage distances and tourist itineraries. For advance assistance with motoring routes and up-to-date road information, visit *www.theaa.com* (for AA members); or the Touring Club Italiano (TCI) *Corso Italia 10, 20122 Milano; www.touringclub.it*

Autostrade

Most major limited-access motorways in Italy are *autostrade* (singular: *autostrada*) toll roads, designated by 'A' in their route number. Rare exceptions are those motorways whose route numbers are prefixed with 'E', which do not charge tolls. On most, you take a ticket as you enter the *autostrada* and pay according to the distance travelled as you exit. You can pay tolls with euros in cash or by VISA credit card.

Breakdowns

The first thing to do if you have a breakdown is to pull over, if possible; then place a warning triangle 100m behind the vehicle (or a passenger with waving arms). Then call *803 116* for road assistance. The tow truck driver will probably not speak English but he will come equipped with a multilingual auto parts manual. You will have to pay for towing and parts. Members of automobile clubs in their own country should be able to arrange for cover. Enquire at your local automobile club about a letter of introduction. If you are not a member of an automobile club that provides this service, it is wise to take out a continental breakdown insurance policy, so that the details will be handled by a multilingual specialist.

Caravans and camper vans (trailers and RVs)

Camping and caravanning are not that popular among Italians, and campsites are not plentiful. But they do exist, especially around popular family tourist areas, such as Lake Garda and the Adriatic coast east of Venice. To book ahead, and to obtain a camping carnet and list of campsites, contact Confederazione Italiana Campeggiatori, *Via Vittorio Emanuele 11, 50041 Calenzano, Firenze; tel: 055 882 391; fax: 055 882 5918; www.federcampeggio.it.* Local and regional tourist offices also offer illustrated directories of campsites or include them in their lodging guides.

The speed limit for caravans in excess of 3.5 tonnes and for camper vans is 100kph on *autostrade*, 80kph on highways and country roads and 50kph in towns. Remember that engine efficiency decreases by about 10 per cent with each 1,000m of altitude, so if you are towing in the mountains, a non-turbo car may not be able to manage the incline.

Documents

Drivers from EU nations need only their own current driving licence; others should have an International Driving Permit (IDP) in addition to their original permit. In practice, it is advisable to carry an IDP even if you are not required to do so, since it translates your own licence into Italian. You can get these in your own country, usually through an automobile club (you usually do not need to be a member). Motorisits without an IDP can obtain a declaration from a local office or the ACI upon presentation of a US or Canadian licence. If driving your own car, you must have its registration and insurance documents in the car at all times. It is also important to get a card from your insurer to prove that you have third-party coverage.

Drinking and driving

Italy has strict limits on the level of blood alcohol a driver can have – 0.08 per cent. To exceed this is to risk stiff penalties. A driver with a high level who is involved in an accident also risks being automatically held at fault.

Driving in Tuscany and Umbria

Touring in Italy is a challenge to even the best driver. Italians drive at outrageous speeds, and can be very inconsiderate. Roads range from state-of-the-art *autostrade* to winding mountain roads not quite two cars wide. The most nerve-wracking problem, apart from Italian drivers, is the number of mountain roads with precipitous drop-offs, some of which have no safety barriers. Avoid these roads in the rain or

Essentials

All automobiles must carry a portable warning triangle to place in the road in case of a breakdown or other traffic-blocking situations. This device is called a *triangolo*. A recently passed law requires wearing a reflective safety vest if you are walking on a motorway. While you are not required to carry one, you will be breaking the law if you must walk to an emergency phone without one. These may be obtained by post from *www.advancedsafetyproducts. co.uk*. If you drive your own vehicle from the UK, you must have headlight converters to adjust the beam to the right.

Petrol = *benzina*
Diesel = *gasolio*
Unleaded = *senza piombo*
Full = *pieno*
Oil = *l'olio*
Water = *l'acqua*

Fines

An estimated 15 per cent of drivers in Italy are stopped for speeding, which is a remarkably low number when you consider the disregard most Italian drivers show for speed limits. On-the-spot tickets are issued and you should be prepared to pay, although you can take your speeding or parking ticket to any post office. Although everything in Italy is flexible, the usual fines are €35–150 for speeds under 10kph over the limit (rarely even

in winter, and at night. In fact, it is wise to avoid night driving entirely, allowing enough time for daylight arrivals.

Traffic jams lasting several hours are not uncommon when an accident blocks an *autostrada* (which is a compelling reason to carry both snacks and drinking water with you). Mountain roads can be narrow and the switchbacks over steep mountain passes will leave you breathless. When choosing a route, be sure to check the map for the tiny chevron marks or inverted brackets that indicate steep grades and passes. Don't be surprised to meet a car rounding a tight corner on a precipitous road with at least half the car in your lane, or to meet motorcycles entirely in your lane. Be alert and defensive at all times, and if you want to look at the stunning mountain scenery, pull into a lay-by. The road needs your full attention at every instant.

The most immediate problem will be for those from left-hand drive countries, such as the UK, Australia and South Africa, since Italians drive on the right. In normal traffic, it will begin to seem natural as you follow other drivers. But at roundabouts or on dual-lane highways, it becomes more difficult, because your natural instincts give you the wrong signals. Be especially alert and continue to remind yourself of this danger.

The most difficult time for some is in starting out in the morning on a road without other traffic. You can drive for some distance without realising that you are on the wrong side. To solve this, attach a card to your keys, with the words 'Drive Right!' printed in large letters. Whenever you leave the car, and need to pocket your keys, remove it and tape it to your steering wheel. That reminds you as soon as you enter your car, at which time you return the card to your keys.

Driving rules

Traffic drives on the right in Italy. The most important rule of the road is to give way to the right. In the absence of a light (*semaforo*), traffic officer or other indication, the vehicle on the right has the right of way, except at a roundabout, where a vehicle in the circle has right of way over entering traffic. This give-way-to-the-right rule does not apply to vehicles entering from driveways, lay-bys or parking spaces, although you should give way to buses leaving bus stops. It is also important to know that a green arrow indicating a left turn means only that the turn is allowed, not that oncoming traffic is stopped by a red light.

The left lane of an *autostrada* is only for passing. Slower vehicles are required to keep to the right. If a driver approaching from behind in the same lane flashes his or her high beams, you are expected to move to the right immediately. Do not pass on the right.

Pedestrians have the right of way on marked crossings, but it is not customary to stop for those on the kerb waiting to cross. To do so is to risk a rear-end collision, since other drivers will not anticipate this.

noticed except in especially hazardous places). Between 11 and 40kph above the limit, the fines are €150–500. Over 40kph in excess means a fine of €500–1,250, plus loss of your driving permit. The good news is that drivers are not jailed for speeding in Italy. EU regulations implemented in March 2007 allow your local vehicle registration authority to 'co-operate' with other authorities throughout the EU, so traffic offenders driving their own cars can receive citations sent to their home address. If you are a non-EU resident and don't pay a fine, the car rental company will bill your credit card or enlist the aid of a debt collection agency. You can run but you can't hide.

Mobile phones

Drivers in Italy are permitted to use only those mobile phones equipped with ear-pieces for hands-free use. Hand-held phones may only be used by drivers who have pulled off the road and come to a full stop.

Fuel

Petrol and diesel are sold by the litre, at fairly high prices. Many stations are self-service, and use credit cards at the pump, but the process can be very difficult to follow if you are not fluent in Italian. Some smaller stations take only cash. Many petrol stations, especially those in rural areas, close during the middle of the day and on weekends and holidays. It is wise to keep your tank as full as possible, especially on weekends. Be sure to check hire cars carefully when refuelling them yourself, and tell attendants if you are driving a diesel car. The nozzles are not different and attendants may not bother to look at the warning before filling your tank.

Information

The best and most up-to-date road maps are issued by Michelin and Automobile Club d'Italia (ACI). Road maps disagree wildly, so it is best to carry several if you plan to do much exploring. One of your maps should show topography; an attractive-looking shortcut may be straight (or not so straight) over a mountain range.

When asking for directions, remember to watch as well as listen: right, left, straight and roundabouts are all described with a wave of the hand. The most common answer is *sempre diritto*, which translates as 'straight ahead' and usually means just that. But it can also mean that the person you asked hasn't any more idea where your destination is than you have, so it's wise to check again before going too far.

Don't expect always to find route numbers on road signs. Instead, know the towns and cities on your route and follow signs from one to the next. Labelling is quite good, especially from major roads. *Autostrade* are usually labelled not by compass points but by the town or city at each end. This can be quite confusing, since the last point may be a tiny village on the Swiss or Austrian border. Before entering an *autostrada*, follow it on the map to know the names at each end.

Lights

Use headlights at all times in rain, fog or poor visibility conditions. Right-hand-drive cars must have their headlight beams modified to prevent blinding oncoming traffic or be fitted with stick-on beam deflectors that make them dip to the right.

Parking

Many parking areas (and streets where parking is allowed) have meter boxes which provide tickets when fed with coins. These are quite simple to use, even without being able to read the instructions,

Speed limits

The speed limit on the *autostrada* is 130kph. Lower speed limits are posted when the road is dangerous or passes through an urban area (usually 100kph, but they vary between 80kph and 110kph) or when construction is under way (usually 60kph) – and you are required by law to slow down.

In towns, the limit is 50kph, and residential areas often post speed limits of 30kph. The maximum speed limit on country roads is 90kph, which may be faster than you would sensibly drive there. Often, they have no verge (shoulder) and you have no margin of error. They go through the centre of villages, where blind turns can hide anything from a parade or street market to a pair of local men discussing politics. Note that in Italy there are more and more roadside speed cameras. If you exceed the speed limit, they record your speed, location and licence plate number so the citation can follow you home.

Seat belts

Seat belts are mandatory for the driver and all passengers, in front or back seats. Those under 12 must be in the back in age-appropriate seats.

although they are often not as easy to find. Put the ticket inside the windscreen, visible from the outside. You may find car parks where your stay is free, but limited to an hour or two. You can buy a paper 'clock' at newsstands, or you can write the time you arrive on a piece of paper.

Parking garages usually have a cashier. Take a time-stamped ticket when you enter. Before leaving, pay for the ticket at the *cassa* (cashier window), drive your vehicle to the exit and insert the ticket to open the gate. Do not expect to find a cashier at the exit (and do expect to find irritated drivers behind you if you get there without the paid ticket).

Security

Although Italy has a very high rate of car thefts and break-ins, the rate is not as bad in northern Italy, especially outside cities. But it is still high and precautions are wise. Try to park in a locked or guarded site or at least in a well-lit, busy place. Don't leave anything in the vehicle that you don't want to lose and don't leave anything at all in plain view when you leave your car. Choose vehicles with concealed luggage compartments and empty those when you stop for the night. When stopping for meals at roadside rest areas, try to park where you can watch your car from the table. Above all, don't leave anything visible that marks your car as belonging to a tourist – road maps, travel guides or brochures all lead thieves to believe that there will be luggage in the boot.

If car windows are open, be careful while stopped for a traffic jam or at intersections. Thieves work in teams, one drawing your attention by approaching the car as if to sell you something while another reaches into open windows to snatch purses and cameras – often right out of a passenger's lap. In case of theft, make a report at the nearest *questura* (police station) and ask for a *denuncia*, a stamped form that you must have for filing insurance claims.

Road signs

Attenzione – watch out
Bivio – crossroads
Deviatzione – detour
Divieto di accesso – no entry
Limite di velocità – speed limit
Parcheggio – parking
Pedaggio – toll
Pericolo – danger
Rallentare – slow down

Senso unico – one-way street
Senza uscita – no exit (cul-de-sac, dead-end)
Sosta vietata/Divieto di sosta – no parking
Strada chiusa – road closed
Vietato il sorpasso – no overtaking

See also p282

ITALIAN ROAD SIGNS

RESTRICTION SIGNS

Maximum speed limit

No Entry,
one way street

No stopping at
any time

No honking

PRECEDENCE SIGNS

Give way

Crossroads with
right of way from
the right

Oncoming traffic
must wait

You have the
right of way

WARNING SIGNS

Roundabout

Signal lights ahead

Double bend,
first curving to
the right

Pedestrian
crossing

GENERAL SIGNS

Snow tyres
required

Stop for
police check

Border between
Italy & other
EU countries

Beginning of motorway (green
background),
or main road
(blue background)

Getting to Tuscany and Umbria

Airlines – UK

Alitalia Tel: 08714 24 14 24; www.alitalia.com

British Airways Tel: 0844 493 0 787; www.britishairways.com

easyJet Tel: 0905 560 7777; www.easyjet.com

KLM UK Tel: 0870 5074 074; www.klm.com

Meridiana Tel: 0845 3555588; www.meridiana.com

Ryanair Tel: in Ireland, 0818 30 30 30; tel: in UK, 0871 246 0000; www.ryanair.com

Fly-drive
Search on www.opodo.com or www.expedia.co.uk

Established tour operators offering fly-drive holidays:

Citalia Tel: 0871 200 2004; www.citalia.co.uk

Cresta Holidays Tel: 0871 664 7963; www.crestaholidays.co.uk

Sunvil Holidays Tel: 020 8568 4499; www.sunvil.co.uk

For up-to-date details of long-distance bus, ferry and rail services, consult the *Thomas Cook European Rail Timetable*, published monthly.

The best travel deals require planning ahead – or for some flight and vacation package options, waiting until the last minute. The Internet is an excellent source of information and booking for airline tickets, car rental, train tickets, ferries and hotels. It is advisable, when booking air fares, to take out cancellation insurance. From among the multitude of Internet sites try *www.cheapflights.co.uk*, *www.flightcomparison.com*, *www.lastminute.com*, *www.bookers.com* or *www.flightline.co.uk*

From the UK

It is much easier to fly from the UK than to drive to Tuscany and Umbria. The advantages of bringing your own car have to be weighed against the high price and added time it takes. Stopping overnight, it takes about three days (about 36 hours if you drive non-stop) to reach Tuscany/Umbria from the UK, using the main north–south motorways. Add together the price of crossing the Channel, tolls, petrol and overnight stays en route and it quickly becomes expensive. However, it might well be worth considering for people travelling as a group of four or more.

London offers many different options. British Airways and Alitalia have flights several times a day to Rome, Milan and Pisa and there are also cheap charter flights to these cities as well as to Bologna and Rimini. Florence's small Peretola airport (car hire available) is handy for Perugia and northern Umbria, too, although there are no regular direct flights from London. Perugia is about two hours away.

Hiring a car requires an extra layer of planning but there are many fly/drive packages on offer from London, Manchester and Birmingham.

Trains

The train has no real advantages for travellers to Italy from the UK unless they want to visit destinations on the way. Contact Eurostar (*tel: 08705 186 186* from the UK; *www.eurostar.com*) for trains to Paris (with overnight connections to Florence for Perugia, Spoleto and Orvieto); Citalia (*see sidebar*) or Trenitalia (*www.trenitalia.it*) for Italian rail tickets and passes; or Rail Europe (*tel: 08705 848 848; www.raileurope.co.uk*). Rail Europe is the best source for rail passes for North American travellers. They sell both single and multiple-country

Channel crossing – UK

Some cross-Channel operators now offer an 'Apex'-type discount for advance bookings. See also www.cheap4ferries.co.uk

Eurotunnel Tel: 0870 5353 535; www.eurotunnel.com

Norfolkline Tel: 0870 1642 114; www.norfolkline.com

P&O Ferries Tel: 08716 645 645; www.poferries.com

SeaFrance Tel: 0871 663 2546; www.seafrance.com

Airlines – North America

Air Canada Tel: 1 888 247 2262; www.aircanada.com

Alitalia Tel: in US, 1 800 223 5730; in Canada, 1 800 268 9277; www.alitalia.com

American Airlines Tel: in the US, 800 433 7300; www.aa.com

Delta Tel: in US and Canada, 1 800 241 4141; www.delta.com

Lufthansa Tel: in US, 1 800 399 5838; in Canada, 1 800 563 5954; www.lufthansa.com

Northwest/KLM Tel: in US and Canada, 1 800 225 2525; www.nwa.com; www.klm.com

United Airlines Tel: in US, 1 800 538 2929; www.ual.com

Right
San Gimignano

rail passes. Note that they must be purchased before departing *(tel: 888 382 7245; www.raileurope.com)*.

Car hire

It is rarely possible to hire a car spontaneously, except in mid-winter. By reserving well ahead, you will usually have the best rate and your choice of car. The best rates are often in a package with airfare, booked through the car-hire company, airline or a reliable travel agency.

Major international hire companies are represented in Italy, with offices in Milan and Pisa, as well as other airports, for pick-up and delivery. Auto Europe offers some of the most competitive rates and offers excellent air-auto packages that include mobile phones and other benefits. Contact them from the UK, Ireland and New Zealand on *00 800 223 5555 5*, in Australia on *00 11 800 223 5555 5* and in the USA on *1 888 223 5555*. Alternatively, visit them on the web at *www.autoeurope.com*. Most companies require a credit card when you claim the vehicle, even if the hire has been prepaid.

One problem with hiring a car in Italy is that you must nearly always purchase the collision damage waiver. Even though some credit cards usually cover this, most do not in Italy, adding another expense to car hire. You can avoid this by leasing a car. Renault Eurodrive has a very smooth system for this for non-EU citizens, and will meet you with a brand-new car at Milan airport. The minimum lease period is 17 days, and the rate for additional days is quite inexpensive. Registration, insurance and all details are included and the rate compares very favourably with hire charges (and without added VAT). Drivers over 70 are not banned, as they are by most car-hire agencies. Contact **Renault Eurodrive**, US *(800) 221 1052 (www.renaultusa.com)*, France *33 1 48 62 37 53*. This plan is not available to residents of Europe.

Before leaving the car park, be sure you have all registration and insurance documents and that you know how to operate the vehicle. Don't plan a long day's driving after a long flight, especially if you are used to driving on the other side of the road.

From North America

Although there are no direct flights to Tuscany or Umbria, many airlines fly daily to Rome and Milan with possible connecting flights to Pisa or Perugia.

Above
The Piano Grande near Norcia

Setting the scene

Geography

The Apennines and the Apuan Alps border Tuscany to the north and northeast. The Apennines – *lo dosso d'Italia* or 'spine of Italy' – continue down through Umbria and form its border with the neighbouring Marche province.

Tuscany's 329km coastline is mostly flat and developed though the population density is much greater to the north than in the south. The peninsula of Monte Argentario was actually an island, until silting joined it to the mainland in the 19th century, while the coastal plain of Maremma consists of reclaimed swampland. South of Siena are the strange clay hills known as the Crete, which look like a grey desert in places. They roll into the verdant hills around the extinct volcano of Monte Amiata and westwards towards the Metallifere mountains, an almost uninhabited area with vast reserves of geothermal energy that provide much of Tuscany's electricity.

Seventy per cent of Tuscany is hilly, with the population concentrated in the lowlands in river valleys like those of the Arno and Tiber. The upper and middle valley of the River Tiber dominates Umbria, bracketed on the east side by the Apennines. It has a number of wide basins that were once lakes, such as the Vale di Umbra, and one that still is, Lago di Trasimeno, as well as plains around Gubbio and Terni, and the spectacular mountain plain, the Piano Grande.

Timeline

800–400 BC Etruscan settlements between the Tiber and Arno rivers – Populonia, Vetulonia, Roselle, Chiusi, Cortona, Arezzo, Fiesole, Volterra, Perugia and Orvieto; Umbrians settle on the left bank of the Tiber and found the cities of Narni, Amelia, Terni, Spoleto, Assisi and Gubbio.

400–350 BC The Golden Age of Etruscan civilisation.

350–250 BC Rome conquers the Etruscans and Umbrians, step by step. As part of their expansion, Romans build *coloniae* – retirement settlements for army veterans – along the strategic *Via Flaminia*, the road built to provide a swift route between Rome and its northern frontiers. Rome adopts Umbrian and Etruscan practices such as foretelling the future by studying birds in flight, forks of lightning or the organs of sacrificial animals.

AD 13–14 The Romans create the provinces of Umbria and Tuscia, left and right of the Tiber.

493–552 After the fall of the Roman Empire, Tuscany and Umbria are invaded and ruthlessly plundered by Goths.

568–71 The Longobards (Lombards) conquer the region and found their own dukedoms in Lucca and Spoleto. The area between Perugia and Amelia remains in Byzantine hands. The Longobards are converted to Christianity.

756 Peppin seizes Byzantine Umbria and gives it to the Pope. This is the beginning of the Papal State, destined to have a profound influence on Italian politics for the next 1,000 years.

774 Charlemagne and the Franks conquer the region. Charlemagne is crowned Holy Roman Emperor. Tuscany and Umbria become provinces of his empire.

1050 Power struggle between the Holy Roman Emperor and the Pope contributes to the growth of autonomous city-states in Pisa, Florence, Lucca, Siena, Arezzo, Prato, Perugia and Spoleto. The rise of guilds and the cloth industry; creation of Europe's first banks.

1063 Pisa beats off the Saracens and develops one of the most important harbours on the Mediterranean.

1125 Florence destroys Fiesole and begins to expand its territory. The Florentines fight wars with the Ghibelline cities of Pisa and Siena.

1210 Rise of Franciscans and Dominicans.

1260 Siena defeats Florence in the bloody battle of Montaperti.

1269 Florence defeats Siena near Colle Val d'Elsa.

1284 Pisa loses out to Genoa in struggle for control of the sea. Building boom of town halls: Prato (1284), Siena (1288), Pistoia (1294) and Florence (1299).

1342 Edward III of England defaults on his loans and ruins the major banking houses of Florence and Siena, setting off an economic crisis.

1348 The plague strikes Tuscany and Umbria, killing almost half of the population. Cities like Siena and San Gimignano never fully recover their importance.

1378 Revolt of the *ciompi* (weavers) in Siena, Lucca, Florence and other cities. The Medici – a wealthy Florentine family – become bankers to the Pope.

1406 Florence conquers Pisa, builds a new harbour in Livorno and wages war with Naples, Milan and Lucca. During a period of unrest in Florence, Cosimo de'Medici sides with the people's party and is driven into exile.

1434 Cosimo Il Vecchio returns to Florence in triumph and remains in power until his death (1464).

Guelphs and Ghibellines and the Middle Ages

'Guelph' and 'Ghibelline' were political factions of this age, supporters of the Pope and the Holy Roman Emperor respectively. The Guelph party was made up of merchants, bankers and members of the trades guilds with growing wealth. They supported the Pope because the papal cause seemed to offer the only hope of release from the imperial yoke. By contrast, the Ghibellines represented the old feudal aristocracy, interested in independence from external control but not in a broad-based city democracy. For them, allegiance to the Emperor was a small price to pay for maintaining a virtual autocracy within their own city-state.

Consequently, there was tension at every level in medieval Tuscany and Umbria: between the Church and Empire; between factions who nominally supported one or the other cause; between merchants and aristocracy; between rival families, and between individual city states, each seeking to extend its control.

1478 War between Florence and the Pope. The Medici prince, Lorenzo the Magnificent, survives an assassination attempt by the Pazzi conspirators.

1501 Michelangelo's *David* graces the square before the town hall in Florence.

1530 The end of Florence as a Republic. The Medici rule as tyrants with the help of Spanish troops.

1540 Perugia falls to Pope Paul III. The Papal State now controls most of Umbria. Its administration is so corrupt and its taxes so high that the Umbrian countryside suffers depopulation.

1555 Florence besieges Siena, starves out its population and puts an end to the last Republic in Italy.

1569 Cosimo I, proclaimed Duke of Tuscany, controls the entire region except for Lucca, Massa-Carrara and the islands.

1590–1790 The dullest period in Italian history with general economic and cultural stagnation.

1798–9 Napoleon occupies Tuscany and Umbria. His sister Elisa rules the Duchy of Lucca from 1805 to 1814.

1814 Under the Treaty of Fontainebleau, Napoleon is banished to Elba. Tuscany is ruled by the Habsburgs, Umbria by the Papal State.

1848 Risorgimento. Italians rebel against the rule of foreigners and the Papal State but the Austrians and Pope regain control.

1860 Unification of Italy. After popular referenda, Tuscany and Umbria join the new state. The name Umbria, which had not been used for centuries, is reintroduced.

1936 Hitler–Mussolini pact.

1940–45 Italy enters World War II as Germany's ally. Heavy fighting between Germans and Italian partisans in the Apennine mountains. Livorno, Pisa, Terni and San Gimignano suffer heavily. Following Italy's armistice with the Allies, in July 1944 the Germans blow up all the bridges in Florence, except for the Ponte Vecchio.

1966 Catastrophic flood sweeps through Florence.

1993 Bomb attack on the Uffizi Gallery in Florence kills four people and causes major damage to the museum and its collection.

1997 A strong earthquake hits Umbria, leaving 30,000 people homeless.

2002 An ambitious engineering project saves the leaning tower of Pisa from the threat of collapse; it is reopened to visitors.

2003 Massive power cut leaves most of Italy in darkness. Authorities blame a malfunction of supply lines from France.

2004 The corruption trial of Silvio Berlusconi, media mogul, AC Milan football club owner and Prime Minister, resumes in Milan.

2005 Premier Silvio Berlusconi is acquitted and Italy enters a recession.

2006 Silvio Berlusconi is replaced by Romano Prodi following election defeat. Italy wins its fourth football World Cup.

2007 Rome's popular mayor, Walter Veltroni, is elected by a wide margin to head the newly founded Democratic Party. Premier Prodi resigns after foreign policy vote loss in Italian senate.

2008 Berlusconi wins the general election and becomes Prime Minister. Berlusconi 'III' (previous terms were in 1994 and 2001) promises to tackle Italy's massive debt and spiralling unemployment.

2010 1,600 years from the fall of Rome.

Art and architecture

Almost everything we know about the Etruscans comes from their tombs and the art and furniture they placed inside them. Although scholars insist that there is nothing 'mysterious' about the Etruscans, lots of writers, artists and New Agers seem to know better. The solitary, semi-wild location of many tombs adds to the effect; it is sometimes difficult to know whether Etruscans, medieval warlords or extraterrestrials deposited a particular pile of red volcanic stone. Almost nothing is known of the Umbrians' culture. They left behind a few portions of city wall built of massive blocks in places like Amelia, and seven bronze tablets found near Gubbio that give lessons in divination and the ritual sacrifice of birds and unwanted neighbours.

Many people in Tuscany and Umbria still live in houses built in the Middle Ages. Their home might have Renaissance or Baroque additions and they may park in an Etruscan tomb downstairs; or perhaps they live in a traditional 18th-century stone farmhouse which animals and farmers shared. In the region's churches and cathedrals, the centuries are just steps apart. Recycled Roman stones support the roof above many an altar painted in the Renaissance.

Romanesque

Florence is celebrated as the cradle of the Renaissance. However, the profile of most historic cities in Tuscany and Umbria is Romanesque and Gothic. The Romanesque style (10th–12th centuries) unites geometry – rectangles, cubes, semicircular arches – with unprecedented ambition to build upwards. Although not directly of Roman origin, many Romanesque *pievi* (parish churches) were built in the countryside on top of sites sacred to Etruscans and Romans. The Pisan Romanesque style was strongly influenced by Byzantine and Islamic architecture. Some of the best early churches are:

Above
The tower of San Pietro
Church in Perugia

- Abbadia San Salvatore (1036) in the Crete
- Sant'Antimo (1100) in the Crete
- San Pietro, Spoleto (façade *c.* 1150–1210)
- Duomo, Sovana (1150)
- Pieve di Romena (1150) near Castello di Romena.

Some of the best Pisan Romanesque churches are:
- Baptistry (1152), Duomo (1063–1180) and Campanile (1173–1350) in Pisa
- San Frediano (1112) and San Michele in Foro (1143) in Lucca
- Duomo (1108–1311) and Sant'Andrea (1180) in Pistoia
- Duomo (1211) in Prato.

Among the best Florentine Romanesque churches are:
- Baptistry (1059–1128) and San Miniato al Monte (1050) in Florence.

Gothic

There are few purely Gothic structures in Tuscany and Umbria. Most Gothic buildings contain Romanesque elements or were built upon or around previous Romanesque buildings. Gothic architecture took a distinctly different form south of the Alps, retaining the dome, using less vertical thrust and giving frescos, rather than stained-glass windows, centre stage. The best examples of this style are:
- Basilica di San Francesco, Assisi (1228–53)
- San Galgano, in central Tuscany (1224–30)
- Duomo, Siena (1225)
- Duomo, Orvieto (1290–1330)
- Duomo, Florence (1294)
- Santa Maria della Spina, Pisa (1323).

Renaissance

The 15th century was a revolutionary period that profoundly changed many aspects of European life – housing, language, warfare, diet, cities, technology and education, for example. Certainly, the Florentines themselves saw this age as a rebirth of classical learning and artistic ideals and called it a *Rinascita* (Rebirth). However, the idea of the Renaissance as a sudden Florentine watershed between the medieval and the modern is essentially a 19th-century theory that has been subject to heavy revision. In fact, the late Middle Ages paved the way for many 'modern' changes to such an extent that a piece of the late medieval period has been appropriated as 'Proto-Renaissance'. Its dominant artistic figure is Giotto (1266–1337), generally considered to be the first artist since antiquity to create realistic representations of people, space and things.

Art historians have picked 1420 to be the magic moment when the Early Renaissance began, the year when Brunelleschi won the contract to put a dome on top of the cathedral in Florence (it was not finished until 1467, after his death). Brunelleschi had already rediscovered linear perspective (the ancients were familiar with it) and his approach to architecture was radically new, although his buildings have Gothic and Romanesque elements, too. Painters Paolo Uccello, Piero della Francesca and Masaccio would make full use of perspective to pioneer the illusion of space and the dimensions of nature on a flat surface. Donatello and Ghiberti incorporated the new principles into sculpture.

The most important figures of the High Renaissance were Michelangelo, Leonardo da Vinci and Raphael. This period spanned little more than a generation, roughly 1490–1520. Admittedly, Leonardo was so busy privately inventing things like the helicopter, bicycle and flame-thrower that he painted little. Raphael, by contrast, was prolific but died young, in 1520. His work possesses in perfect balance the grace and harmony to which Renaissance artists aspired. Michelangelo carried on until 1564 and the incredible age of 89 but by then he had himself broken the Renaissance mould and opened the door to new styles. The best Renaissance buildings are:

- Spedale degli Innocenti (1419–24); Sagrestia Vecchia in San Lorenzo (1419); Cappella dei Pazzi in Santa Croce (1442); San Lorenzo (begun in 1425), all in Florence and by Brunelleschi
- San Marco in Florence, Michelozzo (1437–52)
- Piazza del Duomo in Pienza, Rossellino (1459–62)
- San Biagio in Montepulciano, Sangallo (1513–43)
- Sagrestia Nuova, San Lorenzo in Florence, Michelangelo (1520).

Mannerism

Below
Madonna and Child in Todi's San Fortunato church

The term 'Mannerism', even by the standards of art history jargon, is woolly. It was originally a put-down by Tuscan artist Giorgio Vasari referring to artists who came after Michelangelo and who worked *alla maniera di Michelangelo* (the most hyperactive 'wannabe' was Vasari himself). Michelangelo had given impetus to it: his Medici Chapel (in San Lorenzo) was, in Vasari's words, 'more varied and novel than that of any other master', putting artists 'under a great and eternal obligation to Michelangelo, seeing that he broke the fetters and chains that had earlier confined them to the creation of traditional forms'. The most prominent figures in this school are the painters Pontormo, Bronzino and Rosso Fiorentino and sculptors Benvenuto Cellini and Giambologna. It is ironic that the Tuscan Renaissance bang ended in a Mannerist whimper – a self-conscious, angst-ridden style alien to the classical spirit but with some striking parallels to modern art.

Festivals

The calendar of Tuscany and Umbria is full of festivals. Most are purely local events that celebrate a region's food (mushrooms, *pecorino*, chestnuts, truffles, wild boar, grilled thrush); they offer the perfect chance to eat, drink and make merry with Tuscans and Umbrians. The more famous 'medieval' pageants are a mysterious mix of tourist hype and authentic local tradition – none more so than the most hyped (and insanely crowded) of all festivals, the *Palio di Contrade* in Siena, which nevertheless has deep roots in the city's history and psyche. Some of the seasonal festivals in the region, though adapted to Christianity, have their origins in pagan ritual. One event that stands out in this respect is the *Corsa dei Ceri* in Gubbio. Music, theatre and art festivals fall into a third category. The one with the most cachet is the Festival of Two Worlds in Spoleto but there are many others. The local tourist office is always a good source of information about festivals.

January/February/March
- *Holy Week* in Assisi.
- *Carnevale* in Viareggio. A spectacular Shrove Tuesday parade with floats poking fun at local and national politicians.

April/May
- *Maggio Musicale* in Florence (*Apr–Jun*).
- *Coloriamo i cieli* (Let's paint the skies) in Castiglione del Lago. Every even-numbered year a Kite Festival is held on the banks of Lake Trasimeno (*second Sun in May*).
- *Corso all'Anello* (Ring Race) in Narni. Young men dressed in medieval costume attempt to thrust the tip of a lance through a ring which is suspended on a string between the houses along the Via Maggiore (*first Tue in May*).
- *Calendimaggio* in Assisi. A three-day celebration in commemoration of St Francis with singing, theatre performances, dance, processions, archery and banner-waving (*early May*).
- *Corsa dei Ceri* (Candle Race) in Gubbio. Three gigantic wooden 'candles', each weighing about 50kg and mounted with statues of saints, are carried by young candle-bearers to the Basilica di Sant'Ubaldo, situated on top of Monte Ingino.
- *Balestro del Girifalco* in Massa Marittima (*see page 168*).

June
- *Festival dei Due Mondi* in Spoleto. International prose, theatre, dance and musical performances by leading artists from Europe and the Americas. One of the high points of the Italian social and artistic calendar, you will have to book well in advance if you want to attend any events, or find a hotel room in the city (*Jun and Jul*).
- *Palio della Balestra* in Gubbio. Contests with medieval bows and arrows between Gubbio and Sansepolcro.
- *Calcio Storico* in Florence. Founded in the 15th century with roots in the ancient Roman game of Harpastum, this aggressive form of football/rugby that may have indirectly influenced British football is still played in costume each year in the third week of June.
- *Corpus Christi Day procession* in Camaiore. An ancient procession accented with carpets of flowers (now substituted with coloured sawdust) that decorate the street pavement.

Below
Festive Siena

- *Gioco del Ponte* in Pisa (*see page 146*).
- *Giostra del Saracino* in Arezzo (*see page 186*).
- *Rockin' Umbria* in Perugia. This rock festival has taken place each year since 1986 not just in Perugia, but also in Umbertide and Città di Castello. Although you won't find the rock world's big stars here, you will find promising up-and-coming musical performers (*last 10 days in Jun–first 10 days in Jul*).

July
- *Palio dei barchini* in Orbetello. A boat race dating back to the wedding of the Archduchess of Austria to the King of Naples and the Two Sicilies in 1768.
- *La fiera di Vinci* in Vinci. Festival with historic processions, tournaments, jousting, local crafts and cuisine.
- *International Mercantile Festival* in Certaldo. Street festivals featuring local artists.
- *Pistoia Blues* in Pistoia. Concert series hosting well-known international jazz virtuosi.
- *Palio di Contrade* in Siena (*see page 79*).
- *Umbria Jazz* in Perugia and other cities. One of the most important jazz festivals in Europe (*last two weeks in Jul–first week in Aug*).

August
- *Balestro del Girifalco* in Massa Marittima (*see page 168*).
- *Bravìo delle Botti* in Montepulciano (*see page 106*).
- *Torneo* in Montalcino (*see page 92*).
- *Palio di Contrade* in Siena (*see page 79*).
- *International Ceramics Competition and Exhibition* in Gualdo Tadino. It dates back to 1959 and is attended by well-known ceramicists and exhibitors of widely differing artistic trends (*mid-Aug–30 Sep*).

September
- *Luminaria di Santa Croce* in Lucca (*see page 110*).
- *Gioco della Bandiera* in Volterra (*see page 161*).
- *Giostra del Saracino* in Arezzo (*see page 186*).
- *Todi Festival* in Todi. A wide variety of works in the fields of music, ballet and film produced by young, up-and-coming artists hailing from Italy and abroad.
- *Sagra Musicale Umbra* in Perugia. Highly regarded event in the music world at which 20th-century religious music is performed.

October
- *Sagra* in Montalcino (*see page 92*).

November
- *Rassegna Antiquaria* in Perugia. An exhibition of antiques.

December
- *Celebrazioni di Santo Natale* in Assisi and Amelia. During this time, Christmas concerts are held in many churches and the Nativity scene is portrayed by live animals and actors.
- *Mostra Mercato del Tartufo* in Città di Castello. The entire city is transformed into a heaven for fans of truffles (*24 Dec–6 Jan*).

Highlights

The best of Tuscany and Umbria:
- Archaeology museums: *Chiusi, Florence, Orvieto, Volterra.*
- Art museums: *Uffizi, Bargello* (Florence), *Perugia, Siena, Montefalco.*
- Baptistries: *Florence, Pisa, Pistoia.*
- Beaches: *Castiglione della Pescaia, Vada, Marina di Alberese, Baratti.*
- Castles: *Castiglione d'Orcia, Poppi, Radicofani.*
- Cathedrals: *Assisi, Barga, Florence, Orvieto, Pisa, Siena, Spoleto.*
- Cities: *Florence, Lucca, Siena, Perugia.*
- Etruscan arches: *Perugia, Volterra.*
- Etruscan cemeteries: *Golfo di Baratti, Orvieto, Perugia.*
- Festivals (art and music): *Festival of Two Worlds in Spoleto, Umbria Jazz Festival.*
- Festivals (traditional): *Palio di Contrade in Siena, Corsa dei Ceri in Gubbio.*
- Frescos: *Monte Oliveto (Signorelli, Sodoma), Basilica di Assisi (Cimabue, Giotto), Cappella Brancacci in Florence (Masaccio, Masolino, Filippino Lippi), Chiesa di San Francesco in Montefalco (Benozzo Gozzoli), Collegio di Cambio in Perugia (Perugino), Duomo San Francesco in Arezzo (Piero della Francesca), Palazzo Pubblico in Siena (Ambrogio Lorenzetti).*

Below
Near Lake Trasimeno

- Geology: *Le Balze near Volterra, Larderello.*
- Historic squares: *Bevagna, Castiglione d'Orcia, Lucca, Massa Marittima, Pienza, Perugia, Siena, Volterra.*
- Historic towns: *Montepulciano, San Gimignano, Spoleto, Volterra.*
- Hot springs: *Bagno Vignoni, Calidario in Venturina, Cascate del Mulino in Saturnia, Fosso Biano in Bagni San Filippo.*
- Islands: *Isola Maggiore and Isola Polvese in Lago di Trasimeno.*
- Lakes: *Lago di Trasimeno.*
- Markets: *Arezzo (antiques), Florence (Mercato Centrale).*
- Monasteries: *Monte Oliveto, Sant'Antimo.*
- National Parks: *Parco Naturale della Maremma, Parco Naturale di Monti Sibillini.*
- Palaces: *Palazzo Vecchio, Palazzo Medici-Riccardi (Florence), Palazzo dei Priori (Perugia).*
- Roman ruins: *Carsulae, Ponte d'Augusto in Narni.*
- Wine: *Fonterutoli, Montalcino, Montefalco, Montepulciano, Torrigiano, Volpaia.*

Architecture	●●●●●
Art	●●●●●
Food and drink	●●●●○
Museums	●●●●●
Shopping	●●●●●
Children	●●○○○
Scenery	●●○○○
Nature	●○○○○

Above
Baptistry

Florence

Florentines discovered three-dimensional perspective, football, opera and ice cream – not bad for a city of moneylenders and cloth-makers. Having initiated the Renaissance, Florence still monopolises much of it in the space of a few hundred square metres and the resulting density of tourists rivals Disneyworld. Its architecture has been repeated all over the world in private and public buildings – a sense of *déjà vu* is inevitable. Michelangelo may be the presiding genius but virtually every Italian Renaissance artist of any rank made his mark here. Despite claustrophobia, noise and summer heat, the city still offers sanctuary to the art lover, beginning in its cathedral. Many of the galleries, churches and museums are far from the madding crowd, as are the cloisters of San Lorenzo, Santa Croce and Santa Maria Novella.

Sights

ⓘ APT office *Via Cavour 1; tel: 055 290832/3; fax: 055 2760383; www.firenzeturismo.it, www.comune.fi.it. Open Mon–Sat 0815–1915; Sun 0830–1330.*

ⓑ Battistero € *Piazza del Duomo/San Giovanni; tel: 055 2302885; www.operaduomo.firenze.it. Open Mon–Sat 1200–1900, Sun 0830–1400.*

Battistero
The Battistero (Baptistry) is the oldest building in the city. Its origins are mysterious, but the foundations are probably from the 4th to 8th centuries while the current building – described by art historians as 'proto-Renaissance' – dates from 1059–1128. Medieval Florentines, including Dante (baptised here in 1245), thought it was built by the Romans and it does, in fact, stand at the former intersection of the town's two main Roman roads, and the four bronze doors are aligned with them. The south door (1330–6) by Andrea Pisano depicts scenes from the life of John the Baptist, the patron saint of Florence. Lorenzo Ghiberti worked for almost half a century on the other two doors. He decorated the north door (1403–24) with 28 scenes from the lives of Jesus and the four Evangelists. The east door, however, is his crowning achievement and one of the finest things created during the Renaissance. Its ten gilded panels begin with the creation of Adam and

Museo Nazionale del Bargello € *Via del Proconsolo 4; tel: 055 294883; www.polomuseale.firenze.it. Open daily 0815–1350; closed 1st, 3rd & 5th Sun and 2nd & 4th Mon of every month.*

Campanile €€ *Piazza del Duomo; tel: 055 2302885; www.operaduomo.firenze.it. Open daily 0830–1930.*

Eve, followed by Cain and Abel, the Flood, Noah's drunkenness and other episodes from the Old Testament (the originals are in the Museo del Duomo). Ghiberti's self-portrait is in the fourth panel – the head at the top. Michelangelo, normally a merciless critic, called them the 'doors of paradise'. Inside, the 13th-century mosaics in the apse were a source of inspiration to Dante while writing *L'Inferno* (hell). Look for the Devil with a mouthful of the sinners.

Museo Nazionale del Bargello

The Bargello is strangely neglected in favour of the Uffizi though its collection of sculpture rivals that of any museum in the world. The 13th-century palace, built for sessions of the city council, symbolised the triumph of elected government in Florence. Three centuries later, it stood for the opposite, after Medici tyrants turned it into a prison. The charming courtyard wall was the last thing condemned prisoners saw before their execution. The Bargello's repertoire of nude bodies in stone – twisting, raging, lusting and musing atop their pedestals – expresses a revolution in taste, ie, the Renaissance – and an obsession with the human body. It puts today's cult of the supermodel and Schwarzeneggers to shame for sheer lack of imagination.

The ground floor displays the only bust Michelangelo ever carved, of *Brutus*. The work had distinct Republican overtones because it could be seen as a reference to the assassination of the Medici tyrant, Alessandro I. His *Drunken Bacchus* carries a somewhat different message. The same room contains his *Tondo Pitti* and *David-Apollo* as well as Benvenuto Cellini's bust of *Cosimo I* and Giambologna's *Flying Mercury*. Upstairs is Donatello's homoerotic, under-age *David* – the first nude statue of the Renaissance, and one of the most remarkable works of art in Florence. Other high points include Ammannati's *Leda and the Swan* and Ghiberti's powerful *The Sacrifice of Isaac*. It's easy to overlook, but on the wall of the first floor are two panels submitted by Brunelleschi and Ghiberti in a competition for the commission to do the Baptistry doors. If you have any attention span left, there are still 30,000 odd coins and medallions to look at.

Campanile

Giotto was appointed architect of the cathedral in 1334 but he never got beyond building this tower and then only a third of it. He decorated it with octagonal pilasters and a colour scheme that would later be applied to the cathedral – white marble (Carrara), green marble (Prato) and red marble (Maremma). The reliefs were added over the next century by Andrea Pisano, Luca della Robbia and Donatello. They portray nothing less than the history of humanity, beginning with Adam, and illustrating human progress through crafts, the planets that influence human nature, the seven liberal arts that perfect it and the seven sacraments (originals are in the Museo del Duomo).

Opposite
Giotto's Campanile and the Duomo

Duomo Santa Maria del Fiore

Duomo Santa Maria del Fiore
Piazza del Duomo; tel: 055 2302885;
www.operaduomo.firenze.it.
Open Mon–Wed and
Fri 1000–1700,
Thu 1000–1330,
Sat 1000–1645,
Sun 1330–1645. Free.

Cupola del Duomo €€
Piazza del Duomo; tel: 055 2302885;
www.operaduomo.firenze.it.
Open Mon–Fri 0830–1900,
Sat 0830–1740.

Giardino di Boboli €
Palazzo Pitti; tel: 055 294883;
www.polomuseale.firenze.it.
Open daily Jun–Aug
0815–1930; Apr, May, Sep
& Oct 0815–1830; Mar
0815–1730; Nov–Feb
0815–1630. Closed first/last
Mon of month.

Museo dell'Opera di Santa Maria del Fiore
€€ Piazza Duomo 9; tel: 055 2302885;
www.operaduomo.firenze.it.
Open Mon–Sat 0900–1930,
Sun 0900–1345. If you
want to see the workshop
that is now used to repair
the Duomo, walk around
the corner to Via dello
Studio 23r.

Duomo Santa Maria del Fiore

When it was built, the Duomo was the largest church in the world – 53m long and 38m wide. Today, it is still the fourth largest cathedral in Europe. The overachieving medieval builder, Arnolfo di Cambio, began the Duomo in 1296 at the same time that he was busy with the Palazzo Vecchio and Santa Croce. Filippo Brunelleschi designed the dome (1420–34), the first of its size since the Pantheon in Rome. Climbing to the top of it is one of the most unforgettable experiences of a trip to Florence for its simultaneous views of the city's red-tiled rooftops and a plunging look into the marble canyon of the church interior.

Giardino di Boboli

Instead of a theme park or virtual reality, the 16th-century Medici rulers had this vast fantasy-filled garden to kill time in. The Florentine public didn't get its first peek until 200 years later. Avenues lined with cypresses intersect ensembles of Roman and Renaissance statues and stately cedars of Lebanon shade strange grottoes. Performances of Europe's first operas took place in its amphitheatre. Fountains are ubiquitous, from the fabulous Mannerist Oceanus to secluded, leering fauns that spit water into Roman sarcophagi.

The originals of Michelangelo's *Slaves* once decorated the Grotta del Buontalenti (left of the entrance) until the early 1900s. Copies have replaced them. Deeper inside, beneath the stalactites, is Giambologna's alarmingly endowed *Venus*. The steep climb up from the Pitti Palace to the top of the Boboli Gardens is rewarded with a cinematic view of Florence and the surrounding Tuscan countryside.

Museo dell'Opera di Santa Maria del Fiore

Without seeing this museum, you haven't really seen the monuments of Florence – many of the most impressive pieces of the Battistero, Duomo and Campanile are kept here to preserve them from pollution and vandalism. The 13th-century building behind the cathedral served as its workshop for centuries. This is where Michelangelo sculpted *David* during 1501–4.

Sculptures from the unfinished cathedral façade that was torn down in 1587 line the walls of the ground floor. Central among them is a Madonna (with the glass eyes) by Arnolfo di Cambio, the cathedral's architect. The 80-year-old Michelangelo sculpted the *Pietà* (1548–55) for his own tomb in Rome portraying himself in the figure of St Nicodemus – the old man in a cowl. Dissatisfied late one night, he fell into a rage and tried to smash it. This is the first recorded incident in history of an artist destroying his own work. Christ is scarred by the hammer blows and missing his left leg. Donatello is represented by the early, powerful sculptures of prophets Jeremiah and Habakkuk (1420) and a late Mary Magdalen in wood (1455). There are also pulpits by him and Luca della Robbia, the latter famous for its rows of dancing children. The panels of the restored Doors of Paradise are on the ground floor.

ⓘ Galleria Palatina
€€ *Palazzo Pitti, Piazza Pitti; tel: 055 294883; www.polomuseale.firenze.it. Open Tue–Sun 0815–1850.*

Other museums in Palazzo Pitti open daily 0815–1830, closed first and last Mon of each month, shorter hours in winter.

Palazzo Vecchio €€
Piazza della Signoria; tel: 055 2768224; http:// museoragazzi.comune.fi.it. Open daily 0900–1900 (closes Thu 1400).

Palazzo Pitti

The vast Pitti Palace was built at the edge of Florence by Luca Pitti and greatly expanded by Medici tyrant Cosimo I in his determination to put a little space between himself and liberty-loving Florentines who might try to get up close and personal. He ordered his court architect, Giorgio Vasari, to join the Palazzo to the Uffizi by way of a corridor over the Arno so he could sneak in and out of the Palazzo Vecchio (his former residence) and quickly escape across the river. His paranoid son, Ferdinand I, went a step further and built the Forte di Belvedere above the gardens of the palace – its cannons were aimed at Florence.

The palace contains no less than eight museums (two are closed indefinitely), devoted to fashion, silver, coaches, and so on. The **Galleria Palatina** is one of Europe's great art museums. It has a brace of Caravaggios, 11 paintings by Raphael, 13 Titians and works by Rubens, Tintoretto and Giorgione, to say nothing of the gifted and possibly mad Rosso Fiorentino. Two signature works alone would more than justify a visit: Rubens's *The Consequences of War* and Raphael's *Portrait of a Lady*.

Palazzo Vecchio

The palace is still the City Hall of Florence. It was the work of Arnolfo di Cambio (1299–1314) but Michelozzo created the early Renaissance courtyard in 1453. Two centuries after its completion, Vasari decorated the walls with frescos, now badly faded, of Austrian cities to celebrate a wedding between the house of Medici and an Austrian princess. The clock, added in 1667, still ticks.

Ponte Vecchio

One of Europe's most photographed structures, the 'old bridge' occupies a place used in Roman times as a crossing over the Arno for the *Via Cassia*. Today's bridge was built in 1345. Originally, there were butcher shops and tanners (who dumped their bloody scraps in the river). Ferdinand I wanted the bridge to be more upmarket, reserving its shops for jewellers and goldsmiths, and so it has remained.

War damage

The Germans dynamited all of Florence's bridges except the Ponte Vecchio in 1944 (they blew up houses at each end instead).

Uffizi

Giorgio Vasari designed the Uffizi (offices) for Medici ruler Cosimo I and his bureaucracy in the 16th century. Today, it is Italy's most

Culture shock

Something strange happened to French novelist Stendhal one day in 1817 during a visit to the Uffizi. His heart raced and he began to sweat and tremble. Shortly afterwards, he broke down in tears. After 12-hour days of absorbing art and architecture, anyone could be susceptible to his affliction, now diagnosed as Stendhal Syndrome. In essence, it is a type of nervous breakdown brought on by an overdose of Renaissance culture. Florentine doctors and psychologists treat dozens of cases of *sindrome di Stendhal* each year.

🛈 **Uffizi €€€** *Piazzale degli Uffizi 6; tel: 055 2388651. Open Tue–Sun 0815–1850; reservations (booking charge € per person) Mon–Fri 0830–1830, tel: 055 294883; fax: 055 264406; www.virtualuffizi.com, www.polomuseale.firenze.it.* Booking a ticket means you don't have to wait in line, but it costs a little more.

popular museum (around 1.5 million visitors a year and growing) with 1,000 works of art from the 13th to the 17th centuries displayed in 45 rooms. Its most famous icon, Botticelli's *Birth of Venus* (or *'Venus on the half shell'*) challenges the *Mona Lisa* for the status of world's most recognised painting.

Of all Italy's museums, the plethora of riches here is the most embarrassing. It inspired Mark Twain's stoic boast that he had wandered 'weary miles of picture galleries' in Florence. If your focus is the Renaissance, plan to spend the day in the first 15 rooms without forgetting, however, that the Uffizi is also one of Europe's great international collections, with major works by northern Europeans such as Dürer, Cranach, Brueghel and Rembrandt.

Accommodation and food

Many hoteliers will assure you that 'low season' does not exist in Florence. However, high season climbs even higher in April to June, September and October. Sometimes rates drop 25–50 per cent in winter but it all depends on the hotel. Regardless of the time of year, the city is always packed and people without reservations might have to choose between a night in the train station or the suburbs.

Cantinetta di Verrazzano € *Via dei Tavolini 18r; tel: 055 268590; www.verrazzano.com. Closed Sun.* Very near the Duomo and an ideal place for a break. Excellent for a small meal – a *focaccia* or a sandwich made from *prosciutto di cinghiale* (wild boar) or roasted *porcini* mushrooms washed down with a glass of wine or an espresso. Raspberry and honey *tortini* are luscious.

Hotel Crocini € *Corso Italia 28; tel: 055 212905; fax: 055 210171; www.hotelcrocini.com.* Long established, the Crocini prides itself on being one of the last 'authentic' English-style pensions. It is solidly furnished and located in a quiet residential area. The rooms are spacious for Florence and there is a back garden and parking area. A 10-minute walk from the centre of town.

Mario € *Via Rosina 2/r; tel: 055 218550; www.trattoriamario.com. Closed Sun and Aug.* Lunch-only no-nonsense *trattoria* with generous quality and quantity price ratio, also near the Mercato Centrale. Come early, before it fills up with students.

La Pentola dell'Oro € *Via di Mezzo 24r; tel: 055 241821. Open evenings only, closed Sun and Aug.* Chef Giuseppe Alessi goes tradition one better by serving Renaissance-style dishes – *Piatti Rinascimentale* – and vegetarian meals.

Residenza La Torricella € *Via Vecchia di Pozzolatico 25; tel: 055 2321818; fax: 055 2047402; www.farmholidaylatorricella.it.* Two-night minimum stay. A bed and breakfast in a villa on the outskirts of Florence, run by the attentive and friendly Manetti family. It is an easy drive from the Certosa exit of the A1 *autostrada.* There is public transportation to the city centre.

Trattoria Toscana Gozzi Sergio € *Piazza San Lorenzo 8r; tel: 055 281941. Closed Sun and Aug.* Right off the Mercato Centrale, it is known by the locals simply as 'Da Sergio'. The menu is limited but impeccable. In addition to *bollito misto* (stewed meats) there are lots of things *in umido* (in broth), such as cod, tripe and rabbit.

Il Cibreo €€ *Via dei Macci 118r; tel: 055 2341100 (no reservations). Closed Sun and Mon, last week of Jul and Aug.* This *trattoria* is an annexe to a more expensive restaurant next door. The food is truly outstanding at modest prices. However, it doesn't accept reservations and is always packed. The best tactic is to arrive early, say at 1930. *Anatra ripiena al forno* (stuffed roast duck) is a speciality. One oddity – they don't do pasta.

Hotel Orto de' Medici €€ *Via San Gallo 30; tel: 055 483427; fax: 055 461276; www.ortodeimedici.it.* Centrally located family-run villa with balconies, a frescoed breakfast room and loggia. Breakfast is on a terrace looking out on the church of San Marco. Parking is available in a garage around the corner.

Below
Copy of Michelangelo's *David*
in Piazza della Signoria

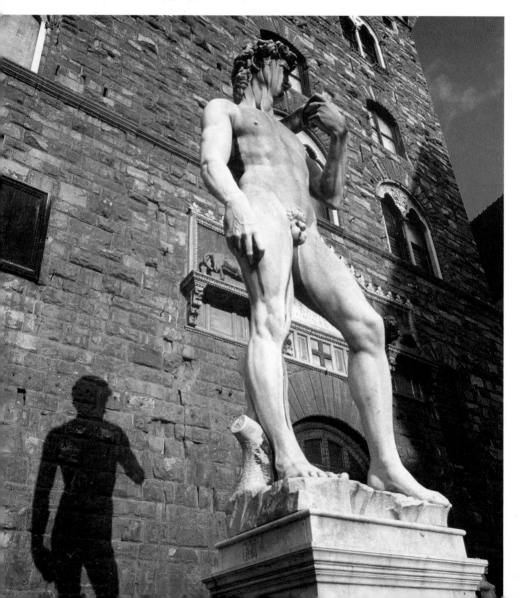

Cucina alla Fiorentina

Florentine cuisine is simplicity itself. *Crostini* are slices of toasted Tuscan bread with chicken-liver pâté, tomatoes or mushrooms, or just dipped in unspeakably good olive oil. Soup often takes preference over pasta: *ribollita* in winter and *pappa di pomodori* in summer. Florentines also like to eat hare, wild boar and pheasant. *Bistecca alla fiorentina* is simply a steak – of local Tuscan beef, from the Valdichiana – marinated in herbs, garlic and the finest olive oil, and cooked to perfection over wood coals. *Tortino di carciofi*, an artichoke omelette, and *funghi alla griglia* (grilled mushrooms) are among the few things for a vegetarian. The more expensive restaurants sometimes have bargain lunch menus. In Florence, in particular, restaurants are likely to charge for *pane e coperto* (bread and tableware) and sometimes for *servizio* (10 per cent). It will always be stated clearly on the menu.

Hotel Royal Firenze €€ *Via delle Ruote 50–54; tel: 055 483287; fax: 055 490976; www.hotelroyalfirenze.it.* One of the more accessible hotels by car which is still central with traditional touches and comfortable rooms. You can drive here directly from the peripheral road between Fortezza da Basso and Piazza della Libertà. It has parking in its courtyard.

Palazzo dal Borgo Hotel Aprile €€ *Via della Scala 6; tel: 055 216237; fax: 055 280947; www.hotelaprile.it.* Eager management and well-appointed rooms in what was the 15th-century Palazzo dal Borgo. It is located near Piazza Santa Maria Novella, 300m away from the train station. The 28 rooms either overlook a garden or have double-glazed windows (ask for the former). Parking in nearby garage.

Enoteca Pinchiorri €€€ *Via Ghibellina 87; tel: 055 242777; www.enotecapinchiorri.com. Closed Sun, Mon and Tue.* Tuscan cuisine with a heavy French accent (explaining perhaps its two Michelin stars). The wine cellar ranks with any in Europe and inspires near-religious awe among connoisseurs.

Below
Eating out in Piazza della Signoria

Hotel J and J €€€ *Via di Mezzo 20; tel: 055 2345005; fax: 055 240282; www.jandj.hotelinfirenze.com.* Few hotels even in Florence have such a beautiful setting: 19 rooms are located off the courtyard of a 16th-century convent and decorated with frescos, wrought-iron beds and fine hardwood furniture. The Duomo is just 500m away. Parking at a nearby garage.

Villa La Massa €€€ *Via della Massa 24, Candeli, on the Arno river 7km east of Florence; tel: 055 62611; fax: 055 633102; www.villalamassa.com.* Absolute luxury in a magnificent 17th-century Florentine villa, now flanked by tennis courts and a swimming pool, that used to be the residence of the noble Pecori Giraldi family. It lies in the Tuscan hills in an expansive park on the banks of the Arno. Ambitious new owners renovated it in 1998. It also has the ever-so-refined Il Verrocchio restaurant. A courtesy bus whisks guests in and out of Florence.

Suggested tour

P There are large car parks near the main train station (Fortezza da Basso) and the cheaper Piazza della Libertà (Parterre). The best chance of finding a space is in the Oltrarno – on the left side of the Arno. Study the signs carefully, making sure they are not for residents only (*ecetto residenti autorizatti*) and that street cleaners are not about to bear down on the spot. Don't park in or near the notorious (for break-ins) Piazzale Michelangelo. For more information, see *www.firenzeparcheggi.it* or contact the **Consorzio Firenze Parcheggi** at *Via G. La Pira 21, tel: 055 272011.*

If Dante were alive today, he would surely add driving in Florence to the punishments of hell! You do not cruise in and out of this city; rather, you bite your lip and run the risk of killing someone, or being killed. Most of the *Centro Storico* is *Zona Blu* (blue zone), meaning that only residents are allowed to park on the streets; cars parked illegally in this zone are towed away (and held for ransom at the Municipal Car Pound, Via Circondaria 17b; *tel: 055 783882).* Hotel guests have the dubious privilege of squeezing through an army of *vespas* and tourist hordes to unload their luggage in the centre; if the hotel has no parking, they must drive right back out again. One could debate the wisdom of spending one's holiday in search of a free parking place in Florence. A cheap and easy alternative for a day trip to Florence is to book a hotel in an outlying town and take the train.

Total distance: 2km.

Time: To see everything on this route would require at least three days; to do it in any less time might trigger the medical condition known as Stendahl Syndrome (*see Culture shock, page 47*). If you have only a day, skip the detours, climb the stairs of the **DUOMO**, walk the walk and, on the way, choose between the **UFFIZI** or **BARGELLO**.

Florence profits from its past but remains a working city engaged in an astonishing range of crafts and trades, particularly shoes, handbags, textiles, nightgowns, bookbinding and art restoration. Most of the work is done in the Oltrarno (left bank of the Arno) in small shops, some the size of a cupboard.

Route: The Piazza del Duomo is the ancient, clotted heart of Florence, where the Roman roads once met. John Ruskin was already comparing it to a crowded bus station a century ago. Begin with a look at the **BATTISTERO** ❶ then visit the **DUOMO SANTA MARIA DEL FIORE** ❷. To appreciate it fully, climb up the steps to the top of the dome. A second, even more dizzying view is possible over the edge of the **CAMPANILE** ❸.

Detour: On the north side of the Duomo, take the Via de'Martelli. After one short block, have a look at the **Palazzo Medici-Riccardi** ❺ and walk into its arcaded courtyard, one of the finest in Florence. This was the family home of the Medici until they moved to the Palazzo Vecchio in 1659. The Palazzo was designed in 1444 by Michelozzo and later much copied by upwardly mobile Florentine merchants. The marble medallions are copies of cameos from the legendary Medici collection.

San Lorenzo ❻ is just a stone's throw away down the Via de'Pucci. The unfinished façade hides one of the most perfectly proportioned buildings of the Renaissance: Filippo Brunelleschi rationalised every centimetre of the space divided between nave and chapels. The bronze reliefs on the pulpit are late masterpieces by Donatello who also decorated the Sagrestia Vecchia. The altar has an annunciation by Filippo Lippi. The entrance to the **Cappelle Medicee** ❼ is behind the church. Michelangelo designed the Sagrestia Nuova as a monumental tomb for the Medici family, achieving a sense of harmony between sculpture and architecture unknown in Western art since classical Greece.

Just a few paces further on is Florence's gastronomic paradise, the elegant 19th-century iron and glass **Mercato Centrale** ❽ (*Via dell'Ariento. Mon–Sat 0730–1400; Sat mid-Sep–mid-Jun until 1700*) – inspired by the market at Les Halles in Paris which no longer exists. It is the town's main market and one of the best places in Italy to buy food or eat lunch – try **Da Nerbone** in the market or **ZaZa** on the Piazza. Both will serve a roast suckling pig sandwich and a glass of Chianti. *Coniglio* or *verdure fritte* (fried rabbit or vegetables) are also classics; braver stomachs will want to try *trippa alla fiorentina* (tripe in tomato sauce) and the tender, almost eggy *lampredotto* (stewed cow's stomach) served in broth (*umido*) or as a sandwich (*panino*).

Back on the main tour, walk around the cathedral past the newly restored **MUSEO DELL'OPERA DI SANTA MARIA DEL FIORE** ❹ where you can see Ghiberti's original Doors of Paradise. Now enter **Via del Proconsolo**, still a pedestrian zone, though you will have to practise the art of dodging taxis and mopeds while craning your neck to see city towers. The **Palazzo Nonfinito** ❾ contains the Museo Nazionale di Antropologia e Ethnologia, the first anthropological museum in Italy and the only one in Florence (founded in 1869, *free admission*). The Romanesque cloister of **Badia Fiorentina** ❿ is a small

Opposite
The Ponte Vecchio

oasis of peace in the middle of Florence. It was here, in the church, that Dante wistfully spied on Beatrice at Mass. The lanes around it are known as the 'Dante quarter'. Opposite the Badia is the grim façade and muscular tower of the **MUSEO NAZIONALE DEL BARGELLO ⓫**. Cross the Piazza San Firenze, a stone canyon of rustication.

Detour: The narrow street of Borgo dei Greci leads into Piazza Santa Croce. You are now entering a neighbourhood where residents actually outnumber tourists and there is a feeling of community in its narrow streets. The largest Franciscan church in Italy, **Santa Croce ⓬**, was the work of Arnolfo di Cambio (but the façade is 19th century). It has been called the Westminster Abbey of Florence. Inside are masterpieces by artists from Giotto to Donatello, and tomb-spotters will quickly alight on Michelangelo, Machiavelli, Galileo and Rossini. Dante's exile finally ended after 500 years when a pompous memorial was built for him in 1863. Few people pay the price of admission to see the **Cappella dei Pazzi** (1430–46) next door, which is now part of a museum – the **Museo dell'Opera di Santa Croce**. It is arguably the most perfect of all the designs created by Filippo Brunelleschi, built according to the golden mean (the principle behind the acropolis in Athens). Brunelleschi was also responsible for the cloister.

Walk right into the imposing Piazza della Signoria and along to the **PALAZZO VECCHIO ⓭**. This was the scene of the Bonfire of the Vanities, when Savonarola convinced Florentines to burn their carnival costumes and licentious paintings only a few short months before they subjected him to the same treatment (after he was declared a heretic). Beneath the three graceful arches of the **Loggia dei Lanzi ⓮** is a most remarkable open-air ensemble – Roman, Renaissance, Mannerist and 19th-century sculpture. Most of the figures are engaged in fighting, rape or decapitation. The name 'dei Lanzi' refers to the Swiss mercenaries of Cosimo I who stood on guard here. The **UFFIZI ⓯** stands at the south end of the square. Follow its length (and the waiting line of tourists) to the **PONTE VECCHIO ⓰**. The bridge is officially monopolised by goldsmiths though most people are taking pictures or snogging or both. Across the bridge, it is just one block further to the **PALAZZO PITTI ⓱**. The **GIARDINO DI BOBOLI ⓲** is behind the palace. From here, buses 36 and 37 return to the central train station.

Also worth exploring

There are sweeping views of Florence and the Arno valley from **Fiesole**, 8km outside the city. It is a refreshing break from congested streets and crowded museums. Fiesole was an Etruscan town and later a medieval rival to Florence until the Florentines destroyed it (on a flimsy pretext) in 1125. The Duomo San Romolo remains, as well as ruined Etruscan walls and an evocative Roman theatre.

0   500m

0   ¹/₄ mile

⇧ **North**

Via Circondaria

Via dello Statuto

Viale Venti Settembre

Viale Govanni Milton

Via Bolognese

Via Don G Minzoni

Via Fra' Bartolommeo

Viale Francesco Redi

Viale Spartaco Lavagnini

Via Filippo Strozzi

Delle Ghiacciaie

Via Filippo Strozzi

Fortezza
da Basso

Via G Dolfi

Via di B C Ridolfi

Via S C d'alessandria

Via delle Ruote

Via Zanobi

Via Bonifacio Lupi

Viale Giacomo Matteotti

Via Cherubini G Modena

Via G Benivieni

Pier Capponi

Via della Fortezza

Piazza della
Indipendenza

Via San Gallo

Via Santa Reparata

Via San Zanoli

Via Camillo Cavour

Lamarmora

Via a Via P A Micheli

Via Gino Capponi

Via Venezia

Benedetto Marcello

Via Pier Luigi da

Viale Belfiore

Via Monaco

Via Cittade

Via I Peri

Via della Fortezza

Via Guelfa

Via Ventisette Aprile

Museo di
S Marco

Giardino
della
Gherardesca

Via Giuseppe Pinti

Porte Nuove

Rosselli

Fratelli

Via Iacopo da Diacceto

Via Luigi Alamanni

Via Faenza

Via Valfonda

Via Cennini

Via Fiume

Via Nazionale

Via Panicale

Via Taddea

Accademia

Museo
Archeologico

Giusti

Borgo

Stazione Firenze
Santa Maria
Novella

Il Prato

Via della Scala

Via B.Rucellai

Via Degliori

Piazza della
Stazione

V S Caterina
da Siena

Via S d'Antonino

Mercato
Centrale

Via de' Ginori

Via Cavou

Via dei Servi

Via Ricasoli

Via degli Alfani

Via della Colonna

Via Laura

Via Garibaldi

Via P.Alazzuolo

V S Lucia N Rosa

Via dell' Abero

Via Canacci

Santa Maria
Novella

Piazza
S Maria
Novella

Cappelle
Medicee

V d Melarancio

San
Lorenzo

Palazzo
Medici-Riccardi

Via de' Pucci

Via Bufalini

Museo dell'
Opera di
Santa Maria
del Fiore

Pergola

Via Nuova Pinti

Via de'Caccini

Via Farini

Montebello

Borgo

Via Benedetta

Via Panzani

V de'Banchi

Piazza
San Giovanni

Duomo

Via dell' Oriuolo

Via S Egidio

Borgo

Via Fiesolana

Via de'Pilastri

Via di Mezzo

Via G Carducci

Amerigo Vespucci

Piazza di
Ognissanti

Via del Porcellana

Via d Sole

Via d'Agli

V de'Pecori

Battistero

Campanile

Piazza del
Duomo

Palazzo
Nonfinito

Badia
Fiorentina

Borgo degli Albizi

Via Pietrapiana

Macci

Piazza
Ghiberti

Ponte
Amerigo
Vespucci

Arno

Via Melegnano

Via del Moro

Via d Spada

V de Campidoglio

V d Trebbio

V Agli

V de'Pecori

Palazzo
Strozzi

Via Strozzi

V d Anselmi

Via Roma

Piazza della
Signoria

Museo Nazionale del Bargello

Via Ghibellina

Ponte alla
Carraia

Lungarno Soderini

Piazza del
Tiratoio

Piazza
di Cestello

Via Borgo San Frediano

L Corsini

Via Vigna Nuova

Via Porta Rossa

Loggia dei
Lanzi

Borgo dei Greci

Via dell' Anguillara

V di Vigna Vecchia

Piazza
S Croce

Borgo
S Croce

Di S Giuseppe

Via dei Malcontenti

Ponte S
Trinite

L degli Acciaiuolo

L Guicciardini

Ponte
Vecchio

d Ninna

Palazzo
Vecchio

Galleria
degli Uffizi

V d Saponai

V d Mosca

V dei Rustici

Via Magalotti

Santa Croce

V P Thouar

Via dei Benci

S Maria
del Carmine

S Spirito

Piazza del
Carmine

Piazza
Piattellina

Via S Monaca

Borgo Stella

Via dei Serragli

Via di S Spirito

Via Maffia

Borgo S Iacopo

Via de'Bardi

Via del Corso

V di Tintori

Via Tripoli

Lungarno della Zecca

Arno

Giardino
Torrigiani

Via del Campuccio

Via Sant Agostino

Via delle Caldaie

Via de' Pitti

Via Toscanella

Via S Felicita

Costa San Giorgio

Lungarno Torrigiani

Via dei Bardi

Piazza
de'Mozzi

Lung Serristori

Lungarno Serristori

Lung Benvenuto Cellini

Viale Francesco Petrarca

Via Romana

Via Guicciardini

Via Maggio

Palazzo
Pitti

Forte di
Belvedere

Via di San Leonardo

Via del Belvedere

Via dei Bastion

Giardino
di
Boboli

Viale G Poggi

Piazzale
Michelangelo

Piazza
Torquato
Tasso

V Giano Dellabella

Val di Pesa, Val d'Elsa and San Gimignano

Ratings

Architecture	●●●●●
Art	●●●●○
History	●●●●○
Scenery	●●●●○
Vineyards	●●●●○
Museums	●●●○○
Shopping	●●●○○
Nature	●●○○○

The resourceful Romans built a road – the *Via Cassia* – through the valley of the Elsa river. The same road, with potholes and detours, became the Via Francigena in the Middle Ages and a war zone between Florence and Siena. The region has a series of major towns, from unprepossessing Poggibonsi to charming Certaldo. The side roads are a different story. They offer scenery to rival neighbouring Chianti, but without tourists. The ridge road leading to Montespertoli cruises a landscape that, from a distance, would have looked scarcely different during the Renaissance. The final destination is San Gimignano, almost as famous for its skyline as New York. The flood of tourists does nothing to diminish its fascination. They just make it hard to find parking.

BARBERINO VAL D'ELSA

ⓘ Pieve Sant'Appiano €
Inside is a fine 12th-century relief of Archangel Michael and the dragon, which once decorated the portal.

Right
Barberino Val d'Elsa city gate

Enter the medieval part of this town through the city gate of Porta Fiorentina from the north or Porta Romana from the south. The Piazza Barberini is a fine medieval ensemble of the Palazzo Pretorio and Romanesque Pieve San Bartolomeo. A small Museo Civico occupies a former hospice for pilgrims. However, the real artistic highlight is a couple of kilometres southwest: the **Pieve Sant'Appiano** is one of the oldest (10th-century) parish churches in the region. A ruined baptistry attests to its former importance.

CERTALDO

ⓘ Pro Loco *Via Boccaccio 16; tel: 0571 652730; www.comune.certaldo.fi.it, www.prolococertaldo.it*

ⓝ Palazzo Pretorio € *Piazza del Vicariato; tel: 0571 61219. Open daily 0930–1400 and 1430–1900.*

The upper part of the city – Certaldo Alto – is a complete medieval town still fully encircled by its defensive walls with a magnificent view of San Gimignano from the Porta Rivellino. In the **Palazzo Pretorio**, built at the end of the 12th century by the counts Alberti, are a lavishly painted Sala delle Udienze and a 1490 fresco attributed to Benozzo Gozzoli that tells the story of Doubting Thomas, sticking his finger into Christ's bleeding midriff. Look for the strange *Tabernacle of the Executed* in the chapel, located near the former prison cells.

Casa del Boccaccio
*€ Via Boccaccio 18,
Certaldo Alto; tel: 0571
664208;
www.casaboccaccio.it. Open
daily 0930–1400 and
1430–1900.*

Giovanni Boccaccio, the greatest medieval Italian writer after Dante, was born here in 1313 and lived here for the last 12 years of his life. By then he had renounced women and literature for prayer and philosophy. 'I have returned to Certaldo,' he wrote, 'and here I have begun to find consolation for my life; and to taste and feel eternal happiness.' In 1944 an Allied bomb all but destroyed the **Casa del Boccaccio**, the house where the poet was born. However, it has been meticulously rebuilt. His simple marble tombstone is buried in the centre aisle of the Chiesa Santi Jacopo e Filippo next door. Modern Italian writers come here occasionally, kneel down and discreetly kiss his feet.

COLLE DI VAL D'ELSA

Pro Loco *Via
Campana 43; tel: 0577
922791; www.comune.colle-
di-val-d-elsa.si.it. Open daily
Jun–Oct 1000–1300,
1400–2000, shorter hours in
winter.*

**Museo
Archeologico 'R.
Bianchi Bandinelli'** *€
Piazza del Duomo 42; tel:
0577 920490. Open
May–Oct Tue–Sun
1030–1230 and
1630–1930, Nov–Apr
Tue–Fri 1530–1730.*

Colle di Val d'Elsa produces excellent glass and crystal ware. There is a glass workshop in the Vicolo della Fontanella (*off Piazza Santa Caterina*). For the history of all things crystal, check out the Museo del Cristallo (*via dei Fossi; tel: 0577 924135. Open Tue–Sun 1030–1230 and 1600–1930, shorter hours in winter*).

Colle is a medieval town of arcaded passageways that seem to swallow up residents and tourists alike. The brooding, monumental Porta Nuova, or Porta Salis, dominates the upper part of Colle. Designed by Giuliano da Sangallo, it is an imposing example of Renaissance architecture, built after a siege in 1479, and is flanked by two cylindrical towers with Guelph battlements.

The Duomo of Colle di Val d'Elsa is adjacent to the Palazzo Pretorio, seat of the well-organised **Museo Archeologico** (lots of Etruscan urns) that occupies a former medieval prison. The Duomo itself is baroque, with a 19th-century façade by neo-classical architect Agostino Fantastici. Inside are two precious works of art – the marble pulpit, decorated with bas-reliefs attributed to Giovanni da Maiano (architect of Siena's cathedral) located in the nave; and a bronze Crucifix above the high altar thought to be by Giambologna. The Via delle Volte is a tunnel 100m long which can be reached by a path branching off from Piazza del Duomo. Locally made blown-glass lampshades arranged in a succession of colours softly illuminate its gloom.

The **Torre di Arnolfo** (*Via del Castello 63*) is, according to tradition, the birthplace of Arnolfo di Cambio, the great Tuscan architect who built the Palazzo Vecchio, Duomo and Santa Croce in Florence. Colle Basso, the lower district, is a 19th-century town with many small workshops and a few modern factories, the sort of place that provides most modern Tuscans with a living.

Above
Colle di Val d'Elsa

SAN CASCIANO

ⓘ Museo di Arte Sacra € *Via Roma 31; tel: 055 8256381; www.san-casciano.com. Open May–Sep Sat 1700–1930 (holidays 1000–1230 and 1630–1930), Oct–Apr Sat 1630–1900 (holidays 1000–1230 and 1600–1900), or by appointment.*

ⓘ Sant'Andrea a Percussina marks the beginning of the Chianti Classico region (*see page 66*). An office of the Chianti Vino Classico Consorzio is located across the street from the Machiavelli Inn and Museum at Via Scopeti 155; *tel: 055 82285; www.chianticlassico.com.* It provides detailed maps showing the location of over 600 Chianti wine estates.

Below
Pressing mats used to produce olive oil

Although mostly a 19th-century town, San Casciano has some remarkable works of art from its medieval days. The 1304 **Santa Maria sul Prato** is one of the most interesting churches in the region and possesses a Crucifixion by Simone Martini, part of a triptych by Ugolino di Nerio and a marble chancel by Giovanni di Balducci da Pisa. The **Museo di Arte Sacra** displays religious art from a church destroyed in World War II. An early work by Ambrogio Lorenzetti takes pride of place alongside an enormous candelabra that was created for Sant'Antimo (*see page 92*) by a French Cistercian monk.

Machiavelli wrote *The Prince* (as well as a series of pornographic farces) while living in exile in the village of **Sant'Andrea a Percussina**, 2km to the north of here. The inn where he lived is still an inn and now bears his name; there is a tiny museum next door only open when the restaurateurs/owners are not making pasta.

San Casciano is known for olive oil rather than wine but the grapes that grow between San Casciano and Mercatale (5km southeast) go towards making two of the most expensive wines in Italy – the so-called 'super-Tuscans' Tignanello (80 per cent Sangiovese, 20 per cent Cabernet) and Solaia (100 per cent Cabernet). The Marchese Antinori, descended from a family of medieval silk merchants, developed them between 1971 and 1979. The family was the first large Chianti producer to depart from the 19th-century Chianti 'formula' (*see page 70*) and launch a completely new wine.

SAN GIMIGNANO

ⓘ Pro Loco *Piazza Duomo 1; tel: 0577 940008; fax: 0577 940903; e-mail: prolocsg@tin.it; www.sangimignano.net. Open Mar–Oct 0900–1300 and 1500–1900, Nov–Feb 0900–1300 and 1400–1800. A Biglietto Cumulativo offers admission to all museums for a single price.*

ⓜ Museo Civico e Pinacoteca €€
Palazzo del Popolo, Piazza del Duomo; tel: 0577 990348; www.museisenesi.org. Open Mar–Oct 0930–1900, Nov–Feb 1000–1730.

Torre Grossa €€ *Palazzo del Popolo, Piazza del Duomo. Open Mar–Oct, same hours as Museo Civico.*

◠ La Buca di Montauto *Via San Giovanni 16; tel: 0577 940407. Picnic supplies include salami from cinghiale (wild boar).*

A town of some 8,000 inhabitants, San Gimignano is flooded by eight million visitors a year. During the Middle Ages, San Gimignano was an important stop on the Via Francigena, the route taken by pilgrims on their way to Rome. It also made a killing in saffron. The plague of 1348 decimated the population and, in 1353, its town council agreed by a majority of one to a Florentine takeover. Its local history involved the usual suspects – Guelphs and Ghibellines – engaged in conspiracy and murder. In those days, Tuscan towns bristled with towers from every *palazzo* – 72 in the case of San Gimignano within the space of a couple of hundred square metres. In places such as Florence, towers were eventually lowered by city ordinances against private warfare. In San Gimignano, by contrast, many of the original towers remain.

Culturally speaking, the town justly calls itself a 'museum of Tuscan art and architecture'. Too small to develop a local style, San Gimignano imported leading artists from Florence and Siena instead.

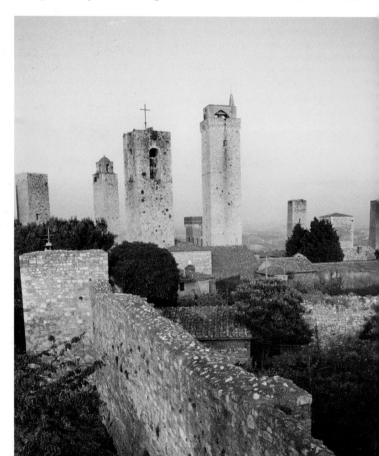

Right
San Gimignano

Collegiata Santa Maria Assunta (and Cappella di Santa Fina)
€ *Piazza del Duomo, tel: 0577 940316. Open Apr–Oct Mon–Fri 0930–1930, Sat 0930–1700, Sun 1300–1700; Nov–mid-Jan and Mar Mon–Sat 0930–1700, Sun 1300–1700; mid-Jan–Feb for religious services only.*

Museo della Tortura €€
Museo Criminale Medioevale, Via Castello 1/3; tel: 0577 942243; www.museodellatortura.com. Open daily 1000–1900. Claiming to be the 'most disturbing exhibition in the world', this museum does offer a convincing anthology of human cruelty.

The **Palazzo del Popolo** (town hall) houses the **Museo Civico e Pinacoteca** with 13th- to 16th-century works from Florentine and Sienese schools and offers access to the **Torre Grossa**, the only one of San Gimignano's towers that you can climb. The 12th-century Duomo was modified by Giuliano da Maiano. The **Collegiata Santa Maria Assunta**, though plain on the outside, conceals a majestic interior that is a revelation of fresco painting. The inner wall of the façade displays the *Martyrdom of St Sebastian* (1465) by Benozzo Gozzoli. Above it is the *Last Judgement* by Taddeo di Bartolo. The medieval equivalent of a snuff movie, it stars devils with green snake penises that rape, sodomise and disembowel the damned. In the **Cappella di Santa Fina**, frescos by Renaissance painter Ghirlandaio depict a woman – Santa Fina, San Gimignano's patron saint – being gnawed by rats. Her finely carved sarcophagus is also in the chapel. In the fresco on the left, Ghirlandaio includes a portrait of himself standing behind a bishop during Mass.

Most tourists tend to overlook the church of Sant'Agostino at the north end of town. Behind its plain Romanesque-Gothic façade is a magnificent collection of art, particularly the vivid fresco cycle about the life of St Augustine by Benozzo Gozzoli (in the apse). There is also a marble altar sculpted by Benedetto da Maiano in the chapel of St Bartolo and two St Sebastians by Benozzo Gozzoli from 1464, one with, and more unusually, one without, arrows. Praying to St Sebastian (or commissioning pictures of him) was the 14th-century idea of treating a plague epidemic. The second painting was executed in a year when the plague didn't reach the city.

Vernaccia di San Gimignano

Vernaccia is a type of grape, not a brand of wine. The word translates roughly as 'belonging here' and it has been cultivated around San Gimignano since the 13th century. The English began drinking it in the 16th century. There are two contrasting types of wine made from the same grape: a mass-marketed, crisp and colourless drink, almost neutral in flavour, that seems ubiquitous at summer parties; and the straw-coloured vintage with a rich flavour that was one of Michelangelo's favourite wines. San Gimignano producers also make lots of Chianti Colli Senesi, which tastes much like Chianti though is rarely as good and never as expensive.

What to drink

Teruzzi & Puthod *Ponte a Rondolino, Località Casale 20; tel: 0577 941076; www.teruzzieputhod.it.* Outstanding oaked Vernaccia, *Terre di Tufia*, and a good Sangiovese.

Giovanni Panizzi *Southeast of San Gimignano near Santa Margherita between San Gimignano and Racciano; tel: 0577 941576; www.panizzi.it.* This local hero of Vernaccia tradition produces exceptional Vernaccia Riserva and Chianti Colli Senesi.

Montenidoli *Southeast of San Gimignano; tel: 0577 941565; www.montenidoli.com.* Elisabetta Fagiuoli produces several interesting wines: *Fiore* (made with soft-pressed grapes), *Tradizionale* (macerated before fermentation) and barrel-aged *Carato*. *Sono Montenidoli* is a blend based on Sangiovese.

Accommodation and food

C'era Una Volta €€ *Via Certaldese 3, Lucardo; tel: 0571 669578. On the road between Montespertoli and Certaldo. Closed Tue; also mid-Jan–mid-Feb.* A country *trattoria* with a view and food 'like it used to be': starters such as *pappardelle al sugo di coniglio* (noodles with rabbit sauce) and *tagliatelle ai porcini* give way grudgingly to main courses such as a *frittura* of chicken, rabbit and vegetables. It is as good a place as any in the area for a *bistecca fiorentina* (one is enough for two people). Even the house wine is a full-bodied Chianti C'era Una Volta.

La Cisterna €€ *Piazza della Cisterna 23, San Gimignano; tel: 0577 940328; fax: 0577 942080; www.hotelcisterna.it.* Former cloister with 17th-century Florentine furniture and fabulous views from (some) rooms of the city and countryside.

Il Frantoio €€ *Via Matteotti 31, Marcialla (near Lucardo); tel: 055 8074244. Closed Mon; also Tue and lunch in winter, last three weeks of Jan and two weeks in Jul and Aug.* Impeccable food served, most of the year, in a garden. From home-made *pasta alla puttanesca* and *gnocchi di patate* (potatoes) to a signature *fritto misto* (lightly breaded and fried meat and vegetables).

Below
The walled city of Certaldo

Osteria Delle Catene €€ *Via Mainardi 18, San Gimignano; tel: 0577 941966, closed Wed.* Before tourism, saffron was San Gimignano's main source of wealth and it finds its way into many recipes of this small *trattoria* – *zuppa medioevale, lingua in salsa allo zafferano* (tongue in saffron sauce) and a flat bread called *torta di farro e zafferano*. The *nana col cavolo nero* (duck with black cabbage) or *coniglio alla Vernaccia* (rabbit in white wine sauce) are just fine without saffron.

Il Paretaio €€ *Strada delle Ginestre 12, Barberino Val d'Elsa; tel: 055 8059218; fax: 055 8059231; www.ilparetaio.it.* A Tuscan ranch that rents six rooms with private bathrooms to overnight guests. Ideal for anyone who likes horse riding and rustic living.

Hotel L'Antico Pozzo €€€ *Via San Matteo 87, San Gimignano; tel: 0577 942014; fax: 0577 942117; www.anticopozzo.com.* Elegant and intimate hotel with exquisite period furnishings.

Osteria del Vicario €€€ *Via Rivellino 3, Certaldo; tel: 0571 668228; www.osteriadelvicario.it.* Built on the site of a 13th-century vicarage with a delightful terrace that has views far and wide. There are five rooms in the main building (best) and six in an annexe down the road.

Suggested tour

Total distance: 142km; detours add 9km and 15km (both return).

Time: Two to three days at a leisurely pace. If you only have a day, concentrate on San Gimignano while still taking time to enjoy the scenery along the way.

Links: This route has the same starting point as that in Chianti Classico (*see page 72*) and runs parallel to it for some distance. You can cross over from Poggibonsi on the serpentine N429 driving east to Castellina in Chianti (and the N222). Volterra is 36km west from Colle di Val d'Elsa (on N68) (*see page 162*).

Route: The easiest way to begin this route is to leave **Florence ❶** (or circumnavigate it) via the *autostrada*, exiting at Firenze-Certosa; at the roundabout, take the *Via Cassia* in the direction of **SAN CASCIANO ❷**. From San Casciano, follow the road for Cerbaia. What follows is a succession of ridge roads, each one more captivating than the last. From Cerbaia, turn left (southwest) to **Montespertoli**, known for its wine fair, the *Mostra del Chianti* (*last Sun in May to first Sun in Jun*). Press on southeast part of the way towards Tavarnelle. At the hamlet of **Lucardo**, follow the road southwest to **CERTALDO ❸**, park in the lower town and walk, or take the funicular, up to Certaldo Alto, the historic part of the city – little changed since Boccaccio lived there in the 14th century. The road out of town is clearly signposted for **SAN GIMIGNANO ❺**.

Detour: Few churches have a more poetic setting than **Pieve di Cellole ❹**, nestled in a hilltop cypress grove off the road to San Gimignano. It was the inspiration of Puccini's opera, *Suor Angelica*. A simple Romanesque building (1193–1238), it is nevertheless striking for the quality of its medieval workmanship.

Leaving San Gimignano, follow the signs for Volterra. The road runs parallel to the Riserva Naturale Castelvecchio, past a prison and ends in a T-junction at Castel San Gimignano. Turn left (east) on the N68. An uneventful road, graced by several rows of birch trees, sneaks up on **COLLE DI VAL D'ELSA ❻**. Below the town, it drops to the Elsa river and lands you in industrial **Poggibonsi ❼**. During the Middle Ages, it was a *città imperiale* – a Ghibelline city – of some importance until one day in 1270 its Guelph neighbours (Florence, San Gimignano and Col d'Elsa) joined forces and annihilated it. If you penetrate that far, there are a couple of fine medieval buildings in its nucleus. Otherwise, follow the signs for the *autostrada* (but don't get on it) and Florence. You will find yourself on the Roman *Via Cassia* again (N2). **BARBERINO VAL D'ELSA ❽** is on this ancient road, at the top of a ridge. **Tavarnelle ❾** was another important stop on the Roman *Via Cassia* and its medieval successor, but most of the houses you see today are from the 18th and 19th centuries. The Santa Lucia al Borghetto was once part of a Franciscan convent.

Below
San Gimignano's Piazza della Cisterna

Detour: Follow the signs for San Donato and take the turn for Sambuca. Just half a kilometre north, the **Badia a Passignano ❿** is clearly marked. The first glimpse – 2km up a farm road – is dramatic. It would be hard to find a more picturesque and solitary corner of Chianti than the hilltop it occupies. The monastery was once one of the most important in Italy, having been founded by Benedictines in the 11th century. The 13th-century church has been done over in baroque style but the refectory still has a Renaissance treasure – Domenico Ghirlandaio's *Last Supper* (*unfortunately only open to visitors on Sun 1600–1800 in summer and 1500–1700 in winter, or by prior arrangement, tel: 055 8071622; www.badia-a-passignano.com*). The monastery has an excellent wine estate, Poggio al Sole, that makes an intense Chianti Classico.

Continue north on the N2 and return to Florence.

Also worth exploring

The Sienese built the fortified town of **Monteriggioni** in 1213–19 along the northern boundary of their territory in the spirit of 'good walls make good neighbours' – 570m of wall topped by 16 towers that Dante compared to 'ugly giants'.

Chianti Classico

Ratings

Scenery	●●●●●
Vineyards	●●●●●
Food and drink	●●●●○
Villas	●●●●○
Architecture	●●●○○
Nature	●●●○○
Shopping	●●●○○
Museums	●○○○○

The region between Florence and Siena is Chianti – or Chianti 'Classico' as it now calls itself, because neighbouring wine regions tend to borrow its famous name. The Chianti hills form a spine supporting a succession of steep valleys. The Chiantigiana road (N222) links them, rising and plunging through groves of silver-grey olive trees, swathes of precisely angled vines, brown chestnut woods and ridges marked by dark cypresses. Most of the castles and villas are secluded and Chianti feels surprisingly empty. Its past was so violent that no one dared to build a city. Florentine and Sienese artists, however, created a blissful mythic Chianti in some of the world's first landscape paintings and its legendary wine completed an identification with the good things in life – Chiantishire to the British. *Altro luogo come il Chianti no c'è* is what Italians say – 'there is no other place like it'.

CASTELLINA IN CHIANTI

La Bottega del Vino di Cantina Orlandi *Via della Rocca 13; tel: 057 7741110; www.enobottega.it.* An outlet for the town's wine co-operative.

The liveliest and most *simpatico* town on the N222 (if you can forgive it for having a fertiliser factory at one end). Furthermore, it has a worthwhile *Centro Storico* up its sleeve. From the long covered street of Via delle Volte, once part of its ramparts, you have a wide view of the green hills that surround it.

GREVE IN CHIANTI

Informazioni turistiche *Viale G. da Verrazzano 59; tel: 055 8546287; fax: 055 8544149; www.comune.greve-in-chianti. fi.it and www.greve-in-chianti. com. Open Mon–Sat 0930–1300 and 1430–1900, shorter hours in winter.*

Greve's main square is the triangular Piazza Matteotti. In the middle stands a dramatic bronze of explorer Giovanni da Verrazzano. In many respects a more able explorer than Christopher Columbus, he explored the actual mainland of North America, Brazil and the mouth of Hudson Bay (New York, at least, honours his memory with a Verrazzano bridge between Staten Island and Brooklyn). An impressive *Sagra dell'Uva* (grape festival) takes place here in September.

⊕ Castello di Verrazzano €€ *Tel: 055 854243; www.verrazzano.com. Open Mon–Fri 1100–1500 (reservations necessary).* Accommodation (two apartments and seven double rooms) is available in the recently restored farmhouse near the castle.

Castello di Uzzano € *Via Fiorentina 5; tel: 055 8544851; www.agricolauzzano.com.* Call ahead for an appointment.

Villa Vignamaggio €€ *Via Petriolo 5.* To visit the villa and wine estate, you must call ahead. *Tel: 055 854661; www.vignamaggio.com*

⊙ Antica Macelleria Falorni *Piazza Matteotti 66–71; www.falorni.it.* An extensive array of cold meats, including various cured hams, wild boar salami, *finocchiona* (fennel salami), *pancetta* ten different ways and *prosciutto* from a local species of pig, the *brada senesi.*

Enoteca del Chianti Classico *Piazzetta Santa Croce 8; tel: 055 853297.* A compendious selection of Chianti wines as well as other local products such as Vin Santo and olive oil.

Entoca Le Cantine *Galleria Delle Cantine 2; tel: 0558 546404. Open daily.* This huge wine shop has over 140 wines available to taste and buy. The shop also houses a museum.

The area's real attractions are the castles and villas in the surrounding hills: the **Castello di Verrazzano** wine estate, which belonged to the famous navigator, is just north of nearby Greti. He might well have asked himself why he ever left this idyllic home as he watched cannibals prepare to slaughter and eat him in 1528 somewhere in the lower Antilles. The medieval **Castello di Uzzano** was converted with ineffable skill into a Renaissance pleasure villa by the 16th-century architect Andrea Orcagna. It is also a fine wine estate and ideal for an afternoon picnic beneath ancient cedars, followed by a romp through the garden's green maze. Some 6km south of Greve and 390m high, **Villa Vignamaggio** is one of the most romantic spots in Chianti. Its charm was nearly milked dry by ex-luvvies Kenneth Branagh and Emma Thompson in the film version of *Much Ado About Nothing*. It is certainly possible that it was in this villa that Lisa Gherardini stood for her portrait in 1503. The result was *La Gioconda* – the Mona Lisa.

IMPRUNETA

Pro Loco *Via Piazza Garibaldi; tel: 055 2313729; www.impruneta. com, www.proimpruneta.rtd.it. Open Mon–Sat 0900–1300 and 1500–1800, Sun 0900–1300 (shorter hours in winter).*

The tourist office has a list of local terracotta workshops.

A working town that has been synonymous with terracotta for centuries, Impruneta was the place where Brunelleschi shopped for tiles for the dome of the cathedral in Florence. The local clay also went into the terracotta tabernacle for the Chapel of the Cross created by Michelozzo for **Santa Maria dell'Impruneta**. Luca della Robbia sculpted the terracotta statues of SS Paul and Luke for the church's Chapel of the Madonna. Impruneta is also known for straw hats and an annual horse and mule fair in October.

PANZANO

Enoteca Il Vinaio *Via S. Maria 22; tel: 055 852603. Closed Tue.* There are bottles from all over Italy at this wine shop, but Chianti takes pride of place. You can eat small bits of this and that while sampling them on the leafy terrace around the back.

Bottega Carlo Fagiani *Via Giovanni di Verrazzano 17; tel: 055 852239; www.carlofagiani.com.* A wizard in leather who produces chic leather goods, handbags, clothing and shoes made to order.

A friendly fortified town high on a 500m hill next to the ruins of a 1260 castle. You can still see its remains behind the Chiesa Santa Maria after climbing up the village street – Via Verrazzano. On the second weekend in September, it is Panzano's turn to host a big wine festival. Panzano is the epicentre of a wine region known as *Conca d'Oro* that produces some of Chianti's best wines.

RADDA IN CHIANTI

Pro Loco *Piazza Castello 6; tel: 0577 738494; www.raddainchiantilife.com. Open daily 1000–1245 and 1500–1900.*

Above
Panzano

Left
Chianti farms

Tiny, picture-perfect Radda, straddling a ridge between the Pesa and Arbia valleys in the wooded Monti del Chianti, was the capital of the *Lega del Chianti* in 1475. The League also included Castellina and Gaiole. It still has an impressive Palazzo del Podestà, a ruined castle, walls and two towers. Today, it caters to wine tourists with places to taste and buy excellent local wines such as *Vignale* (*Piazza XX Settembre 23* in the hotel of the same name) and *Vigna Vecchia* (*Sdrucciolo di Piazza*). The famous Sangiovese wine, *Le Pergole Torte*, is made by winemaker Signore Sergio Manetti in Monte Vertine, a small fortified village 3km north of Radda (*tel: 0577 738009; fax: 0577 738265; www.montevertine.it*). The estate's wine, grappa and olive oil all sell out fast. The castle-village of **Volpaia** (another 3km north) is even more perfect than Radda and boasts an even better wine – *Castello di Volpaia*.

Accommodation and food

Volpaia *Piazza della Cisterna I, Radda in Chianti; tel: 0577 738066; www.volpaia.com.* The unlikely setting for modern art exhibitions, mounted in September in the early Renaissance Commenda di San Eufrosino, a former pilgrim hospice. *Free.*

There is almost no industry, light or otherwise, in Chianti Classico. Some traditional crafts are still going strong: the production of terracotta, utensils in olive wood, woven wicker baskets, wrought iron and blown glass for wine-flasks and demijohns.

The area known as Chianti Classico has no major towns to speak of (Greve in Chianti hardly qualifies). There is a lot of *agriturismo* with a range of accommodation though much of it is at the luxury end of the spectrum. Towns along the *Via Cassia* such as Colle di Val d'Elsa have more options and a wider range of prices.

Carloni € *Via G Puccini 24, Gaiole; tel: 0577 749549. Closed Wed.* Simple restaurant on the outskirts of Gaiole. Great local food and wine.

Casa La Mura € *2km south of Panzano; tel/fax: 055 852138.* The gracious and warm-hearted Ciapini family lets several well-equipped apartments among their olive groves. They are available by the night when it is not high season.

Nerbone € *Piazza Matteotti Giacomo 22, Greve in Chianti; tel: 055 853308; closed Tue.* A small place with slow service where workers and tourists rub elbows over Tuscan comfort food: soup, sausages, stews and *lampredotto* (stewed cow's stomach).

Badia a Coltibuono €€ *Across from the abbey, Gaiole in Chianti; tel: 0577 749031; www.coltibuono.com. Closed Mon.* Gourmet food cooked the Luisa de Medici way and served, in summer, on the leafy terrace of this former monastery.

Villa Vignamaggio €€€ *Via Petriolo 5, Greve in Chianti; tel: 0558 54661; fax: 0558 544468; www.vignamaggio.com.* Sleep here in the footsteps of Mona Lisa – her former villa is now an *agriturismo* (Tuscan country lodging). The five-star luxury includes swimming pools, a Jacuzzi® and tennis courts. You've probably seen the garden already, in Kenneth Branagh's film of *Much Ado About Nothing*.

Chianti cuisine is based on 'poor' but savoury dishes: *ribollita* (a 'twice-cooked' vegetable and bread soup), minestrone, grilled meats, tripe and fried zucchini flowers and the famous *cantucci* biscuits accompanied by the dessert wine, Vin Santo.

Opposite
Badia a Coltibuono

Chianti

The Latin poet Fluvio Testi said that Tuscan wine 'kisses you and bites you and makes you shed sweet tears'. In Chianti itself, it was medieval monks at Badia a Passignano and Badia a Coltibuono who advanced the cause of the big red wine. Chianti in the strictest sense of the word, however, was 'invented' in 1835 when Bettino Ricasoli came up with a modern 'formula' based on the traditional Sangiovese grape and a special fermentation process to give it more depth.

The 1960s were the low point in the long history of Chianti; in those days, low-grade Chianti drunk from a straw-covered flask – the *fiasco* (!) – caused many a hangover. But Chianti winemakers have made an extraordinary comeback in the space of a generation and are realising its potential to be, again, one of the world's great wine regions. Areas such as Castellina, Gaiole and Radda are the source of heady red wines that only get better with time.

Suggested tour

Chianti is a region where it is hard not to lose your way. The wine estates, castles and abbeys are scattered through a surprisingly rural region where vineyards alternate with bare hillsides, dense stands of wood and shrub, and alleys of cypresses with puzzling signs at the entrance. A good map is essential. Try to get *Il Chianti* (1:70,000) from a local tourist board or the APT in Florence.

Below
Chianti country

Total distance: 115km; detours add 20km, 10km (both return) and 8km (last detour is an alternative route that rejoins the N408 south).

Time: One could follow this route as an idyllic way of getting from Florence to Siena in a single day; or explore it during an extended *soggiorno* in the hills of Chianti Classico; or sell up, move here and, like American author Frances Mayes, write a book about your 'life-transforming experience'. Where the humbler pursuits of driving and wine-tasting are concerned, count on everything taking twice as long as you would imagine.

Links: The route runs parallel, in places, to the route of the previous chapter and has the same starting point.

Route: It is hard to find your way out of **Florence ❶** on the N222, because the signs command the driver to make simultaneous left and right turns (even Italian roads are subject to the laws of physics). It is far easier (or less fiendishly difficult) to get on the *autostrada* and exit at Firenze-Certosa; from the roundabout, take the *Via Cassia* in the direction of San Casciano and, after 1km, the narrow road towards **IMPRUNETA ❷**; in only five minutes, you will be cruising the hills of Chianti. The road joins the elusive N222 after Impruneta; press on to **GREVE IN CHIANTI ❸** . This particular stretch is full of sudden bottlenecks in the form of villages, cyclists and heavily wooded blind turns. In other words, it is utterly charming.

Detour: Upon entering Greve from the north, there is a tiny road that veers up to **Montefioralle ❹**, an almost perfectly oval fortified village with a panoramic walk that triggers the 'wannalivehere' Tuscan fantasy. For centuries, until the conquest of Siena, this was a Florentine military outpost that guarded the route north. Amerigo Vespucci – the explorer from whom America got its name – was born here in 1451 (while mapping the coast of Brazil, he thought he was in the seas of southern Asia; only later did he realise his mistake).

An even narrower road (with a traffic light for the one-lane stretch) takes you through a dreamy, hilly tableau of olive trees and vineyards towards **Badia a Passignano ❺** (*see page 64*). It eventually turns into a quality dirt road that twists through more vineyards on its way to the 11th-century abbey. On the way back, you will cross an intersection with a road signposted for Panzano. If you take it, you won't be sorry. It has sweeping views east of Chianti's hills and west of the Val di Pesa. You can either backtrack to Greve or skip it.

A couple of wide curves soar up to the lower end of **PANZANO ❻**, which occupies a narrow ridge. As in so many places, the interesting part of town is at the top of the hill. A rigorous amount of hairpinning will take you to **CASTELLINA IN CHIANTI ❼** .

Detour: Just five minutes south of Castellina is the village of **Fonterutoli ❽**, famous for the wine estate of the Mazzei family and for some of the best olive oil in Tuscany. The Castello di Fonterútoli (*tel: 0577 73571; www.fonterutoli.it*) has an earthy Osteria with a small wine bar where you sample the estate's wine before buying it.

Turn east on to the N429 and drive 10km to **RADDA IN CHIANTI** ❾. From there, drive further east (ignoring the N408 south) up into the heavily forested hills. On a ridge (628m) in the middle of an oak forest, **Badia a Coltibuono** ❿ moulders in profound peace, only rarely disturbed by modest tours. The abbey was founded almost a thousand years ago, in 1050, and Lorenzo the Magnificent was often a guest here in the 15th century. Its wine estate and restaurant are now popular among foodies and occasionally used as a venue for upmarket cooking classes by cookbook author Luisa de Medici.

There is not much to **Gaiole in Chianti** ⓫ itself. No one ever even bothered to build a wall around it; it served rather as a marketplace for the surrounding area. However, it is completely surrounded by castles, monasteries and quirky mountain villages. You could easily spend a couple of weeks ferreting them all out.

Detour: The area around Gaiole was the historic fault line between the territories of Florence and Siena. Some 3km south of Gaiole, the beginning of the Strada dei Castelli (Castle Road) is indicated by unmissable signs. The **Castello di Meleto** ⓬ was, in its 13th-century heyday, an almost impregnable place behind its cylindrical towers. The 'formula' for Chianti was created by Barone Bettino Ricasoli at **Castello di Brolio** ⓭ in 1835: a mixture of red (Sangiovese and Canaiolo) with an itsy bitsy bit of white (Malvasia and Trebbiano) grapes. The castle and wine estate now belong to Seagrams and its wines don't quite live up to its tradition.

Follow the signs for **Siena** to get back on the N408 and arrive in Siena after about an hour.

Also worth exploring

The hill of **Monteaperti** lies just off the N326. Sienese Ghibellines and Florentine Guelphs demonstrated once and for all that Tuscany was not big enough for both of them here on 4 September 1260. It was the bloodiest battle fought on Italian soil in the Middle Ages. A simple pyramid in a cypress grove recalls the event. Siena was victorious, killing 10,000 Florentine soldiers and capturing 15,000. The painter Duccio celebrated the victory with an impressive *Maestà* in the cathedral of Siena (now in the museum of the Duomo Nuovo). It was, however, a short-lived triumph. The Pope excommunicated the entire population of Siena while Guelph armies destroyed its forces in the decade that followed. Merchants with Guelph sympathies took power in Siena and pursued a policy of peace. The decades of their rule were marked by a period of great prosperity and artistic achievement.

Siena

Ratings

Architecture	●●●●●
Art	●●●●○
Food and drink	●●●●○
Museums	●●●●○
Children	●●●○○
Shopping	●●●○○
Nature	●●○○○
Scenery	●●○○○

Siena and Florence, the two cities that fought bitterly in the Middle Ages to control the destiny of Tuscany, remain worlds apart. Siena is a place where the Renaissance never triumphed – an isolated hilltop floating in a Gothic time warp. Incredibly, its major monuments were built in a mere six decades between the 13th and 14th centuries, until the Black Death came to town in 1348 and swept away two-thirds of the population. Its lifeblood ebbed with the decline of the Via Francigena, the route of trade and pilgrimage to Rome. Florence conquered Siena in 1555 after a terrible siege, putting an end to the last Republican government in Italy. In 1956, Siena reasserted its liberty by saying 'no' to the 20th century and barring traffic from its ancient core.

Sights

ⓘ Informazioni turistiche *Piazza del Campo 56; tel: 0577 280551; fax: 0577 270676; www.terresiena.it. Open daily 0900–1900.*

ⓑ Battistero di San Giovanni € *Piazza San Giovanni; tel: 0577 283048; www.operaduomo.siena.it. Open Mar–May and Sep–Oct 0930–1900, Jun–Aug 0930–2000, Nov–Feb 1000–1700.*

Battistero di San Giovanni
The Battistero (Baptistry) di San Giovanni (built in 1316) sits behind the Duomo where the crypt should be. The white marble façade and its three large doorways were added later (1382). The interior seems to rotate inexorably towards the magnificent baptismal font, attributed to Jacopo della Quercia. It also bears works by Donatello and Lorenzo Ghiberti. Many other works add to the sensory overload: bronze figures by Giovanni di Turino and Goro di Neroccio as well as frescos by Vecchietta (*c.* 1450), Michele di Matteo Lambertini and Benvenuto di Giovanni. The sumptuous cross-vaulted ceiling invites much craning of the neck but, fortunately, there are wood-framed mirrors that allow you to contemplate its reflection in your lap.

0 200m
0 150 yards

North

Porta
Camollia

Via di Biagio di Montluc

Via Ricasoli

Via di Camollia

Via Campansi

Via Giuseppe Garibaldi

Via della Stufa Secca

Via dei Monnanini

Viale Sardegna

Viale Giuseppe Mazzini

Viale Don Giovanni Minzoni

Via Simone Martini

Via Simone Martini

Porta
Ovile

Via Baldassarre Peruzzi

Viale Armando Diaz

Viale Rinaldo Franci

La Lizza

La Lizza

La Lizza

Piazza della
Libertà

Viale Venticinque Aprile

**Stadio
Comunale**

Viale del Mille

Viale Curtatone

Piazza
Giacomo
Matteotti

Via della Sapienza

Via di Vallerozzi

Via dei Rossi

S Francesco

Piazza
S Francesco

Piazza
Salimbeni

Banchi di Sopra

**Oratorio di
San Bernardino**

orte di
Barbara

S Domenico

**Casa di Santa
Caterina**

Via di S Caterina

Via dei Termini

Via delle Terme

Via Banchi di Sopra

Via Sallustio Bandini

Porta
Fontebranda

**Battistero di
San Giovanni**

Croce del
Travaglio

Fonte Gaia

Banchi di Sotto

**Piazza del
Campo**

Via di Pantaneto

Via dei Pispini

Porta
Pispini

ia Esterna di
Fontebranda

**Ospedale di
Santa Maria
della Scala**

Via del Fosso di S Ansano

Duomo

**Museo
dell'Opera
Metropolitana**

Casato di Sotto

Via di Città

**Palazzo
Pubblico**

Via del Porrione

Piazza
del
Mercato

Via di Salicotto

Via S Martino

Via dei Pispini

Via Roma

Via Paolo Mascagni

**Pinacoteca
Nazionale**

Via S Pietro

Via Giovanni Dupré

S Agostino

Via di Fontanella

Porta
Laterina

Pian dei Mantellini

**S Maria
del Carmine**

Via delle Cerchia

**Orto
Botanico**

Via Pier Andrea Mattioli

Porta
Roma

Via Girolamo Gigli

Strada di Certosa

Via S Marco

Via delle Sperandie

Porta
S Marco

Via Massetana

Porta
Tufi

Via Enea Silvioni
Piccolomini

🏛 **Duomo** *Piazza del Duomo 8; tel: 0577 283048; www.operaduomo.siena.it. Open Jun–Aug Mon–Sat 1030–2000, Sun 1330–1730 (inlaid marble floor uncovered); Mar–May and Sep–Oct Mon–Sat 1030–1930, Sun 1330–1730; Nov–Feb Mon–Sat 1030–1830, Sun 1330–1730. Entrance to cathedral free, cupola €.*

Libreria Piccolomini € *Piazza del Duomo (inside the cathedral). Same opening hours as the Duomo.*

Museo dell'Opera Metropolitana €€ *Piazza Duomo 8; tel: 0577 283048; www.operaduomo.siena.it. Same details and opening hours as Battistero.*

Duomo

The Duomo Santa Maria (cathedral) of Siena is at the highest point in the city (346m). A tale of two styles, it was begun in 1200 in Romanesque fashion, then, in 1258, Cistercian monks (who also worked on the monastery of San Galgano) took over and built the transept, dome and choir in a revolutionary new Gothic style. The great sculptor Giovanni Pisano worked on the marble façade between 1284 and 1297. The campanile was finished in 1313.

The interior, in the form of a Latin cross, with a nave and two aisles divided by Romanesque pillars and arches, is highly evocative. There is a cornice of the nave and presbytery overpopulated with 172 busts of popes above and 32 busts of emperors below. The floor is divided into 52 panels of inlaid, etched and coloured marble representing various tales. Unfortunately, many are under wraps on any given day. In the left (north) transept is the cathedral's greatest work of art, the pulpit (1266–8) by Nicola Pisano, only fully appreciated after multiple drops of the coin in the illumination strongbox. The **Libreria Piccolomini** has a lavish Renaissance interior and is covered in frescos (1502–9) by Pinturicchio that tell the life story of Anea Silvio Piccolomini, the poet who became Pope (*see Pienza, page 100*).

Duomo Nuovo (Museo dell'Opera Metropolitana)

The cathedral is only a small part of the Duomo Nuovo (new cathedral) planned by the city fathers in 1316, which might have been completed had not the plague intervened. The sheer ambition of the Sienese builders bordered on lunacy. Their idea was to use the existing cathedral as the transept of a gargantuan new edifice that would surpass anything in Pisa or Florence. The cathedral choir was moved to the east and the baptistry constructed as part of the foundation while work commenced on the enormous façade and three naves.

The **Museo dell'Opera Metropolitana** occupies rooms obtained by closing the first three spans of the right aisle of the Duomo Nuovo. The sculptures, paintings, gold objects, illuminated manuscripts and hangings come mostly from the Duomo: works by Giovanni Pisano, Jacopo della Quercia and, its crowning glory, Duccio's glorious *Maestà*, the supreme masterpiece of the Sienese school, painted between 1308 and 1311. You are allowed to climb to the very top of one of the walls of the Duomo Nuovo for a dizzying view over the roofs of Siena and a chance to imagine what might have been the strangest cathedral in Italy.

Palazzo Pubblico

Henry James called this building 'Siena's Declaration of Independence' and it is one the finest examples of Gothic architecture in Italy. However, the building does not dominate the square but, rather, forms part of its harmony – one of the achievements of Sienese architecture. The 'Sienese' arch used on the town hall and other buildings in Siena looks Gothic but was probably an import from the Orient. The black and white coat of arms of the town of Siena – the Balzana – is above the tympana of the doors and windows. Its other symbol appears on a granite column – a she-wolf and twins Romulus and Remus.

One entrance leads to the courtyard of the Podestà (mayor); the other leads to the rooms where the paintings of the **Museo Civico** are now kept, including the fresco cycles by Ambrogio Lorenzetti depicting Good Government and Bad Government. Jesus, Mary, angels and saints float in a tender *Maestà* by Simone Martini in the Sala del Mappamondo (globe room); however, they cohabit the room with a portrait of *condottiere Guidoriccio da Fogliano*. Between the end of the 14th century and the beginning of the 15th century the interior of the palace was altered. The Sala del Risorgimento was created in honour of Vittorio Emanuele II and filled with the heroic works of Sienese artists such as Amos Cassioli, Piero Aldi and Cesare Maccari.

The **Torre del Mangia**, one of the most striking towers in Italy, looks like a cross between a spear, a lily and a hypodermic needle. It rises from the lowest point of the Piazza del Campo alongside the Palazzo Pubblico to a height of 102m (including the lightning rod), a lasting symbol of power once wielded by the Palazzo Pubblico. Built between 1325 and 1348 (additions in 1680), it is of red brick with a travertine belfry.

Piazza del Campo

Siena's historic centre, perhaps the most beautiful square in Italy, is sunk between the three hills on which the city is built and encircled by the red brick and stone façades of medieval houses. The scallop-shaped square was the original nucleus of Siena, built to stem the rainwater and to reclaim the ground, formerly a marketplace that sloped downhill. A document from 1196 shows that it included today's piazza and the part known as the Mercato (market). Later a large wall was built to separate the two parts and the Campo acquired its characteristic form while the first buildings were erected. Gradually the Campo took on the full functions of a square, a public meeting place, and became the centre for social, civil and religious life. It is paved with nine bands of travertine fanning out across the square. The Palazzo Sansedoni is a complex of medieval houses joined into one palace by Agostino di Giovanni in 1339. Its façade curves around the Piazza. The windows are of the same type as those of the Palazzo Pubblico in accordance with the city's 13th-century building code.

Most often seen as a feature of doors and windows, a 'Sienese' arch consists of a pointed arch with a decorative *archivolt* (underside), which itself sits on the *architrave* (lintel) of a lower arch.

Museo Civico €€
Palazzo Pubblico,
Piazza del Campo;
tel: 0577 226230;
www.comune.siena.it/
museocivico. Open daily mid-Mar–Oct 1000–1900;
Nov–mid-Mar 1000–1800.

Torre del Mangia €€
Palazzo Pubblico, Piazza del Campo; tel: 0577 226230;
www.comune.siena.it/
museocivico. Open daily mid-Mar–Oct 1000–1900,
Nov–mid-Mar 1000–1600.

In July and mid-August, the legendary Palio takes place on the Piazza del Campo, a horse race, in which every *contrada* (district) of Siena enters a horse in the race (after having it blessed in church). The colourful festival has existed since the Middle Ages, when each neighbourhood took part in the defence of the city.

Opposite
Siena's Duomo

Pinacoteca Nazionale €€ *Via San Pietro 29;*
tel: 0577 281161;
www.spsae-si.beniculturali.it.
Open Tue–Sat 0815–1915,
Sun–Mon 0830–1330.

Ospedale di Santa Maria della Scala €€
Piazza del Duomo 2; tel: 0577 224811;
www.santamariadellascala. com. Open daily 1030–1830.

Left
Siena's Piazza del Campo

Below
The Oratorio di Santa Caterina

Pinacoteca Nazionale

Siena's famous art gallery is partly housed in the Palazzo Buonsignori, donated by the nobleman Niccolò Buonsignori, and in the adjacent Palazzo Brigidi, belonging to the Province of Siena. If there is a drawback, it is the sheer number of Madonnas. If you try to look at every one, you may find yourself wishing, blasphemously, that the New Testament had never been written. Begin with the best: the *Madonna of the Franciscans* by Duccio di Buoninsegna (1255–1319), the great altarpiece by Pietro Lorenzetti (dated 1329), the refined Madonnas by Ambrogio Lorenzetti and the *Madonna and Child* by Simone Martini. Also the *Città sul Mare*, again by Ambrogio Lorenzetti, regarded as one of the first landscape paintings in modern history.

Among 15th-century works, look for the paintings of Giovanni di Paolo, the comforting Madonnas of Neroccio di Bartolomeo Landi and Francesco di Giorgio Martini, and the stylised compositions of Matteo di Giovanni. In the collection of masterpieces donated by the nobleman Spannocchi, two are of particular interest: the *Self-Portrait* by Albrecht Dürer (1514) and the *Nativity* (1521) by Lorenzo Lotto.

Ospedale di Santa Maria della Scala

A hospital founded in the 9th century, Santa Maria was in operation until the 1980s (Italo Calvino, the author of *Invisible Cities*, died here in 1985). Most of the present building dates from the 13th and 14th centuries. It is now being transformed into a cultural centre and museum complex.

The frescos by Domenico di Bartolo in the great hall – Sala del Pellegrinaio – are one of the artistic glories of Siena and offer fascinating insights into the blood and guts reality of 15th-century hospitalisation. It also portrays orphans in different stages of their lives, from childishly naughty to subdued and apprenticed young men and marriageable women (with small dowries provided by the hospice). There is a frescoed chapel by the artist Vechietta and another one underground – the Oratorio di Santa Caterina della Notte – where Siena's patron saint had visions and ecstasies.

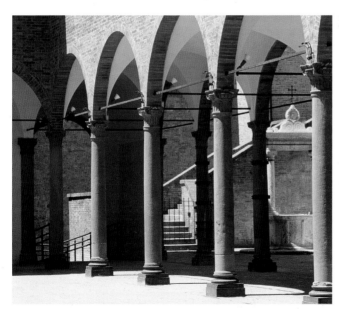

Accommodation and food

Drogheria Manganelli *Via di Città 71; tel: 0577 280002. Open 0900–1945.* Gourmet delicatessen with regional specialities at elevated prices – olive oil, honey, wine, truffles, marmalade, vinegar.

Consorzio Agrario *Via Giuseppe Pianigiani 9; tel: 0577 226589; www.capsi.it.* The second largest supermarket in the *Centro Storico* (the largest is the new Conad located inside the nearby Centro Commerciale Galleria Metropolitan off Piazza Matteotti). It carries a large selection of wine, olive oil, *charcuterie* and other goods.

La Chiacchiera € *Costa San Antonio 4; tel: 0577 280631.* For an informal, delicious but inexpensive meal, there isn't a better place in Siena but it is hard to get a table and service is often slow. The best strategy is to come early.

Grattacielo € *Via dei Pontani 8; tel: 0577 289326. Closed Sun.* A humble place with just a couple of tables and a low ceiling (hence the name, 'skyscraper') where the owner hands over plates of sausage, cheese and ham across the counter along with *vino della casa* – the authentic and delicious Sienese version of a quick lunch.

Antica Trattoria Botteganova €€ *Via Chiantigiana 29; tel: 0577 284230; www.anticatrattoriabotteganova.it. Closed Mon.* Creative variations on Tuscan classics and a Michelin star are the big draw for foodies. It is located on the road to Chianti.

Hosteria del Carroccio €€ *Via del Casato di Sotto 32; tel: 0577 41165. Closed Wed in winter. No credit cards.* Down a street just off the Piazza del Campo. The menu here changes every week and is based on fresh ingredients, Sienese tradition and owner Renata's fancy. Make reservations.

Pasticceria Nannini €€ *Via Massetana Romana 42–4; tel: 0577 283072.* The Italian rock singer Gianna Nannini grew up in Siena. Her family owns a chain of shops here that make Siena's most celebrated nosh – the chewy *panforte*.

Pensione Palazzo Ravizza €€ *Pian dei Mantellini 34; tel: 0577 280462; fax: 0577 221597; www.palazzoravizza.it.* The queen of Siena's hotels has 30 elegant rooms in a restored palace, spectacular views and a garden (ask for a room overlooking the garden). But it is hard to reach by car if you don't know the city.

La Taverna del Capitano €€ *Via del Capitano 6/8; tel: 0577 288094.* Easy to find, this traditional restaurant is on a broad street near the

Cucina Senese

The Sienese season their food more heavily than the Florentines and rely even more on roasting and grilling. Typical dishes are *ribollita* (a 'twice-cooked' vegetable and bread soup), minestrone, grilled meats, tripe and fried zucchini flowers. The classic dessert is *cantucci* (almond biscuits) accompanied by the dessert wine, Vin Santo. *Panforte* is a famous Sienese speciality, a cake of candied fruit, almonds, honey and orange peel compressed into a chewy, dense, delicious mass that they say never goes bad. *Ricciarelli* are biscuits made of almonds, egg white, sugar and vanilla. Tourism in Siena has had its culinary side effects and it is now possible, in the fast-food places on the Via Banchi di Sopra for example, to eat a truly lousy meal.

cathedral. The menu usually includes things such as *panzanella di farro* (spelt, dried bread, herbs and vegetables), *pappardelle* (broad noodles) with meat sauce, an outstanding veal cutlet and, on Friday, cod cooked Tuscan style.

Villa Liberty €€ *Viale Vittorio Veneto 11; tel: 0577 44966; fax: 0577 44770; www.villaliberty.it.* Charming, intimate and only a short walk from the centre. It has 12 rooms in a restored art nouveau townhouse with marble and parquet floors, and is easy to reach by car with parking in front. You should insist on a room overlooking the garden.

Below
Festive Siena

Suggested tour

Total distance: 2km.

Time: Two days should be a minimum for Siena. Distances are deceptively short in Siena relative to the number of its *palazzi*, museums and other things to see. If you are limited to a single day, concentrate on the two poles of the city – the Piazza del Campo and the Piazza del Duomo – and try to take in either the Pinacoteca Nazionale or the Museo dell'Opera del Duomo. The latter has a fabulous view of the city that rivals that of the town hall's famous tower and there are no queues.

Route: From the *terrazza* of the church of **San Domenico** ❶, you can take a long look at the city's two highest hills, occupied by its cathedral and town hall. The vast brick structure of San Domenico looks more like a warehouse than a church. Behind the unfinished façade, deep in the cavernous interior, is a chapel where the mummified head of St Catherine holds court, accompanied by a finger and the chain that she used to beat herself with. She is one of the most famous women in church history and the subject of chapel frescos by Sodoma that depict vivid scenes in which she faints, casts out demons, and pleads for a young man facing execution. Back outside, walk down the Via della Sapienza.

Detour: Turn right into Corta San Antonio and follow the sign to the **Casa di Santa Caterina** ❷ (*open daily mid-Mar–Oct 0900–1230, 1500–1800; Nov–mid-Mar 0900–1230 and 1530–1800; www.caterinati.org*). St Catherine was born here on a backstreet, into a dyer's family. In her lifetime, she would dictate letters to popes and kings and helped bring about the return of the papacy from Avignon to Rome. The house attracts a mix of tourists and pilgrims. The rooms where Caterina Benincasa lived have been transformed over the centuries (but her hair shirt is still there). The inner Superior Oratory, known as '*della Cucina*', has a magnificent majolica floor beneath a coffered ceiling. A Renaissance loggia leads through a modern annexe to the Oratory of the Crucifix.

The Via Banchi di Sopra is Siena's throbbing, claustrophobic shopping street where locals and tourists vie for space, particularly during the evening *passeggiata*. It is worth taking a moment to contemplate the world's oldest bank still in operation – the Monte dei Paschi di Siena – housed in the Gothic Palazzo Salimbeni and two adjoining Renaissance palaces on **Piazza Salimbeni** ❸. The bank was founded by the city in 1472 to provide cheap loans to sheep farmers. The Piazza Tolomei has the first of many Sienese she-wolf statues. The city council met in the church on the square, San Cristoforo, before the completion of the Palazzo Pubblico. The Palazzo Tolomei (1205–67) was the proud headquarters of yet another medieval bank.

Opposite
Siena's Piazza del Campo

The **Croce del Travaglio** ❹ is the meeting point of three streets, Banchi di Sopra, Banchi di Sotto and Via di Città. Squeeze through the Vicolo di San Pietro to PIAZZA DEL CAMPO ❺. You will find yourself standing next to the 14th-century **Fonte Gaia** ❻ (happy fountain), which flows on the highest point in the square. Nineteenth-century copies have replaced the magnificent original reliefs (1414–19) by Jacopo della Quercia. The PALAZZO PUBBLICO ❼ occupies the lowest point in the square and its **Torre del Mangia**, perhaps the finest medieval tower anywhere, rises up to a dramatic height, as if it is going to take flight.

Return to the Croce del Travaglio and go left into the Via di Città, a street of medieval and Renaissance palaces such as the Palazzo Patrizi (No 75) and, best of all, the **Palazzo Chigi-Saracini** (No 82) with a curved façade built of brick and stone. Inside the entrance is a statue of Pope Julius II. Diagonally opposite is the **Palazzo Piccolomini**, built by Bernardo Rossellino for the sister of Pope Pius II (hence its other name, the Palazzo delle Papesse). It is now an art gallery.

Turn right when you run into another she-wolf column – this is the Via del Capitano. Walk past the 13th-century Palazzo del Capitano and its nine Sienese arches; after a few more paces, you will step into the Piazza del Duomo, which is the highest point in Siena, 30m higher than the Campo. It is only logical to visit the DUOMO SANTA MARIA ❽ first. Many believe it to be the most beautiful Gothic building in Italy. However, save time for the **Museo dell'Opera Metropolitana** ❾ located in the ruins of the DUOMO NUOVO – Siena's most ambitious work in progress that was never to be. If at all possible, climb to the top. The square's two remaining attractions are the BATTISTERO DI SAN GIOVANNI ❿ and the OSPEDALE DI SANTA MARIA DELLA SCALA ⓫.

Retrace your steps from the Piazza del Duomo down the Via del Capitano to the Piazza Postierla and walk down its continuation, the Via San Pietro. The **Palazzo Buonsignori** ⓬, containing the PINACOTECA NAZIONALE, is on the left.

Also worth exploring

Fortezza Medici (**Forte di Santa Barbara**) is located near the Piazza San Domenico. The Medici fortress built by Cosimo I (1555) has since become a park with magnificent views. The Enoteca Nazionale displays 600 wines from all over Italy in the glowing arches of the fortress's brick cellar. Upstairs is a bar where you can savour them.

0   200m

0   150 yards

Via Simone Martini

⇧
North

Porta
Camollia

Viale Sardegna

Viale Giuseppe Mazzini

Viale Don Giovanni Minzoni

Via Biagio di Montluc

Via di Camollia

Via Campansi

Via Ricasoli

Via Giuseppe Garibaldi

Viale Armando Diaz

Via Simone Martini

Via della Scuffia Secca

Porta
Ovile

Viale Rinaldo Franci

La Lizza

La Lizza

Via dei Montanini

S Francesco

Via di Vallerozzi

Via Baldassarre Peruzzi

Piale della
Libertà

Viale Venticinque Aprile

**Stadio
Comunale**

Piazza
Giacomo
Matteotti ✉

Piazza
S Francesco

**Oratorio di
San Bernardino**

orte di
arbara

Viale del Mille

Viale Curtatone

Via della Sapienza

Piazza
Salimbeni

Via dei Rossi

❸

Via dei Termini

Banchi di Sopra

① **Casa di Santa
Caterina** ②

Via di S Caterina

Via delle Terme

Via Sallustio Bandini

S Domenico

Croce del
Travaglio ④

Banchi di Sotto

Porta
Fontebranda

**Battistero di
San Giovanni**

❻ Fonte Gaia

**Piazza del
Campo**

⑤

Via del Porrione

Via di Pantaneto

Via dei Pispini

Porta
Pispini

Via Esterna di
Fontebranda

Duomo S Maria ✕ ⑩

⑨

Via di Città

ℹ

⑦

**Palazzo
Pubblico**

Via di Salicotto

Via S Martini

**Ospedale di Santa
Maria della Scala** ⑪

⑧

**Museo
dell'Opera
Metropolitana**

Casato di Sotto

Piazza
del
Mercato

Via Roma

Via del Fosso
di S Ansano

**Pinacoteca
Nazionale**

Via S Pietro

⑫

Via Giovanni Dupré

Porta
Roma

Via Paolo Mascagni

Pian dei Mantellini

S Agostino

Via di Fontanella

Strada di Certosa

Via Girolamo Gigli

Porta
aterina

Via delle Cerchia

**Orto
Botanico**

Via Pier Andrea Mattioli

**S Maria
del Carmine**

Via S Marco

Via delle Sperandie

Porta
S Marco

Via Massetana

Porta
Tufi

Via Enea Silvio
Piccolomini

The Crete

Ratings

Art	●●●●●
Castles	●●●●●
Monasteries	●●●●●●
Scenery	●●●●●
Vineyards	●●●●●
Architecture	●●●●○
Nature	●●●●○
Museums	●●●○○

The hillsides south of Siena are an undulating sea of clay in which thickets of oaks and *maquis* seem to float like islands. The fields have been adapted with terrible labour for use as farm and pastureland. The haunting landscape, called the *crete senese*, forms the background of many school of Siena masterpieces. All historical epochs have left their mark. There are Etruscan Cities of the Dead, and medieval castles and monasteries. Even the road system is ancient, once forming part of the Roman *Via Cassia* and the medieval *Via Francigena*. Further south, the Crete gives way to Monte Amiata, an extinct volcano and the highest peak (1,739m) in southern Tuscany.

ABBAZIA DI MONTE OLIVETO MAGGIORE

Abbazia di Monte Oliveto Maggiore €
On the N451 between Buonconvento and Asciano at 273m; tel: 0577 718567; www.monteolivetomaggiore.it. Open daily 0915–1200 and 1515–1800 (until 1700 in winter). The monks produce an excellent herbal spirit – Flora di Monte Oliveto – from 26 herbs grown in the monastery garden. It can be purchased in the pharmacy, where 17th-century vases are still used for keeping the herbs.

The solitary Benedictine monastery, still occupied by monks, has one of the most beautiful cloisters in Tuscany. Bernardo Giovanni Tolomei, a Sienese nobleman, renounced the world and founded the abbey in 1313. Beyond the fortified outpost, which is decorated with fine della Robbia terracottas, a cypress avenue leads to the abbey's late Gothic church, much altered during an 18th-century baroque face-lift. The abbey complex also comprises a library, guesthouse, cloisters, chapels and gardens. The intarsia (inlaid wood) of the choir stools (1503–5) unfolds a series of imaginary cities and dream landscapes – all in perspective – created with chips of oak, chestnut, olive, acorn and walnut (if it is too dark, ask the caretaker to switch on the lights).

One of the monastery's three cloisters is decorated with a magnificent series of frescos that tell the life of St Benedict in 36 panels. Five were painted by Luca Signorelli and the rest by Giovanni Antonio da Bazzo, or 'Sodoma'. Vasari claims that he 'earned' his nickname. The young painter certainly didn't lack self-confidence; he

inserted his self-portrait next to that of the saint in the third episode, more or less demanding equal time. For a young man, he understood a lot about temptation, corruption, greed, voluptuousness, gluttony and forgiveness: though employed by monks, he depicted them freely in his art.

ASCIANO

Asciano is the largest town in the Crete and an important centre of sheep farming and cheesemaking that remains within its medieval fortified walls. Few tourists bother to stop here, which is part of its charm. Surprisingly, it has three worthwhile museums. The main street, the Corso Matteotti, lined with neoclassical *palazzi*, ends in the Piazza della Basilica, embellished by a 15th-century fountain. The Basilica di Sant'Agata stands across from it. Nearby, housed in the restored 13th-century Palazzo Corboli, is the **Museo Archeologico e d'Arte Sacra** with several important works from the Basilica and other churches of the area. Of particular interest are the wooden panel paintings of the Sienese school (14th–15th centuries) with a stunning archangel by Ambrogio Lorenzetti and a Madonna with child by Duccio.

The museum also contains an interesting collection of Etruscan art and artefacts excavated in the nearby necropolis di Poggio Pinci (7th–4th centuries BC). The **Museo Amos Cassioli** has a collection of 60 paintings and numerous drawings by Amos Cassioli (1832–92), the master of Risorgimento melodrama, and his son Giuseppe (1865–1942), both interesting for a look at 19th-century Italy.

Brunello di Montalcino

Brunello di Montalcino is one of the world's most famous red wines. Unlike Chianti, it is made from a single type of grape – Brunello, a clone of Sangiovese Grosso – and aged for four years. Rosso di Montalcino, aged one year, packs a similar punch and is good for uncomplicated drinking. On a different note, Moscadello is a soft, lightly sweet white wine. Producers to look for:

Il Poggione *South of Castel Sant'Angelo; tel: 0577 848412; www.ilpoggiolomontalcino.com*

Col d'Orcia *South of Castel Sant'Angelo; tel: 0577 80891; www.coldorcia.it*

Talenti *Main road just to the north of Castel Sant'Angelo; tel: 0577 844064.*

Lisini *Dirt road between Sant'Antimo and Castel Sant'Angelo; tel: 0577 864040; www.lisini.com*

Opposite
Crete Sienese scenery

CASTIGLIONE D'ORCIA

Rocca a Tentennano € *Via Francigena; tel: 0577 88401. Open Easter–Oct 1000–1300 and 1500–1800, Nov–Easter Sat/Sun only 1000–1300 and 1430–1630.*

13th-century human rights

Another feudal family of Castiglione, the Tignosi, did an extraordinary thing in 1207. They granted rights – in writing – to the town's population. This unheard-of document – the *Charta libertatis* – is one of the most important in medieval Italian history.

From its perch above the Val d'Orcia, Castiglione was strategically important for many centuries. It is first mentioned in a historical document in 853 and later belonged to the powerful Aldobrandeschi family that controlled a chain of castles on the Via Francigena. The town has a dipped-in-amber medieval square, the Piazza II Vecchietta, with a fanciful baroque fountain in the middle. There is a Palazzo Comunale with school of Siena frescos, and the earthy Romanesque Chiesetta di Santa Maria Maddalena, which hides behind a 17th-century façade. Its star attractions are paintings by Pietro Lorenzetti, Simone Martini and native son Il Vecchietta.

From the church, it is just a short walk to the ruined Aldobrandeschi castle, the pentagonal Rocca d'Orcia, now a park. It has a panoramic view of Castiglione and Monte Amiata. For an even more extraordinary view, guaranteed to upset acrophobes, climb to the top of the town's second castle, the trapezoidal **Rocca a Tentennano**, which was built by the hyperactive Salimbeni family in the late 13th century. A hundred years later, the fortress was used by them for a last stand during their confrontation with the city of Siena that ended with the surrender of Cocco Salimbeni in 1419. He was exiled and his castle remained an important military outpost until seized by the Florentines in the 16th century. In both cases, betrayal rather than force breached the fortress defences.

MONTALCINO

ⓘ Pro Loco
Costa del Municipio 8;
tel: 0577 849331;
www.prolocomontalcino.it;
www.comunedimontalcino.it.
Open Tue–Sun 1000–1300
and 1400–1800.

ⓝ Rocca € (access to
the ramparts, courtyard
free) Piazzale della Fortezza;
tel: 0577 849211. Open
Apr–Oct daily 0900–2000,
Nov–Mar Tue–Sun
0900–1800.

Museo Civico e
Diocesano d'Arte Sacra
€€ In the former Convento di
Sant'Agostino, Via Ricasoli
31; tel: 0577 846014.
Open Tue–Sun Apr–Oct
1000–1300 and 1400–1750,
Nov–Mar 1000–1300 and
1400–1740.

ⓢ Torneo/Sagra Feasts
celebrating the start
(Torneo) and the end
(Sagra) of the hunting
season. Aug and Oct.

Above
Montalcino's Rocca

The splendid panorama of the Sienese hills from Montalcino – as far as the mountain of Amiata – is an impressive site. It might have looked a bit different to the last of the Sienese Republicans (600 families) who holed up here in 1555 in the **Rocca** (fortress) and held out against the Florentines for four more years. To honour their memory, the procession at Siena's Palio di Contrade is always led by the Montalcino delegation. Today, the fortress is regularly besieged by coach-loads of tourists, who patrol the town for 45 minutes, buy a bottle of wine and press on to rupture the peace of nearby Sant'Antimo monastery.

The street across from the fortress leads into the Via Ricasoli and past the Gothic marble portal and rose window of the Romanesque church of Sant'Agostino. Its former convent houses a well-endowed **Museo Civico e Diocesano d'Arte Sacra** displaying works by Sodoma, Sano di Pietro and Luca di Tommè, five pictures by Bartolo di Fredi (1380) and one of the earliest known works of Sienese art, a crucifixion by an unknown artist. Downhill from the fortress, the curious little Piazza del Popolo is dominated by the Palazzo Comunale (or dei Priori), which is vaguely reminiscent of Siena's famous town hall. The square also has a number of fine Renaissance buildings with double loggias.

SANT'ANTIMO

ⓝ Abbazia di
Sant'Antimo *Tel:*
0577 835659;
www.antimo.it. Open
Mon–Sat 1015–1230 and
1500–1830, Sun
0915–1045 and
1500–1800. Free.

Proud and solitary, the abbey of Sant'Antimo is arguably the most beautiful Romanesque church in Tuscany and one of the region's finest examples of 13th-century monastic architecture. It is surrounded by fields, forest and olive groves. The present church, dating back to the 12th century, has a simple façade crowned with small arches, a massive square bell tower in the Lombard style with a 12th-century bell, and a semicircular apse. The interior – essentially a Romanesque basilica – has a nave and two aisles separated by piers and pillars whose capitals are carved with lions and mythic beasts. A lot of alabaster was used in the building of the abbey and it adds strange effects of light. The abbey, restored at the beginning of the century, is the seat of a community of canons who officiate with Gregorian chants several times a day.

Accommodation and food

Cantina

Conveniently, at Montalcino there is an **Enoteca della Fortezza** (wine bar and shop) right inside the fortress (not the place to buy in bulk). You can have a drink with a view at the **Fiaschetteria Italiana** or with the locals and football on the telly at the **Bar Mariuccia**; both are on the Piazza del Popolo.

Abbazia di Monte Oliveto Maggiore € *Tel: 0577 707652; fax: 0577 707644.* For those wishing to make a retreat, from Easter to October you can stay overnight in simple rooms in the abbey guesthouse and eat with the monks. The abbey also has a café open at lunchtime that serves good *panini* (sandwiches) and a *menu turistico*. In summer, there are tables outdoors.

Fattoria Taverna dei Barbi €€ *7km on the road to Sant'Antimo just after La Croce; tel: 0577 841111; www.fattoriadeibarbi.it. Closed Tue evening and Wed.* A family-owned *agriturismo*, wine estate and restaurant with a compendious assortment of local wine and dishes such as *porcini*, *pici* or *parpadelle*, followed by sizzling grilled meat. Accommodation includes apartments near the 12th-century Villa Colombini along with two others in old farmhouses close to the taverna. All are furnished with Cinelli family furniture.

Porta al Cassero €€ *Via Ricasoli 32, Montalcino; tel: 0577 847196; closed Wed.* Just two blocks from the fortress, a small establishment run by an uncle–nephew team. Home-made pasta, tripe in saffron or *scottiglia* (stew) and pungent *pecorino* cheese from Pienza paired with good house wine or a bottle of Brunello, Rosso or Moscadello.

Suggested tour

Food of the land

Local food and drink in the Crete includes *pici* (handmade thick spaghetti) with hare and garlic sauce and wines like Brunello of Montalcino and Vino Nobile di Montepulciano (*see page 98*). The best Tuscan cheese comes from the Crete. The forests of Monte Amiata also play a major role in Crete cuisine providing chestnuts, raspberries, mushrooms, wild asparagus and game. Traditional biscuits and cakes are more or less the same as in Siena – *ricciarelli*, *cavallucci*, *copate* and *panforte*, the dense, sweet cake that never goes bad.

Total distance: 83km; detours to Monte Amiata and Abbadia San Salvatore add 60km; detour to Castel Sant'Angelo adds 16km.

Time: If you skip the detours and don't indulge in much wine-tasting, this tour of the Crete can be completed in a moderately ambitious day. Adding detours, walks and wine to the equation expands it to at least three days.

Links: The first of two routes that explore the Crete (*see page 105*).

Route: From **Siena ❶** take the N326 and turn on to the N438 to get on the road to **ASCIANO ❷**. After the village of Taverne d'Arbia, you will get your first real look at the landscape of the Crete. From Asciano, there are two roads that lead in the right direction. Either one will do and both are scenic but the one at the entrance to Asciano is more direct.

It is a lonely few kilometres to **ABBAZIA DI MONTE OLIVETO MAGGIORE ❸**; however, unless you spend the night or join the order, you will never have the abbey to yourself. It is usually beset by a couple of coach-loads of tourists. The next stretch of road is perhaps the best of the entire day. The rolling hills have been worked over the centuries into a landscape that seems timeless, embroidered by cypress-lined ridges, hillside farms and isolated stone villas. **Buonconvento** ❹ is directly on the ancient *Via Cassia* and sits behind walls that the Sienese built in the Middle Ages (its Museo d'Arte Sacra contains fine works that other Sienese painted).

The road to **MONTALCINO** ❺ appears about 2km outside of town. To really appreciate the hill-town, zigzag to the very top and the Rocca (paid parking is available). The abbey of **SANT'ANTIMO** ❻ is just 13km to the south, and a right-turn down a dusty road.

Detour: On the road to Sant'Antimo, there is an immediate right fork that leads to Castel Sant'Angelo. It is a wide and well-maintained dirt road that penetrates deep into the heart of Brunello vineyards. Many wine estates along the road have signs saying *vendita diretta*, inviting you to taste and buy wine.

At the end, turn left on the paved country road and carry on to **Castel Sant'Angelo** ❼ where a couple of sharp curves climb to its main piazza. The town feels like a miniature version of Montalcino without the tourists. The Romanesque church of San Michele is well worth a look, followed by a visit to the friendly cantina across the square. The owner will wave lists and unfurl maps of local vintages, telling you everything you want to know while pouring glasses of intense Brunello.

South of Sant'Antimo, the prosperous realm of Brunello quickly gives way to the solitary foothills of Monte Amiata. The hamlet of Monte Amiata in the Orcia valley (not to be confused with the mountain) is just a whistle-stop on a neglected railway. A couple of uphill curves end in a fork in the road near Ansidonia.

Detour: If you just can't get enough of mountain driving and medieval monasteries, turn south on the N323 and get ready for the 22km ascent of **Monte Amiata** ❽. The actual summit is a bit of an anticlimax thanks to a tacky complex of bars, car parks, ski runs and hotels. It doesn't detract, however, from the spectacular glimpses of sea to the west, Lake Bolsena to the southeast, and the towers of villages that encircle the mountain (the best lookout is the statue known as the Madonna delle Scout).

The **Abbadia San Salvatore** ❾ is just 8.5km further southeast. The Romanesque monastery was constructed of brown trachite, a sombre contrast to Sant'Antimo's travertine and alabaster. The Cistercians built the 11th-century abbey church on top of a vast and eccentrically decorated 8th-century crypt. The town itself, an ensemble of Renaissance and Gothic buildings, seems an odd place for a budding winter sports capital but that is how it sees itself. From the abbey, it is easier to rejoin the route by driving east to the N2 and turning north.

A further 12km of driving, mostly on mountain ridges, leads to **CASTIGLIONE D'ORCIA** ❿. It overlooks, at a distance, the *Via Cassia*, last seen in Buonconvento.

The Crete and Val d'Orcia

Ratings

Architecture	●●●●●
Castles	●●●●●
Scenery	●●●●●
Thermal springs	●●●●●
Vineyards	●●●●●
Nature	●●●●○
Museums	●●●○○
Shopping	●●●○○

The scenic Orcia valley was one of Italy's historic fault-lines, forming the medieval frontier with the Papal State. Two of the most memorable towns in Tuscany occupy the hills above it: ancient, airy Montepulciano and Pienza, a Renaissance pope's utopia. Strongholds such as the Rocca at Radicofani, by contrast, are dramatic examples of feudal one-upmanship. Chiusi, lying just off the modern *autostrada* near the border of Umbria, was a mysterious Etruscan capital and efficient Roman colony. The Crete has attracted health tourism for at least 2,000 years in places such as Bagni San Filippo and Bagno Vignoni. The hot springs of the region have been channelled into modern thermal baths but you can still soak in naturally steaming ponds and sulphurous cascades deep in the woods.

BAGNO VIGNONI

🅗 **Terme di Bagno Vignoni** € *Piazza del Moretto 32; tel: 0577 887365; www. termedibagnovignoni.com. Open Jun–Sep Mon–Sat 0800–1300 and 1600–1900. The baths are located behind the Hotel Posta-Marucci. Open 1300. You can soak for free in pools at the edge of town.*

In the middle of Bagno Vignoni is a steaming pool (51°C) instead of a piazza. Etruscan and Romans bathed in it. The Russian director Andrej Tarkowski used it as a setting for *Nostalgia*, an eerie film about an exiled, hydrophilic Russian poet who tries to walk across the water. The Renaissance Palazzo Piccolomini was a residence of master architect Bernardo Rossellino who built Pienza for Pope Pius II. It is now the Hotel Le Terme.

In ancient times, the medical benefits of the hot springs were attributed to water nymphs. In the Middle Ages, physicians boiled the maidenhair ferns growing on its edge and had their patients drink the liquor for 40 days, to flush the 'melancholy' out of their systems so that it wouldn't concentrate in any one organ – say the spleen – for too long. It was even known to cure the 'French disease'. Lorenzo the Magnificent soaked his rheumatic body here in the company of the humanist philosopher Pico della Mirandola.

CHIUSI

i **Pro Loco** *Piazza Duomo 1; tel/fax: 0578 227667; www.terresiena.it. Open in summer Mon–Fri 1000–1300 and 1530–1830, Sat–Sun 1000–1300; in winter daily 1000–1200.*

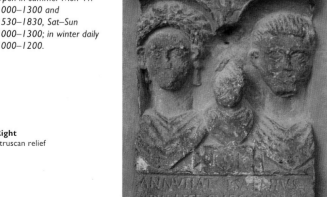

Right
Etruscan relief

The origins of Chiusi date back to the first millennium before Christ. In the 6th century BC, *Clevsin* or *Chamars* (as the Etruscans called it) was one of the 12 most important cities in the Etruscan federation. Under King Porsenna, Chiusi reached its peak when the Etruscans fought and defeated the Romans.

⓵ Museo Archeologico Nazionale € *Via Porsenna 93; tel: 0578 20177. Open daily 0900–2000. Charge includes admission to tombs.*

Tomba della Pellegrina *€ Guided tours Tue, Thu & Sat 1100–1200 and 1600–1700, maximum of 50 visitors per day, via the Museo Archeologico Nazionale.*

Catacombe Santa Mustiola €€ *Tel: 0578 227667. The only Christian catacombs ever discovered in Tuscany are located just outside of Chiusi; the tombs include a children's cemetery. The Museo della Cattedrale on the Piazza del Duomo arranges guided tours (tel: 0578 226490, Jun–mid-Oct daily 1100 and 1730; mid-Oct–May Mon–Sat 1100, Sun 1100 and 1630). Dress warmly and bring a torch.*

The Duomo San Secondiano, one of the earliest churches in Italy, is supported by 18 marble columns taken from Roman temples after the city's destruction by Goths. The altar rests on a Roman mosaic (the mosaics in the apse are 19th-century imitations of Byzantine work).

The **Museo Archeologico Nazionale**, for all its merit, is a masterpiece of disorganisation: signs placed next to display cases refer to objects that are not in the museum; the only texts are written in academic jargon that suffers further in translation; and a photocopy of a tomb gets top billing while a rare – and very real – tomb painting is half-hidden on a wall in the back. There are many cinerary urns and most of them have inscriptions; one of the most famous is the urn of Larth Sentinathes' Caesa, discovered in the grave of Pellegrina. The sculpture is represented by numerous *cippi* (remarkable is the one with wedding scenes) and by some sphinxes, xoana and lions which were placed as guardians of the graves. There are Roman pieces, too. Don't miss the powerful head of Augustus.

Chiusi was one of the most important centres for Etruscan art and, in the 19th century, produced – for the second time – finely crafted 'Etruscan' urns, vases and figurines. These fakes became the major local industry. Their quality was such that even museums and expert collectors were fooled. The museum displays some of these remarkable copies next to Etruscan originals. It also organises tours of the two Etruscan tombs near Lago di Chiusi – the Tomba del Leone and the **Tomba della Pellegrina**. The latter has been left as it was discovered, with some of the funerary urns and sarcophagi in the odd positions they were left in by tomb raiders centuries ago.

Vino nobile

The wine of Montepulciano was already held in high esteem in the 14th century. The style of today's Nobile di Montepulciano, however, only goes back a few decades. It is based on a different variety of Sangiovese than Chianti, the *Prugnelo Gentile*, which is mixed with Canaiolo (and sometimes Mammolo) and small amounts of white Malvasia and Trebbiano. By law, a Montepulciano wine is only *nobile* if it has aged two years (three if it is a *riserva*). Rosso di Montepulciano is younger and less expensive. Sangiovese-Cabernet blends are becoming very fashionable. To taste some of these wines, drop into the **Enoteca del Consorzio del Vino Nobile di Montepulciano**, *Piazza Grande 7; tel: 0578 757812; www.vinonobiledimontepulciano.it. Mon–Fri 1100–1300, 1500–1900 and Sat 1500–1900 in summer, by appointment in winter.*

Wine producers to look for

Poliziano *Via Fontago 1, Montepulciano Stazione; tel: 0578 738171; www.carlettipoliziano.com.* A wine estate with a grand tradition, Vino Nobile cru Vigna Asinone is its flagship wine. Also, Elegia (Sangiovese/Cabernet) and Vin Santo.

Avignonesi *Estate Le Capezzine, Valiano di Montepulciano; tel: 0578 724304; www.avignonesi.it.* The Avignonesi brothers make a fine Grifi (Sangiovese/Cabernet), Marzocco (barrique Chardonnay) and acclaimed Vin Santo.

Poderi Boscarelli *Via di Montenero 28, Cervognano, 5km east of Montepulciano between Cervognano and Aquaviva; tel: 0578 767608; www.poderiboscarelli.com.* Small wine estate with intense wines with lots of aroma. Boscarelli is a compelling Sangiovese/Cabernet blend.

MONTEPULCIANO

Pro Loco *Via di Gracciano nel Corso 59/a; tel: 0578 757341; www.prolocomontepulciano.it & www.comune. montepulciano.si.it*

Palazzo Comunale *€ Piazza Grande 1; tel: 0578 757034. Open Mon–Sat 0900–1800; Tower 1000–1800.*

Duomo Santa Maria Assunta *€ Piazza Grande. Open daily.*

Madonna di San Biagio *€ Via di San Biagio 14. Open daily Jul–Aug 0900–1900 (closed 1230–1500), Sep–Jun until 1800.*

Below
The walls of Montepulciano

At 605m, Montepulciano is one of the highest situated cities in Tuscany, straddling the Chiana and Orcia valleys. Legend has it that the famous Etruscan king Lors Porsena founded the town. Etruscans dug deep beneath the city and their chambers were later used as wine cellars. Architecturally, it is a fascinating mix of Sienese Gothic and Florentine Renaissance architecture. The ring of fortifications was erected in 1511 based on designs by Antonio da Sangallo the Elder at the behest of Cosimo I.

A long, arduous street, the Corso, winds its way from the main square up to the Piazza Grande, the highest point in the city. The **Palazzo Comunale** dates to 1243, but was massively rebuilt by the Florentines in 1393 who gave it a face-lift based on plans by Michelozzo, as well as a symmetrically placed tower. The building has three floors; the upper one is made as a battlement and has some similarities with the Palazzo Vecchio of Florence – a 14th-century court with loggias placed one upon another. The view from the top of the tower takes in the surrounding region and, on a clear day, Siena is visible 65km to the north. The impressive Palazzo Nibili-Tarugi, built entirely with travertine, is on the northern side of the square. The **Duomo Santa Maria Assunta** is late baroque, resting on the foundations of a Romanesque church and retaining its bell tower. Behind its unfinished façade is a harmonious interior with a luminous, gilded triptych on the main altar, the Ascension of Mary (1400) by Sienese painter Taddeo di Bartolo.

Perhaps the most remarkable building in Montepulciano sits in a solitary setting just outside the city gates. The Renaissance masterpiece of **Madonna di San Biagio** (1518–45) is based on designs by Antonio da Sangallo the Elder and much influenced by St Peter's in Rome. It is built entirely of travertine on a Greek-cross plan and surmounted by a central dome. The front of the church, facing north, is flanked by two bell towers. The inside repeats the Doric lines of the exterior. Near the main altar there is a huge marble missal-cover made by Giannozzo and Lisandro Albertini.

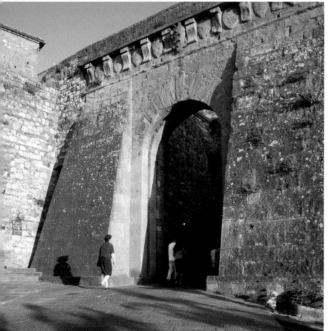

PIENZA

ℹ Informazioni turistiche *Palazzo Comunale, Corso Rosellino 59; tel: 0578 749071; www.portalepienza.it & www.pienza.info*

Museo Palazzo Piccolomini € *Piazza Pio II 2; tel: 0578 748392. Open mid-Mar–mid-Oct Tue–Sun 1000–1830, mid-Oct–mid-Mar Tue–Sun 1000–1630.*

Sant'Anna in Camprena *Tel: 0578 749404; www.scuolacamprena.it. Open daily. 7km north of Pienza, off the road to Castelmuzio. Benedictine monastery founded in the 14th century, with frescos by Sodoma. It provided a setting for The English Patient and offers accommodation and Italian courses.*

Pienza is in the capital of Tuscany's cheese zone. Many of its shops sell delicious local *pecorino* made from sheep's milk. The *Fiera del Cacio* – an annual cheese fair and festival – takes place on the first Sunday in September.

The scholar and humanist Aenea Silvio Piccolomini became Pope Pius II in 1458. It wasn't enough for him to build a cathedral in his birthplace, Corsignano. He wanted to turn it into utopia, a *Città Ideale*, and name it after himself. He recruited Leon Battista Alberti to create plans and Bernardo Rossellino to carry them out. The result, though never finished, was one of the most beautiful cities built during the Renaissance, a harmonious ensemble of buildings constructed of honey-coloured travertine that glows at dusk and dawn. It was the stage set for Zeffirelli's *Romeo and Juliet* long before the film crew of *The English Patient* arrived. Piazza Pio II is its core, a trapezoidal square based on the ideas of Humanistic Renaissance culture.

At the main side of the Piazza is the cathedral of Santa Maria Assunta, built over the spot where the ancient Pieve di Santa Maria was situated. The papal coat of arms adorns the façade. Inside, you can pace its Latin cross of travertine columns, similar to the Hallenkirchen (hall churches) of central Europe. Two altarpieces, by Giovanni di Paolo and Matteo di Giovanni, compete for attention with an *Assunzione* by Vecchietta, a *Madonna con Bambino* by Sano di Pietro and a marble altar, probably by Rossellino. Under the apse there is a crypt, actually the church of San Giovanni, where it is possible to find some portions of Romanesque sculptures that decorated the ancient Pieve di Santa Maria; there also is a magnificent font designed by Rossellino.

On the left of the cathedral is the **Palazzo Piccolomini** (1459–62), inspired by the Palazzo Rucellai in Florence. It has a nearly squared plan with ashlar-worked façades. The three floors have mullioned windows between pilasters and views of the Val d'Orcia and Monte Amiata. Nature and architecture were meant to coexist harmoniously in the *Città Ideale*. The court is surrounded by an elegant arcade with arches placed over columns with Corinthian capitals. The Palazzo is now a museum with the library of Pope Pius II and a collection of papal paraphernalia.

RADICOFANI

Rocca di Radicofani € *Tel: 0578 55867. Open daily 1030–1930.*

Opposite
Wellhead and cathedral façade in Pienza's Piazza Pio II

On a visit to Radicofani, Charles Dickens described the region as 'barren, as stony and as wild as Cornwall in England'. Perhaps that is why the only English pope in history, Nicholas Breakspear of St Albans (1100–59) – better known as Adrian IV – chose the site for his fortress. This **Rocca**, sitting at 766m on a hill above town, was used in later centuries by the notorious Ghino di Tacco. His name is mentioned with fear and loathing by both Boccaccio and Dante.

The town has a pair of interesting churches, the Romanesque San Pietro and the Renaissance Sant'Agata. Both have glazed terracotta

Opposite
Bagno Vignoni

Below
The portal of Collegiata
di Orsenna

work by the Andrea della Robbia school. On the road from Radicofani to Siena is an abandoned-looking Medici villa called Palazzo La Posta with an imposing fountain. For a couple of centuries, it was one of the few hotels in the region between Siena and Rome, serving people on the Grand Tour.

SAN QUIRICO D'ORCIA

Collegiata di Orsenna € *Via Dante Alighieri; tel: 0577 897236; www.comunesanquirico.it.* *Open daily 0830–2000.*

Each year in June (on the third weekend), San Quirico remembers its moment in history with a *Festa del Barbarossa*, which involves a lot of medieval pageantry, flag-waving and longbow competitions.

High on its hill, San Quirico began its history as an Etruscan settlement (its original name, *Osenna*, is Etruscan for 'water', or 'brook'). From the beginning of the 11th century, it became an important stop for pilgrims on their way to Rome as well as for Holy Roman Emperors. Frederick I (Barbarossa or 'red beard') came to Italy in 1154–5 to pick up the Imperial Crown. He and his army encamped at San Quirico because it was the last town before the boundary of the Papal State. Pope Adrian IV sent three cardinals to meet him and they struck a deal: the Pope gave him the crown; in return, Barbarossa hanged the Pope's nemesis, a monk named Arnaldo of Brescia. Unlike his friend Peter Abélard (lover of Héloïse), Arnaldo had put his actions where his words were and organised a rebellion against papal greed and warmongering.

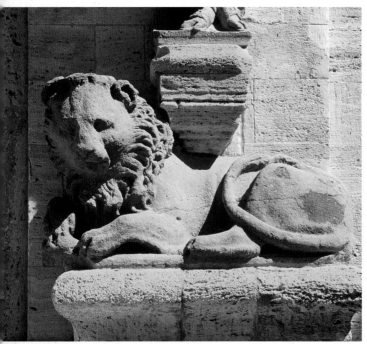

The town's single artery is the Via Dante Alighieri with the tiny 11th-century Romanesque Chiesa Santa Maria Assunta at the south end and the baroque Palazzo Chigi (1679) at the north end. Facing the *palazzo* is the **Collegiata di Orsenna** – famous for its carved portals. The *portale di mezzogiorno* (south door) is carved with enigmatic symbols and mythic beasts in mostly Romanesque style, with a few hints of Gothic. It is attributed to Giovanni Pisano. Inside, the choir stools have magnificent intarsia work, based on designs by painter Luca Signorelli that were originally created for one of the chapels of Siena's cathedral.

Accommodation and food

Antico Caffè Poliziano € *Via di Voltaia nel Corso 27, Montepulciano; tel: 0578 758615. Closed Wed.* This art-deco café/bar has an art gallery, magnificent view and, in July, a jazz festival.

Osteria del Leone € *Via dei Mulini 3, Bagno Vignoni; tel: 0577 887300. Closed Mon.* Right across from the old Bagni Vignoni bathhouse, this simple *trattoria* offers a blackboard rather than a menu – just a short list in chalk of seasonal dishes such as pasta with a sauce of rabbit or boar, *anatra all'uva* (duck with grape sauce) and *scottiglia di pollo* (chicken stew with herbs).

Parco delle Piscine € *Via del Bagno Santo 29 (9km from Sarteano); tel: 0578 26971; fax: 0578 265889; www.parcodellepiscine.it. Open Apr–Sep.* 'Camping' with a difference. There are three swimming pools, hot springs, a bar-restaurant and tennis courts. Reservations advised for summer.

Santo Pietro € *Strada Statale 146, No 29 on the road between Pienza and Montepulciano; tel and fax: 0578 748410; e-mail: santo.pietro@libero.it. Open Mar–Dec. Three-day minimum stay, half board only.* Fine views and lots of bucolic bliss at this *agriturismo*. The farm of Felice d'Angelo and Giulia Scala provides the wine, olive oil and vegetables for their guests' dinner.

La Solita Zuppa € *Via Porsenna 21, Chiusi; tel: 0578 21006; www.lasolitazuppa.it. Closed Tue.* A dozen kinds of soup: try chestnut and lentil, courgette and fresh basil.

Le Terme € *Overlooking the Basin of St Catherine, Bagno Vignoni; tel: 0577 887150; fax: 0577 887497; www.albergoleterme.it.* Unforgettable location but the interior is disappointing. Reservations a must.

Castello di Ripa d'Orcia €€ *Via della Contea 1/16, Ripa d'Orcia, 5km south of San Quirico d'Orcia; tel: 0577 897376; fax: 0577 898038; www.castelloripadorcia.com. Open Mar–Nov; two-day minimum stay.* The Aluffi Pentini family offers six rooms with private bathrooms in their castle (at the end of a gravel road out of Bagno Vignoni) with all sorts of comfort without compromising its medieval character. There are sweeping views from its terrace down the Val d'Orcia, a swimming pool and tennis court. It also has a good restaurant (*closed Mon*).

Il Chiostro €€ *Corso del Rossellino 26, Pienza; tel: 0578 748402; fax: 0578 748440.* As the name suggests, this is a former Franciscan cloister with vaulted rooms, frescos and coffered ceilings; a swimming pool, parking and a dazzling view.

La Frateria di Padre Eligio €€€ *Convento San Francesco, Cetona; tel: 0578 238261; fax: 0578 239220; www.lafrateria.it. Closed Nov.* St

Francis would not approve, but if you want to splurge, go ahead and reserve one of the six luxurious double rooms in this converted monastery, now one of Tuscany's top hotels.

Suggested tour

Total distance: 94km; detours add 14km (to Cetona) and 4km (to Bagni San Filippo) (both return).

Time: Three days would be a reasonable amount of time for this tour. The itinerary can be done in a day if you drive most of the time and don't dawdle in castles, hill-towns or vineyards. There might even still be time for a quick soak in the thermal springs.

Links: This route can readily be combined with the route of the previous chapter. Chiusi is only about 10km from Città della Pieve, in Umbria (*see pages 213–14*).

Above
Hilltop Pienza

Bravìo delle Botti
Eight divisions
(*contrade*) of Montepulciano
roll heavy barrels up a hill
in an attempt to win a
painted cloth. Last Sun
in Aug.

Route: From **MONTEPULCIANO ❶**, proceed to **Chianciano Terme ❷** – one of the most important thermal spas in Italy, celebrated for its waters since the Roman period. It was the centre for a cult of Apollo and another temple was devoted to Diana. Today, the spas are rather clinical, in keeping with their serious medical role in the treatment of liver and rheumatic problems.

Detour: For an alternative route from Montepulciano, take the small, desolate road at Croce di Febo and drive through an almost unpopulated stretch of the Crete brushing past the hamlets of **Castelluccio** and **La Foce**; from Sarteano (10km), turn northeast to Chiusi.

Carry on 13km to **CHIUSI ❸** where there is free parking in a field at the edge of town (*you have to drive into the centre first to get there*). After retrieving the car, drive to **Sarteano ❹**, another medieval town with an Etruscan past.

Detour: Turn left (south) on the road to **Cetona ❺**, at the foot of Monte Cetona. The village is an oval-shaped maze built around a formidable fortress. The Chiesa Collegiata has a fresco of the ascension of Mary by Pinturicchio. The **Parco Archeologico Belverde ❻**, 5km north of Cetona, is an idyllic natural park with a small museum displaying Stone Age finds.

Continue on the N478 for the next 18km. It crosses the upper valley of the Orcia river.

Getting out of the car: After 8km, there is a road leading to the hamlet of **Fonte Vetriana**. The trail from there that climbs up to Monte Cetona is one of the most rewarding hikes in Tuscany.

The village of **RADICOFANI ❼** seems high enough but a brutally steep road twists even further up to the **Rocca** (720m), the most famous castle in southern Tuscany. After hairpinning back down the hill (in low gear), proceed towards Siena.

Detour: Almost immediately after getting on the N2, you will see signs for **Bagni San Filippo ❽**. There is not much to the place except a turn-of-the-20th-century spa and a handful of modest hotels at the edge of the forest. The thermal waters here range from 25° to 52°C. Signs will direct you further up the valley to **Fosso Bianco**. This is surely one of the most surreal waterfalls in Italy. The cascade of thermal water has left brilliant white deposits that look like hummocks of snow and icicles. It has many inviting pools of hot, milky water to soak in.

The N2 rejoins the valley of the Orcia river at the village of **BAGNO VIGNONI ❾**, clearly signposted just 1km off the road. **SAN QUIRICO d'ORCIA ❿** is a hop, skip and 5km up the N2. From there return to the N146 going east in the direction of **PIENZA ⓫** (*parking just outside the walls*). It is another 12.5km back to Montepulciano.

Also worth exploring

San Casciano dei Bagni is a medieval town on the southern slopes of Monte Cetona, not far from the meeting point of the provinces of Tuscany, Umbria and Lazio. The town, which attracts few foreign tourists, is surrounded by a natural park of hundred-year-old oaks, chestnuts and pines. At its core is a narrow maze of ancient streets intersecting with a Romanesque church and bell tower. The town's hot springs bubble with indubitable therapeutic properties. Not far from the town, in fact, flow 42 thermal springs, at a blissful bathtub temperature of 37–43°C.

Lucca

Ratings

Architecture	●●●●●
Shopping	●●●●●
Villas	●●●●●
Food and drink	●●●●○
Parks	●●●●○
Children	●●●○○
Museums	●●●○○
Nature	●●○○○

Lucca rivals any city in Italy for fascination and beauty. One century flows into the next – and right up to the present – as you walk past shops with medieval and art nouveau façades, cross a Roman amphitheatre turned piazza and stroll along the magnificent 16th-century ramparts that are now a pleasure garden. This is 'the Tuscany that still lives and enjoys, hopes and works' (Henry James). Lucca is located in a plain at the foot of the high Apuan Alps and separated from the Tyrrhenian coast by a green border of pine forest and a line of low hills. Thanks to its impenetrable walls, Lucca remained an independent city until the 19th century, long after most other Tuscan cities had become part of the Grand Duchy of Tuscany under the control of Florence.

Sights

ⓘ APT office *Piazza Santa Maria 35; tel: 0583 919931; www.luccatourist.it. Open daily Apr–Oct 0900–2000, shorter hours in winter.*

Pro Loco *Piazzale Verdi; tel: 0583 442944; www.comune.lucca.it*

ⓗ Duomo San Martino € *Piazza del Duomo; tel: 0583 957068. Open daily Mar–Oct 0700–1900, Nov–Feb 0700–1700.*

Anfiteatro Romano

The Roman amphitheatre (2nd century AD) is now underground beneath this strange piazza and its former exterior is a street – Via dell'Anfiteatro. You can see one of the original arches at No 32. The amphitheatre was elliptical in shape and had two levels of 55 arches, one on top of the other.

Duomo San Martino (Opera del Duomo)

Bishop Frediano commissioned the building of the church of San Martino in the 6th century and the edifice advanced to the status of cathedral in the 8th century. Another bishop of Lucca and Pope Alexander II rebuilt it a couple of centuries apart. On the latter version, Guidetto da Como created its façade: a series of loggias resting on pillars and an atrium packed with bas-reliefs (1233) depicting the four stories of St Martin, the dispute with the Aryans and the

Ilaria del Carretto
€ *Sacrestia del Duomo;*
tel: 0583 490530. Open
Apr–Oct Mon–Fri
0930–1745,
Sat 0930–1845,
Sun 0900–1000 and
1300–1745; Nov–Mar
Mon–Fri 0930–1645, Sat
0930–1845, Sun
0900–1000 and
1300–1700.

Museo della Cattedrale
€ *Piazza del Duomo; tel:*
0583 490530;
www.museocattedralelucca.it.
Open daily Apr–Oct
1000–1800; Nov–Mar
1000–1400.

Martyrdom of San Regolo. The great sculptor, Nicola Pisano, added a Nativity and Deposition. The porch is decorated with the tasks of the 12 months of the year, from giving a girl roses to slaughtering a pig.

Inside, the cathedral's pride and joy is the Volto Santo (Holy Face), an ancient wooden statue of a bearded Christ on the Cross, fully dressed, with a feminine face – said to have been carved by St Nicodemus. The people of Lucca have worshipped it for centuries. The cross is rumoured to contain relics – hairs of Christ, a phial of blood and, believe it or not, Our Lord's prepuce.

The marble figure of **Ilaria del Carretto** is Lucca's greatest monument. Ilaria, the 19-year-old wife of nobleman Paolo Guinigi, died in childbirth at the beginning of the 15th century. Short of freezing her head, there is nothing more sculptor Jacopo della Quercia could have done to immortalise her. The beautiful young woman seems to have fallen asleep on a cushion. At her feet is an alert lapdog, a symbol of fidelity. Other important works in the cathedral include: *Last Supper* by Tintoretto or his school (16th century) in the third altar; *Madonna with Child* by Domenico Ghirlandaio (15th century) in

The **Volto Santo** is carried out of the cathedral every year for the Luminaria di Santa Croce on the evening of 13 September. The crucifix is wrapped in its best silver and gold brocade, and paraded by candlelight through the *Centro Storico* by citizens of Lucca in medieval dress.

Every third Sunday of the month, there is a large antique market in front of the Duomo.

The 4km circuit of Lucca's walls can be done on a hired bicycle. Lucca is one of the few Italian cities that likes to 'get on its bike'. **Cicli Bizzarri** *Piazza Santa Maria 32, tel: 0583 496031;* **Antonio Poli** *Piazza Santa Maria 42, tel: 0583 493787.*

San Michele in Foro € *Piazza San Michele; tel: 0583 48459. Open daily 0800–1200, 1500–1800.* To the right of the church is the Palazzo Pretorio, by Civitali, with a loggia containing busts of illustrious city citizens. On the left, the Palazzo del Decanato takes up the whole side of the square. Behind the tower are perfectly preserved 14th-century houses.

Opposite
Duomo San Martino

the sacristy; *Resurrection* by Giambologna (16th century) in the so-called Freedom Chapel at the top of the left nave; *Madonna and Child between Two Saints* by Fra Bartolomeo (16th century) in the Madonna of the Sanctuary Chapel; and *Holy Apostle* (1416) by Jacopo della Quercia (in the left transept). There is also much fine work by Matteo Civitali, Lucca's best sculptor, including the pulpit, baptistry font and the tombs of Domenico Bertini and Pietro da Noceto in the south transept.

The cathedral museum, **Museo della Cattedrale**, next door was opened in 1992 as an act of piety and PR by a local bank. It is full of objects relating to the cult of the Volto as well as cathedral treasures: liturgical vestments, choir books, silver objects, paintings and statues.

Le Mura

Lucca is one of the few towns in Italy with a set of defensive walls perfectly intact (for what it is worth, they are, according to *Guinness World Records*, the largest completely preserved set of walls in Europe). The 4km circuit of wall was started in 1554 and took nearly a century to complete. Twelve metres high, it consists of 11 curtain walls, 10 bastions and 1 platform, called San Frediano. The base is 30m thick. On the bastions, the little barracks still stand that once housed guards or munitions. One hundred and twenty-four cannons defended the city until the Austrians removed them in 1799.

The walls of Lucca were so intimidating that no one ever dared to besiege the city. The only assault it was ever called on to withstand was the great flood of 1812 when the Serchio river overflowed its banks and turned the plain around Lucca into a lake. Maria Luisa Bourbon, acting on the suggestion of Napoleon's sister, Elisabeth Baciocchi, transformed the ramparts into a public garden. It is thanks to her that the people of Lucca take their *passeggiata*, the ritual evening walk, beneath the ancient plane, oak, lime and chestnut trees.

Piazza San Michele

The Piazza San Michele stands on the site of the former Roman forum. The church of **San Michele in Foro**, first mentioned in a document of AD 795, was rebuilt in the 11th century and completed in its present form in the 14th century. The brilliant white façade is a dreamy fusion of Gothic and Romanesque styles beneath a triumphant statue of St Michael the Archangel slaying a dragon (13th century).

'For the first time I now saw what medieval builders were and what they meant,' was the reaction of John Ruskin. The adjoining bell tower is the highest in Lucca. The façade is a hard act to follow (and the medieval builders ran low on funds) so the interior is less impressive. In one corner is a Madonna and Child by sculptor Matteo Civitali (it was once part of the façade). There is a glazed terracotta Madonna and Child attributed to Andrea della Robbia and a crucifix by Berlinghieri from the end of the 12th century. However, the real

Basilica di San Frediano € *Piazza San Frediano; tel: 0583 493627. Open daily 0830–1200 and 1500–1700.*

San Giovanni e Reparata € *Piazza San Giovanni; tel: 0583 490530. Open daily mid-Mar–Sep 1000–1800, Oct–mid-Mar Sat–Sun 1000–1700.*

Taddeucci *(Piazza San Michele 34; tel: 0583 494933)* is the best place to buy the local speciality, *buccellato*, a raisin and aniseed cake. The shop has an untouched 19th-century interior of wood panels and mosaic tiles.

Centre of government

Lucca was already an important city when Caesar, Pompey and Crassus met there in 56 BC to form Rome's first triumvirate, and it became even more important when, under the Lombards, it formed the centre of government of the surrounding region.

highlight is the luminous panel by Filippino Lippi, son of the more famous Filippo.

Basilica di San Frediano

The oldest church in Lucca was named after the Irish saint and Lucca's first bishop, Fredianus. The mosaic façade, a kaleidoscopic Ascension of Christ, is by the picturesquely named Berlinghiero Berlinghiera. The church faces the wrong direction, east, because it was built next to a city wall. Inside, it is a monumental basilica with some of the capitals recycled from the nearby Roman amphitheatre.

The single most impressive object is the Romanesque Fonta Lustra near the front, a baptismal font upon which an anonymous artist sculpted Moses crossing the Red Sea, pursued by Egyptians in medieval armour. There is another baptismal font, still in use, carved by Matteo Civitali in 1489. The Cappella Trenta has an altar by Jacopo della Quercia. In the left nave, frescos by Amico Aspertini depict the arrival of the Volto Santo in Lucca.

The unmissable right-hand chapel is one of the most popular places to pray in Lucca – in the presence of the mummified St Zita. She accepted that bending the rules is all in a saintly day's work. A servant born in 1218, she stole bread on the job to give it to the poor and lied about it when caught in the act. But the lie became truth when the scraps of bread miraculously turned into roses.

San Giovanni e Reparata

Few basilicas in Tuscany have a longer tale to tell than this one, from Roman times to the Middle Ages. It is a surreal experience to wander among the bits and pieces of Roman baths, pillars, mosaics and shops (180–100 BC) beneath the floor of the present church and then to re-emerge into natural light and look up at the baroque coffered ceiling. The stones are a vast puzzle, presented in a meticulous multicoloured map that the guardian will sell or loan out. The church dome was built in 1390 and represents a brave attempt to solve the problem of supporting such a structure, using a circle on top of a square. Brunelleschi studied it before beginning work on the cathedral in Florence.

Via Fillungo

This narrow street is lined with medieval palaces and towers and shops with *fin de siècle* or art nouveau façades: the jeweller Chioccetti (No 20); the shoe store graced with sexy art deco nudes dating from the time when it was the Profumeria Venus (No 65); Puccini's favourite place to chain-smoke, the Caffè di Simo (No 58); Carli (No 95), in business since 1655 selling jewellery, ancient coins and antique watches; and the jeweller Pellegrino (No 111). There is also a small art nouveau passage (No 102).

Opposite
San Michele in Foro

ERITHRAEA

Accommodation and food

Don't even think of coming to Lucca without a reservation. If you just arrive on a weekend or in high season, you might have to drive far before you sleep.

Osteria Baralla € *Via Anfiteatro 5–9; tel: 0583 440240. Closed Sun.* An atmospheric bar/inn right off the Roman amphitheatre, popular with students, where you can eat anything from a *crostini* (toasted bread with liver pâté or tomatoes) to a full traditional meal.

Piccolo Hotel Puccini € *Via di Poggio 9; tel: 0583 55421; www.hotelpuccini.com.* A simple, friendly hotel with nostalgic, 19th-century flourishes but no 21st-century parking. Located just off Piazza San Michele in Foro.

Buca di Sant Antonio €€ *Via della Cervia 1/5; tel: 0583 55881; www.bucadisantantonio.com. Closed Sun and Mon.* A rustic place that is always crowded with people hungry for traditional dishes such as *zuppa al farro* (soup made with chicken stock, lentils and spelt) and home-made pasta such as *tortelli al sugo.*

Hotel Stipino €€ *Via Romana 95; tel: 0583 495077; fax: 0583 490309; www.hotelstipino.com.* The best hotel immediately outside the walls (well, a five-minute walk from Porta Elisa), Stipino also has private parking. The owner is always busy, good-naturedly fussing over the housekeeping, his guests and his grandchildren. However, the rooms on the street are loud unless the double-glazed windows are kept shut (a disadvantage in summer) so ask for a room at the back.

Locanda di Bacco €€ *Via San Giorgio 36; tel: 0583 493136. Closed Tue.* Near Piazza San Michele and its magnificent Pisan-Romanesque church. The best of everything the region has to offer: soup made with farro (spelt), pasta, chickpeas, beans and sausages; mushrooms and chestnuts in season. There is a bottle of deep-green Lucchese olive oil on every table.

Universo €€€ *Piazza del Giglio 1; tel: 0583 493678; fax: 0583 954854; www.universolucca.com.* The location is ideal, just inside the city walls and near the cathedral. It has an evocative, if faded, *belle-époque* atmosphere, its own parking and a good restaurant.

Suggested tour

Total distance: 3.5km.

Time: Although compact, Lucca is not the sort of place you can easily reduce to an afternoon or even a long day. Two days is better. If time is short, walk a part of the walls, visit the Duomo and focus on the Piazza San Michele in Foro and the Via Fillungo.

Links: The route SS12 through the Garfagnana and Alpi Apuane begins and ends in Lucca (*see page 124*). It is also the starting point for the route on *page 135*.

Route: Enter Lucca from the Piazzale Risorgimento through the **Porta San Pietro** ❶, the city's oldest gate. Turn left into the Via F Carrara and then right into the Via Vittorio Veneto to reach the **Piazza Napoleone**. There is a grotesque memorial to Princess Maria Luisa in the middle of the square and one of Garibaldi in the adjoining Piazza del Giglio. Walk past the latter statue and squeeze through a short lane into the Piazza San Giovanni to come face to face with **SAN GIOVANNI E REPARATA** ❷. Walk into the next piazza – the Piazza San Martino, dominated by the **DUOMO SAN MARTINO** ❸ and the **Palazzo Arcivescovile**. Exit the cathedral and veer right past a group of houses abutting the Duomo – built on the former colonnade of its

❶ While you are permitted to drive within the walls, you will probably regret it. There are small, paying car parks in: Piazza San Ponziano, Piazza Santa Maria Bianca, Piazza della Manifattura and Piazzale San Donato; but they fill up quickly (tourists must park within the blue lines as those delineated by yellow lines are for residents only). The free car parks just outside the walls are a better option (Via delle Tagliate or the Macelli area beside the hospital).

Left
Café in Lucca

Below
Le Mura, Lucca's defensive walls

13th-century cemetery. The door to the cemetery is still preserved and leads to the treasures of the **Museo della Cattedrale** (Cathedral Museum). Continue up the same street (Via delle Trombe) a couple of paces and duck left into the atmospheric **Via del Battistero**. Proceed to Piazza San Giusto and turn right into Via Cenami. After one block it meets Via Roma. Turn left and walk into Piazza San Michele. Circle around **SAN MICHELE IN FORO ❹**, turn left into Santa Lucia then immediately right into Chiasso Barletti, an almost sunless lane which intersects with **VIA FILLUNGO ❺**. From here, join the eternal parade of this fascinating street. The walk now follows, roughly, the route taken by the annual candlelit procession of Lucca's prize relic, the Volto Santo (Holy Face), and, in reverse, the silent procession of Napoleon's sister, Elisa Bonaparte Bacciochi, when she entered the city as princess in 1805.

Detour: At the Piazza dei Mercanti take the Via Sant'Andrea to the **Torre Guinigi ❻**. Bizarrely, it is crowned with holm oaks. However, the people of Lucca claim that all of their towers once sprouted trees. Climb the tower for a memorable view of the rooftops of Lucca and the marble-veined peaks of the Alpi Apuane to the north. On the way up and down you can study the shoe marks on the whitewashed staircase walls, some as high as 2m up. No, it's not a Euro-funded art project, just a local, acrobatic form of graffiti.

Carry on down Via Fillungo to Piazza Scalpellini. Duck under the arch to the right and walk into the middle of the **PIAZZA ANFITEATRO ROMANO ❼**. Exit the piazza through the gate on the opposite side (the small figure above it to the left is St Frediano). On the other side of the gate is Via dell'Anfiteatro. Follow the curve left until you reach Via Fillungo, walk left a few paces and take the first right to reach **SAN FREDIANO ❽**. After going inside, retrace your steps and, facing the church, walk left around it. Once behind it (having crossed Piazza del Collegio) take the ramp to the right of the wall. Begin your *passeggiata* along **LE MURA ❾** (city walls) going right.

Detour: Descend from the walls at the bastion of Baluardo San Salvatore, dropping down into Via della Quarconia, to reach the **Villa Guinigi ❿**.

The Villa Guinigi was built by Paolo Guinigi in 1408 in a style that still displays some characteristics of Gothic architecture. The villa is now seat of the **Museo Nazionale di Villa Guinigi** (€; *tel: 0583 496033. Open Tue–Sat 0830–1930, Sun 0830–1330*). The museum houses important Roman and Hellenistic finds to remind the visitor how old Lucca really is. However, it is the medieval period that predominates with Romanesque, Gothic and Renaissance sculptures. There are many fine pieces by della Quercia and Matteo Civitali. Paintings range from the 13th to the 19th century. Among them are a crucifix by Berlinghieri (13th century), two lovely altarpieces by Ugolino Lorenzetti and works by other Lucchese and Sienese masters.

Continue along the walls to the **Orto Botanico Comunale** (Botanical Garden) **⑪** (€; *Via del Giardino Botanico 14; tel: 0583 442160. Open Tue–Sun May–Jun 1000–1800; Jul–mid-Sep 1000–1900; Apr and mid-Sep–Nov 1000–1700; Nov–Mar 0930–1230 by reservation only*), laid out by Elisa Baciocchi.

Also worth exploring

The **Museo Nazionale di Palazzo Mansi** (€ *Via Galli Tassi 43; tel: 0583 55570; www.villelucchesi.net. Open Tue–Sat 0830–1900, Sun 0830–1330*) is worth a visit for the building alone, which is a rococo riot inside, culminating in the sumptuous *Camera degli Sposi* overflowing with Lucca-style embroidered silk. The Palazzo's Pinacoteca Nazionale has some 80-odd paintings, including a portrait of a pouting Alessandro de' Medici by Pontormo and one of Cosimo I by Bronzino. There are also works by Tintoretto, Fra Bartolomeo, Andrea del Sarto, Sodoma and Beccafumi.

Garfagnana

Ratings

Caves	●●●●●
Geology	●●●●●
Mountains	●●●●●
Nature	●●●●●
Scenery	●●●●●
Food and drink	●●●●○
Architecture	●●●○○
Museums	●○○○○

The Garfagnana is as far from Chiantishire as you can travel, and still be in Tuscany. The mountainous region was once notorious for witches and its landmark is a grotesque medieval bridge supposedly built by the devil. Except for the hill-town of Barga, there isn't much here for the medievalist but it is a paradise for the walker, naturalist and spelunker. The Serchio river has cut a dramatic course between the heavily forested Apennines on the east and the geologically older Apuan Alps to the west. Although both ranges are beautiful, the Alpi Apuane stand out as one of the most original landscapes in Italy. Its peaks appear snowy because of the gleaming white fissures left by quarrying marble. Narrow roads switchback between the white-veined summits, plumbing forests of chestnuts and skirting alpine meadows.

BAGNI DI LUCCA

ℹ **Informazioni turistiche** c/o Chiesa Anglicana; tel: 0583 805745; fax: 0583 809937; www.provincia.lucca.it & www.alpiapuane.com. Bagni di Lucca organises an annual opera festival that takes place from late Jul to early Aug.

Right
Bagni di Lucca

This little spa town has seen better days, for example, when literary types such as Shelley, Byron and Heinrich Heine stayed here. However, it is still a good place for people who like to wallow in faded elegance. In springtime, the surrounding sub-alpine meadows are covered with wild flowers. The casino has the oldest gaming licence in Europe, though it is not of much use since it is semi-permanently closed for restoration.

BARGA

Pro Loco *Piazza Angelio 3; tel: 0583 723499.*

Duomo San Cristofano €
Open daily.

It has been a long, strange trip for Barga. It evolved from Roman fort to Lombard castle-town to Lucchese bishopric and became a gleam in the expansionist eye of the Medici, who ruled it from Florence for centuries. In the hard times after World War II, more people emigrated from Barga per capita than any other town in Italy.

The impressive **Duomo San Cristofano** dominates not only the town but also the surrounding valley. Architecturally, the cathedral is a Romanesque masterpiece. The lion-mounted pulpit inside is one of the most important medieval works of art in Tuscany (attributed to Guido Bigarelli), rivalling more famous work in Pisa. It evokes an early Christianity with eccentric figures portraying the familiar stories of the birth of Jesus, Adoration of the Magi, and so on. The enormous wooden figure in the choir is St Christopher, patron saint of travellers.

The people of Barga have no doubt prayed to him often in the last century as they boarded ships for America, Argentina and Scotland. The town is proud of its expatriates and its links to Scotland, in particular. Don't be surprised if you stumble across a fish and chips festival or a Highland marching band.

CASTELNUOVO DI GARFAGNANA

ℹ **Pro Loco** *Piazza delle Erbe 1; tel: 0583 641007; e-mail: prolococastelnuovogarf @virgilio.it; www.turismo. provincia.lucca.it, www. castelnuovogarfagnana.org. Open Mon–Sat 0930–1300 and 1530–1900, shorter hours in winter.*

It was Castelnuovo's fate to be both an important base for Italian partisans during their guerrilla war against the German occupation and a part of the retreating Germans' line of defence. Allied bombing destroyed much of it. However, it is a friendly town that offers provisions and resources for all sorts of excursions into the surrounding mountains. The Renaissance poet Ariosto, author of *L'Orlando Furioso*, complained bitterly about his job as governor of this modest fortress. His former study is open to the public.

PARCO NATURALE DELLE ALPI APUANE

ℹ **Centro Accoglienza Visitatori** *Piazza delle Erbe 1, Castelnuovo di Garfagnana; tel/fax: 0583 644242; www.parcapuane.toscana.it and Via Corrado del Greco 11, Seravezza; tel/fax: 0584 756144; www.parks.it. Both centres open daily Jun–Sep 0900–1300 and 1500–1900, Oct–May 0900–1300 and 1530–1730.*

The Apuan Alps, the mountain range between the Serchio valley and the Versilian Riviera, only became a Parco Naturale in 1992, after much agitation and petition gathering. Now the struggle is on to give it the more protected status of Parco Nazionale. There is a good network of trails leading up to Pania di Croce (1,858m) and Monte Forato (1,223m), and the range of vegetation is amazingly wide.

Within the park are hundreds of kilometres of trails marked out by the local chapters of the Italian Alpine Club (CAI). The vast complex of caves beneath these mountains is a spelunker's paradise. The deepest, Antro del Corchia, reaches 1,210m underground. Marble quarrying has contributed to the strange appearance of the mountains by leaving enormous open gashes. It remains important to the local economy and is not likely to stop anytime soon.

PIETRASANTA

🏛 **Museo Civico di Marmo** € *Via XX Settembre 85, Massa Carrara; tel: 0585 845746. Open Jul–Aug Tue–Sat 1000–2000, May–Jun & Sep 1000–1800, Oct–Apr 0900–1700.*

Museo dei Bozzetti *Via Sant'Agostino; tel: 0584 795500; fax: 0584 795588; www.museodeibozzetti.com. Open Sep–Jun Tue–Sat 1400–1900, Sun 1600–1900; Jul and Aug Tue–Sun 1830–2000 and 2100–2400. Free.*

Few tourists ever bother to visit Pietrasanta (blessed stone) and the other marble towns in the region with the partial exception of Carrara. Pietrasanta still practises the industry that was behind much of the great art in Tuscany. Once the marble quarried here was turned into heroic statues by Renaissance sculptors, but today the lion's share of the marble is earmarked for kitchens, kitsch and export to the Middle East.

The history and mining of marble is documented in the **Museo Civico di Marmo** while the **Museo dei Bozzetti** displays 280 works (dating from the beginning of the 20th century to the present time), created by artists from all over the world. The sketches (on a small scale) and the patterns (in actual size) represent the original idea before the work is executed. The museum, housed in the huge cloister of Sant'Agostino, also hosts travelling exhibitions.

PONTE DELLA MADDALENA

**⊘ Ponte della
Maddalena** *Near the
hamlet of Borgo a Mozzano.*

Above
The Ponte della Maddalena
(Devil's Bridge)

Previous page
The Parco Naturale delle Alpi
Apuane

The 93m-long bridge thrusts a bizarre parabolic stone arch 19m above
the Serchio river, supported by three smaller arches. The existing
bridge was probably built in the 13th century. Locals also call it the
Ponte del Diavolo (devil's bridge) since, presumably, only he would
build it – in one night, according to the legend. Another legend claims
that Satan merely helped in return for the first eight legs to cross the
bridge (he was more interested, one assumes, in the souls attached to
them). The architect, to fulfil his part of the bargain, sent chickens
and a dog over the newly completed bridge.

Accommodation and food

Accommodation in this region is among the least expensive in Tuscany.

Albergo La Posta € *Piazza Antelminelli 2, in the village of Coreglia Antelminelli; tel: 0583 78027.* Rooms with a view (but shared bathroom) in an airy mountain village, with places to park and an earthy *trattoria* downstairs. The price is about the same as a campsite.

Da Giaccò € *Via di Arni 2, Camaiore; tel: 0583 667048.* In the heart of the Apuan Alps on the reservoir of Lake Isola Santa, this *trattoria* has a small terrace for summer eating but is perhaps at its best in autumn when they serve home-made pasta with truffles, *capretto alla brace* (grilled goat) and *funghi* (mushrooms), grilled on polenta. For dessert, there are puddings made with mountain raspberries and chestnut flour.

Albergo Roma €€ *Via Umberto I 110, Bagni di Lucca; tel and fax: 0583 87278.* A great hotel for romantics where Puccini used to be a regular. Most rooms have balconies overlooking its park and views of the Apennines.

Locanda Le Monache €€ *Piazza XXIX Maggio 36, Camaiore; tel: 0584 989258; fax: 0584 984011; www.lemonache.com.* An inn/tavern on the ancient Via Francigena, the road used by pilgrims on their way south to Rome. They dish out a fine *frittura* of delicately fried meat and vegetables and standards such as *bistecca fiorentina*. Otherwise, the short menu depends on the season – minestrone with mushrooms, perhaps, or *coniglio* (rabbit) *alla cacciatora*.

Villa Libano €€ *Via del Sasso 6, Barga; tel: 0583 723059; fax: 0583 724185; www.hotelvillalibano.com.* The best address for Barga with a leafy garden, outdoor restaurant, swimming pool and stunning views of the Apuan Alps.

Ristorante La Mora €€€ *Via Sesto di Moriano 1748, in the village of Ponte Moriano, 9km north of Lucca on the N12; tel: 0583 406402; www.ristorantelamora.com.* Often described as Lucca's best restaurant. A former coach station that has earned a Michelin star, La Mora triumphs with local ingredients such as eel and trout, pigeon, lamb and goat.

Suggested tour

Total distance: 127km; detours add 10km (return) to Villas Reale and Mansi, 20km (return) to Coreglia Antelminelli, and 26km to the gorge of Orrido di Botri.

Time: This route can be appreciated as a long, interesting mountain drive. Getting out of the car to climb a peak in the marble mountains or descend into its caves would extend it to a couple of days or more.

Links: This route does not overlap with any other. However, it would be easy to combine it with a drive down the coast (*see page 154*).

Route: From **Lucca** ❶, drive north along the meandering Serchio river on the N12.

Below
Duomo San Cristofano, Barga

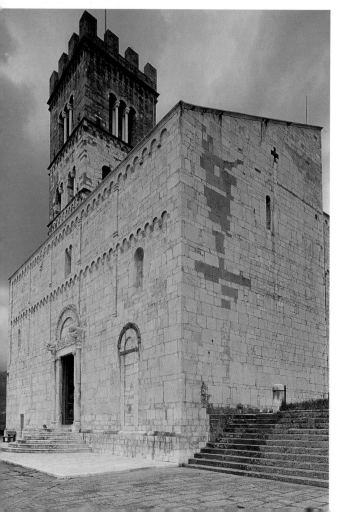

Detour: The village of Marlia is signposted to the right after only 6km. From there, follow the signs for Villa Reale. The nobility and merchants of Lucca have always invested their money in land. Their villas allow you to compare 16th-century conspicuous consumption with the 18th- and 19th-century varieties. One of the best is **Villa Reale** ❷ (*open for guided tours only Mar–Nov Tue–Sun 1000–1200, 1500–1800, with tours beginning each hour; or by booking, tel: 0583 30108; www.parcovillareale.it*). The former summer residence of Elisa Bonaparte Bacciochi, it also belonged to the king of Italy, Vittorio Emanuele, hence its claim to be 'royal'. The main draw is a legendary baroque garden at the back with green rooms formed of clipped shrubs, potted citrus trees, a vast pool embroidered with flowers, statues of Harlequin and Columbine, and trick fountains that spray water on unsuspecting visitors. The Renaissance villa was redecorated in First Empire style by Elisa and she had another garden, English-style this time, laid out in front.

The **Villa Mansi** ❸ (*open Tue–Sun 1000–1300, 1500–1800; tel: 0583 920234; www.villamansi.it*) is only 2km away, in the direction of Segromigno. The baroque villa is in a perfect state of preservation and filled inside with Pompeii-style Mannerist décor and imposing porcelain and plate. The garden is a somewhat less impressive motley of styles – French, Sicilian and English.

The **PONTE DELLA MADDALENA** ❹ spans the Serchio river near Borgo a Mozzano. Further up the valley, take the right fork in the road towards **BAGNI DI LUCCA** ❺ into a long, leafy funnel of plane trees. Just before the edge of town to the left, a remarkable 19th-century bridge, the Ponte delle Catene (1840–60), spans the Lima river (a kind of Brooklyn Bridge in miniature).

Getting out of the car: Scale the road that rises from Bagni di Lucca above the valley of the Lima river to the high mountain village of Montefegatesi (842m). It then plunges down to a spectacular wild canyon – the Riserva Naturale dell'Orrido di Botri. The gorge has a couple of well-marked trails and nesting eagles, which you are more likely to hear than see. The adventurous mountain road continues to Abetone via the pass of Face a Giovo (1,647m).

From Bagni di Lucca, return to the Serchio river road and follow the N445, continuing northwest in the direction of Barga.

Detour: The mountain village of **Coreglia Antelminelli** ❻ is 10km off the N445 up a steep and scenic road. It has the curious little **Museo della Figurina di Gesso e dell'Emigrazione** (*Palazzo Vanni, Via del Mangano 17; tel: 0583 78082; open Jun–Sep Mon–Sat 0930–1230*). The production of plaster of Paris figures goes back to the 17th century here. The craftsmen, known as *figurinai*, fell on hard times and were eventually forced to emigrate to places all over the world – hence the juxtaposition of themes. If it happens to be closed, ask at the Pro Loco (*Via Roma 8*) and they will open it.

There is free parking at the entrance to Porta Reale in **BARGA** ❼. The steep walk up to its cathedral leads through a maze of houses built on the slopes over many centuries. The church terrace has one of the finest views in Tuscany sweeping over the woods of the Apennines and across the Serchio valley to the flinty crest of Pania di Croce (1,858m) in the Alpi Apuane.

Getting out of the car: Cross the Serchio river at Barga to Gallicano and press on west for 9km to reach the **Grotta del Vento** ❽ at the foot of Pania di Croce. It is one of the largest stalactite caves in Europe. There are three different tours several times daily lasting one, two or three hours that venture progressively deeper into the cave (*all three tours daily Apr–Sep and Sun year round; Oct–Mar Mon–Fri only the first tour is available; tel: 0583 722024; www.grottadelvento.com*). They explore its crystal-incrusted lakes, natural curtains of alabaster and

Above
Marble quarry in the Alpi
Apuane

subterranean waterfalls. The third tour, taking in the entire cave, involves a dizzying climb down into an abyss that leaves you clutching at the handrails. Dress warmly regardless of the time of year. The normal temperature is 10°C.

Continue on the N445, skirting the Serchio river until you reach **CASTELNUOVO DI GARFAGNANA ❾**. If it isn't lunchtime, this is the best town (along with Seravezza) to find maps and information about outdoor activities. From here, take the road that leads through the narrow valley of Túrrite Secca (be careful not to get on the road to Careggine by mistake) and you will find yourself driving through the heart of the **PARCO NATURALE DELLE ALPI APUANE ❿**.

Getting out of the car: Several trails of the Garfagnana trekking circuit pass near the small lake of **Isola Santa ⓫**. A rewarding but brutally steep trail climbs 8km (return) to the summit of Monte Sumbra (1,764m). An easier walk leads towards Lago di Vagli.

After the reservoir of Isola Santa, choose the left fork at the hamlet of Tre Fiumi. Shortly afterwards, you will pass an abandoned marble quarry (belonging to Henraux). Through a massive fissure in the rock gleams a vast, neatly carved expanse of grey-veined marble. (A rusty sign, now fallen to the ground, warns that you set foot on the area at your own risk.) The road passes through a natural rock tunnel. When you burst into the light at the exit, pull over for a look at **Monte Altissimo**, where the illusion of snow is striking. It's like a ski resort with a couple of inviting *pistes* running down the middle. (There is a road leading up to the quarry but it is strictly off-limits and signs in multiple languages warn of multiple dangers including falling rock and the use of explosives.)

A long descent now begins, through perhaps the most beautiful stretch of the Apuan Alps. For the next 45km, you will be travelling in the footsteps of Michelangelo. He spent the two most frustrating years of his life in the region (1518–20) engaged in road engineering and the transport of marble (because his patron, Pope Leo X, had a disagreement with the marble suppliers of Carrara). Quarrying marble has always been a hazardous occupation; the road is lined with small chapels in memory of those who have died in mining accidents. One of them records the death of 22-year-old Giulio, followed by his father Carlo, 15 years later.

Outside **Seravezza** ⑫, a left fork in the road heads to **PIETRASANTA** ⑬ although the rusted blue sign only mentions '...SANTA'. If you miss it, it is no big deal. The next major left turn (south on the N1) also takes you there. However, when leaving town, avoid the N1, instead following the signs for **Camaiore** ⑭. From there, a pleasant country road leads back to **Lucca** with views, to the left, of the Alpi Apuane.

Also worth exploring

For people who plan ahead, there is a village worth seeing – at the bottom of Lago di Vagli. The village of **Fabbrica di Carregine** was evacuated and flooded by a newly built reservoir in 1953. Every ten years the reservoir is drained for cleaning and the village rises from the protean muck as if by miracle. The last time this took place was in 2004. The former residents and a few curious tourists stand on the shore and watch.

Parco di Pinocchio
ingresso

Ratings

Children	●●●●●
Thermal springs	●●●●●
Architecture	●●●●○
Shopping	●●●●
History	●●●○○
Museums	●●●○○
Scenery	●●●○○
Nature	●●○○○

Lucca to Florence

The lower valley of the Arno river forms a broad green trough, a notable exception to Tuscany's hilly geography. It has a dense concentration of agri-business, light industry and people. The A11 *autostrada* – one of Italy's main traffic arteries – covers the distance (74km) between Lucca and Florence in 40 minutes, unless there is a traffic jam. People who prefer travel to transit, however, will find that the valley's historic towns are rewarding for their art and architecture. Pistoia's marketplace has scarcely changed since the Middle Ages and Prato has something for both the art historian and the fashion victim. The valley's byways quickly lead to places where there is neither industry nor tourism, such as the deep woods and high mountain valleys of the Apennines, dotted with castles and medieval villages.

MONTECATINI TERME

🛈 **APT office** *Viale Verdi 66/68; tel: 0572 772244; fax: 0572 92761; www.montecatini.turismo. toscana.it*

🔘 A funicular € begins a few hundred metres above the spa and climbs up the mountain to **Montecatini Alto**, an ancient fortified town.

The most elegant spa in Tuscany and the largest in Italy, Montecatini has played host to the Medici, Verdi, the Duke of Windsor, Spencer Tracy, the Shah of Iran and Princess Grace of Monaco. They all came here to cure their livers and upset stomachs, putting themselves and their organs under the care of doctors, dieticians, masseurs and polished hoteliers. While the place still pulls a few rich and famous, it is becoming more scientific and less chic. The traditional thermal treatment of the liver, digestive tract and disorders of a creaking metabolism are now supported by modern medicine and rehabilitation. Therapy might mean simply gulping the water, taking salty baths and being massaged; or, more ambitiously, mud baths, inhalations, physiotherapy and medical gymnastics. If that doesn't restore the 'psycho-physical balance', there are also naturally hot 'sweat-caves' in nearby Monsummano Terme.

Montecatini's eight spas are set in the vast, well-manicured Parco delle Terme. Since 1926, the entire complex has belonged to the State.

Below
Pescia's market

The most elegant of them is Tettuccio. If the spa looks familiar, perhaps it is because you've seen it before in Fellini's film *8 1/2*. The central protagonist, Marcello Mastroianni, oscillates between his soft-porn fantasy world and real-life encounters in the spa with wife and friends among neoclassical marble pools, fountains and loggias.

PESCIA

ℹ **Informazioni turistiche** *Via Pasquinelli 54; tel: 0583 978205; www.comune.pescia.pt.it*

Italy's flower capital, Pescia harvests a couple of million blooms daily from its rows of vast glasshouses; it is also a major producer of olive oil and asparagus. The Piazza Mazzini is a historic, elongated square on the east side of the Pescia river packed with shops, bakers and bars.

The parish of Pescia is mentioned for the first time in a 10th-century document as being a religious complex of remarkable importance. The cathedral was, however, completely rebuilt in the baroque style in 1726. Among its treasures are a triptych by Luca della Robbia and, in the Cappella Turini, a copy of *Our Lady of the Canopy*, by Raphael (the original was appropriated by Ferdinand, Duke of Tuscany, and is now in the Pitti Palace in Florence). The altar of the austere church of San Francesco reveals the earliest known portrait of St Francis, painted in 1235, only a decade after his death.

PISTOIA

ℹ APT office *Piazza del Duomo 1; tel: 0573 21622; fax: 0573 34327; www.comune.pistoia.it, www.pistoia.turismo.toscana.it*

Ⓓ Duomo San Zeno € *Piazza del Duomo. Open daily.*

Capella di San Jacopo € *Piazza del Duomo; tel: 0573 25095. Open daily 1000–1230 and 1500–1730.* If the chapel is locked and no church service is under way, ask the church guardian to open it. He might insist on locking you in, but will return, sooner or later.

◔ The annual *Giostra dell'Orso* is a knight's tournament in Renaissance dress (25 July), in which each knight has to kill the figure of a bear – Pistoia's heraldic animal – with a heavy lance in the presence of his lady.

Pistoia Blues An international blues festival held every July. *E-mail: info@pistoiablues.com; www.pistoiablues.com*

Above
Pistoia's market

Opposite
Pistoia's Duomo San Zeno

The Romans founded the city of Pistoia in the 2nd century and it was near here that Rome's famous conspirator, Catiline, lost his life in battle. In the Middle Ages, Pistoia was caught between the overlapping spheres of influence of Florence and Pisa, until the former took over in 1254. Pistoia had a reputation for all sorts of evil-doing, promoted mostly by the Florentines who blamed them for splitting Florence into factions of Bianchi (Whites) and Neri (Blacks). In any case, Pistoia was the place where you could get the latest weapons, such as the *pistole*, originally a combination dagger and hand-held gun.

The city's Piazza del Duomo is the secular and religious rolled into one: the cathedral, bell tower and baptistry, and the Palazzo del Comune, Palazzo Pretorio and Palazzo Vescovile are all here. The **Duomo San Zeno**, founded in the 5th century, is one of the oldest in Tuscany. The present building dates mostly from the 12th century. An unusual porch was added to the façade in 1311. The central pillars form the opening of a barrel vault decorated with vivid coffers of shiny, pastel-painted terracotta by Andrea della Robbia (15th century). The interior is simple and imposing with a nave and two aisles divided by columns. The entrance wall has a font sculpted by Benedetto da Maiano. On the wall of the right aisle is the tomb of poet Cino da Pistoia, a contemporary and friend of Dante. The monument to Cardinal Niccolò Forteguerri is by Verrocchio and pupils.

The most remarkable object is the luminous silver altar of the **Cappella di San Jacopo**. Generations of artists worked on it in gold and silver between 1287 and 1456 and created 628 figures. It is interesting to compare the figures on the left side, by Brunelleschi and Leonardo di Giovanni, to the nine principal scenes from the saint's life on the front, sculpted centuries earlier. Opposite the cathedral is the octagonal baptistry built in only 20 years, starting in 1338, of green and white marble.

Just two blocks off the square, the Ospedale del Ceppo is perhaps the world's most beautiful functioning hospital. It was founded in 1277 and expanded during the 1348 plague. Its storybook 15th-century frieze in glazed terracotta by Giovanni della Robbia shows the Seven Merciful Works of founder St Buglioni. It is well worth seeking out Sant'Andrea as well. Inside is a pulpit sculpted by Giovanni Pisano (1301), and on the right in a niche, his statue of Sant'Andrea.

PRATO

ℹ **Informazioni turistiche** *Piazza Santa Maria delle Carceri 15; tel:/fax: 0574 24112; www.prato.turismo.toscana.it. Open Mon–Fri 0900–1300 and 1400–1830, Sat 0900–1330 and 1400–1800.*

🖼 **Museo del Tessuto** *€ Viale Santa Chiara 24; tel: 0574 611503; www.museodeltessuto.it. Open Mon–Fri 1000–1800, Sat 1000–1400, Sun (free) 1600–1900.*

Museo dell'Opera del Duomo *€€ Piazza del Duomo 49; tel: 0574 29339. Open Mon, Wed–Sat 0930–1230 and 1500–1830, Sun 0930–1230.*

Centro per l'Arte Contemporanea Luigi Pecci *€€ Viale della Repubblica 277; tel: 0574 5317; www.centropecci.it. Open Wed–Mon 1000–1900.*

Prato, the second largest city in Tuscany, has been in the shadow of Florence for all of its history. It even suffered the indignity, in 1351, of being sold to its wealthy neighbour by absentee rulers from the Neapolitan House of Anjou. Then, as now, the town's main concern was producing and selling cloth. Today, Prato accounts for the lion's share of Italian textile production and provides cloth to the big names in Italian fashion.

The 6,000 exhibits at the **Museo del Tessuto** (Textile Museum) are a useful introduction to Prato's business and a homage to damask, silk, brocade, velvet and even polyester. However, Prato is a historic and artistic city as well as a commercial one. Its star attraction is the 13th-century cathedral of **Santo Stefano**, inspired by Pisa and Lucca in its use of limestone and green marble, which gained cathedral status in 1653. It still attracts pilgrims from all over the world to see a precious relic – Mary's girdle, which she threw down to St Thomas on her way to heaven. The outdoor pulpit on the right corner of the façade was purpose-built to show it off (designed by Michelozzo with panels sculpted by Donatello). The girdle is actually kept in the 14th-century Cappella della Cintola at the beginning of the left-hand aisle.

One of the signature paintings of the Renaissance is in the choir. The fresco of *Herod's Banquet* is the work of native son Fra Filippo Lippi, a priapic monk and great painter. He seduced a nun in a Prato convent, and immortalised her as a sensual, black-eyed Madonna in many paintings. Thin veils billow around the body of Salome as she does her veiled dance – Botticelli's beauties owe much to her (he was Lippi's apprentice); in the meantime, the head of John the Baptist arrives on a platter like the *pièce de résistance*. Architecturally, the interior is a muscular Romanesque style, lightened by the two-colour scheme, used here for the first time indoors.

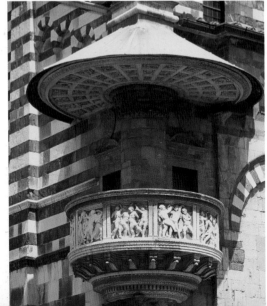

The **Museo dell'Opera del Duomo** has the (weathered) original Donatello panels from the pulpit of the sacred girdle and *The Death of Jerome* by Filippo Lippi. On the edge of town, near the Firenze-Mare *autostrada* exit, is Prato's progressive modern art museum and cultural centre, the **Centro per l'Arte Contemporanea Luigi Pecci**, created by the industrialist Signor Pecci in memory of his dead son.

Opposite
Prato's Piazza del Comune

Left
The cathedral's external pulpit

Accommodation and food

Flora Hotel € *Via Cairoli Benedetto 31, Prato; tel: 0574 400289; www.hotelflora.info.* A family-run hotel located in Prato's historic centre with comfortable rooms and helpful staff. Florence is just half an hour away by train.

Lo Storno € *Via del Lastrone 8, just off Piazza Sala, Pistoia; tel: 0573 26193. Closed Sun and Mon–Wed evenings.* There is a wonderful price-quality ratio at this small *trattoria*. The menu is limited (no *antipasta* and only two house wines) but delicious and changes almost daily depending on what's fresh in the market and the whim of owner-chef Aldo Bugiani.

Below
Montecatini Terme spa

La Vecchia Cucina di Soldano € *Via Pomeria 23, Prato; tel: 0574 34665. Closed Sun and in Aug. No credit cards.* A good place to try the local *minestra di pane* (vegetable soup), *sedani repieni* (stuffed celery) – a signature Prato dish – and *biscotto di Prato*, a hard biscuit that is often dipped in wine or coffee.

Il Convento €€€ *Via San Quirico 33, Pistoia (Pontenuovo district), 4km in the direction of Prato; tel: 0573 452651; fax: 0573 453578; www.ilconventohotel.it.* Pistoia's best hotel – 23 rooms in a former Franciscan convent with an excellent restaurant.

Il Pirana €€€ *Via Giuseppe Valentini 110, Prato; tel: 0574 25746. Closed Sat lunch and Sun.* One of the top fish restaurants in Tuscany. The décor is postmodern.

Shopping in Prato's factory outlets

Some of Prato's *fabbriche* (factories) sell clothing directly and the savings can be substantial. Their hours vary and are subject to change. Some of them will only accept cash.

Lanificio Cangioli *Via del Bisenzio a San Martino 6; tel: 0574 693925; www.cangioli.it. Open Mon and Sat 0930–1230, Tue and Thu–Fri 1530–1830. No credit cards.* Specialists in cashmere.

Maglieria Artigiana *Via A. Einstein 36–39; tel: 0574 8974479; www.maglieriaartigiana.it. Open Mon–Fri 0930–1300, 1500–1900, Sat morning by appointment only. Credit cards accepted.* Classic designs and a broad range of colours.

Maglificio Denny *Via Santa Gonda 3/7; tel: 0574 592350; www.denny.it. Open Mon–Fri 0900–1300, 1500–1930; Sat 0930–1300 by appointment. Credit cards – VISA, MasterCard accepted.* A vast selection of knitwear is sold here – pure wool, merino, Shetland and cashmere or blends with natural and synthetic fibres.

Milior M-Wear *Via Pistoiese 755/D; tel: 0574 81811; www.milior.com. Open Tue and Wed 1530–2000, Thu and Fri 1200–2000, Sat 1000–1300 and 1600–2000.* Affordable, knitted designer clothing and accessories.

Suggested tour

Total distance: 74km; detours add 22km (return) to Villa Torrigiani, 4km to Collodi (return); 35–60km, depending on circuit, for La Svizzera Pésciatina; 44km to Abetone, Montagna Pistoiese.

Time: This route could be considered as an alternative to the *autostrada* for reaching Florence. Or you could stay in one of the towns for a couple of nights and visit Florence by train, reserving the car for excursions into the Apennines and spending the money you save in Prato on a cashmere sweater.

Links: Lucca is also the starting point for a tour of the Garfagnana (*see page 124*).

Route: The N435 road from **Lucca** ❶ (*see page 108*) to Pescia is often congested and runs the gauntlet of roadside light industry and retail. You could have your hair cut, cat spayed, shoes and tyres replaced, and furniture re-upholstered many times over in the first couple of kilometres.

Below
Collodi's Villa Garzoni

Detour: Take the left fork at Borgonuovo after 9km. Drive to the village of Camigliano and follow the signs from the village to **Villa Torrigiani** ❷.

A long avenue of cypresses leads from here to one of the most famous Medici villas in Tuscany (€, *open Mar–mid-Nov 1000–1230, 1500–1830, mid-Nov–Dec groups by appointment only – tel: 0583 928041. Closed Tue and Jan–Feb*). The villa was the 16th-century dream home of the Buonvisi family. Alfonso Torrigiani remodelled it in the 18th century and created an English garden. The baroque garden is the biggest draw with occasional demonstrations of trick fountains used for 18th-century soak-the-guest water games.

The road leaves the plain as the N435 approaches Pescia, near the foothills of the Apennines.

Detour: 4km before Pescia, the road to **Collodi** ❸ is clearly marked.

Wooden Pinocchio puppets dangle by the hundred from souvenir stands in a bend in the road just before the **Parco di Pinocchio** €€ (*tel: 0572 429342; www.pinocchio.it; open daily 0830–dusk*). The theme park re-creates 21 scenes from the adventures of Pinocchio in mosaics, mazes and statues (no virtual reality yet). The author, Florentine Carlo Lorenzini, wrote the celebrated children's story in 1881, and adopted the name of his mother's village, where he had spent part of his childhood, as a pseudonym.

The town's other star attraction is the fabulous garden of the Villa Garzoni, a man-made Eden planted in the 17th century and inhabited by topiary animals and strange terracotta creatures. It is one of the finest baroque gardens in Italy. Above the garden is the medieval hamlet of Collodi that has stupendous views and relatively few visitors – perhaps because it is a steep (but short) uphill walk.

The road twists into **PESCIA** ❹ and then out again after crossing the river of the same name.

Detour: Only a few kilometres north of Pescia, above the local paper mills, is so-called La Svizzera Pesciatina (the Pescian Switzerland), a rugged and heavily forested range of hills and mountains divided by two high valleys. Monte Battifolle (1,109m) is their highest point. Ten tiny, fortified villages dating from the 11th century dot the area, all of them with walls and castles at least partly intact. Few tourists make their way up here and the facilities are limited so inquire in advance about accommodation. **Pietrabuona** ❺ (**Pro Loco** *Via del Campanile 7, tel: 0572 429342; fax: 0572 429342*) is normally the starting point for a tour of the area, which usually includes **Castelvecchio** ❻ and Pontito, and **Vellano** ❼ as the final destination.

Once you reach **MONTECATINI TERME** ❽ , follow the signs for Parco delle Terme. After the leafy park, the road to **Montecatini Alto** ❾ zig-zags 5km and several hundred metres up to the mellow old hill-town that overlooks the Val di Nievo. On the way back down, stop at the first intersection, follow the signs for Serravalle (passing a co-operative that sells local olive oil on the right) and descend into the Val di

Nievo. At the end of the valley is the unmistakably medieval profile of
Serravalle ⑩, where you will rejoin the N435. The *Centro Storico* has
several well-preserved towers (and an optimistic tourist office that calls
it 'a miniature San Gimignano'). The road to **PISTOIA ⑪** is
uneventful except for the occasional traffic jam and a couple of fine
old villas that seem stranded by the roadside. There is a car park near
the *Centro Storico* and, generally, parking is available on the street as
well (but check the signs).

Detour: The mountains above Pistoia – the Montagna Pistoiese – are
reached via the N66, N632 and N12. This is the route Hannibal and
his elephants travelled on their way to crush the Romans at Lake
Trasimeno (the elephants didn't make it: *see page 217*). The area is
popular for skiing in winter and trekking in summer. The highest peak
is Cimone (2,165m). **Abetone ⑫** is the main ski resort.

From Pistoia, follow signs for Montale and Montemurlo to **PRATO ⑬**.
The road between Prato and Florence is almost solid light industry so
one might as well take the *autostrada* to get to **Florence ⑭**.

Also worth exploring

The town of **Vinci**, as in Leonardo (1452–1519), is 24km south of
Pistoia along a charming road that climbs over Monte Albano. The
great artist, scientist, inventor, architect and engineer was born out of
wedlock in the nearby village of Anchiano. The **Museo Leonardiano €**
(*tel: 0571 56055; www.leonet.it/comuni/vincimus; open daily 0930–1800*)
has a fascinating collection of his inventions – the bicycle, an
armoured tank, helicopter, swing and suspension bridges, a parachute
and machine guns – that never made it any further than his
sketchpad. Vinci is in the middle of a nature reserve and the starting
point for many rewarding hikes.

Pisa

Ratings

Architecture	●●●●●
Art	●●●●●
History	●●●●○
Seafood	●●●●○
Museums	●●●○○
Children	●●○○○
Shopping	●●○○○
Nature	●○○○○

Few cities, even in Italy, have known such a burst of creativity as Pisa in the 11th century. The Pisans expelled Saracen invaders and launched a new era in trade and commerce. They did the same for architecture and sculpture, contributing to the rebirth of the classical spirit in Italy. The Renaissance itself might have taken place in Pisa rather than Florence had it not been for the city's disastrous naval defeat of 1284 and the silting up of its port. The group of medieval buildings in Pisa's Campo dei Miracoli (Field of Miracles) is one of the most remarkable in the world. Its Leaning Tower, as Charles Dickens observed, leans enough 'to satisfy the most demanding tourist'. However, there is another Pisa, where few tourists go: the *Centro Storico*, not a museum but a throbbing city, humming with traffic and thousands of university students.

Sights

ⓘ Informazioni turistiche *Piazza del Duomo; tel: 050 560464; www.comune.pisa.it. Open Mon–Sat 0900–1800; Sun 1030–1630.*

ⓑ Campo dei Miracoli
www.opapisa.it. All sights are open daily Apr–Sep 0800–2000, shorter hours in winter. Combined tickets may be purchased to cover all or some of the sights (€–€€).

Battistero
The reason for a separate baptistry here, as in Florence, was the early Christian taboo against an unbaptised person setting foot in the Lord's house. Begun in 1152, it was essentially the work of the father and son team of Nicola and Giovanni Pisano. The hexagonal pulpit by Nicola Pisano (1260) launched a new style of sculpture in Italy. The building has remarkable acoustics. If you test it by snapping your fingers in the centre, a loud echo replies.

Campanile (Torre Pendente or Leaning Tower)
Surely the most bizarre fact about the Leaning Tower is that most of it was built after it had started to lean. The Pisans who began this tower in 1173 only completed 10m before things went awry. The 13th-century architects made the best of it by lengthening the south-side columns by 70mm, giving it a slight banana shape. This is

North

0   400m
0   300 yards

Via Ugo Rindi

Via Lucchese

N12

Via di Pratale

Via Piave

Via Luigi Bianchi

Strada Statale

Via San Zeno

Via Vittorio Veneto

Via Filippo Buonarroti

Via Angelo Batelli

Duomo
Santa
Maria
Assunta

Via Contessa Matilde

S FRANCESCO

Via S Giovanni Bosco

mposanto
numentale

Via Card Pietro Malfi

Battistero

Campanile
(Torre Pendente)

Palazzo
della
Carovana

Piazza
Martiri
della Libertá

S Caterina

Via Mario Canavari

Museo
dell'Opera
del Duomo

Via Camneo

Piazza
Manin

Campo dei
Miracoli

Via S Lorenzo

S Francesco

Via E de Amicis

Museo
delle
Sinopie

G Carducci

Via S Maria

Via Giuseppe
Garibaldi

Via di Faggiola

Oberdan

Via San Francesco

Piazza
dei
Cavalieri

Via Ulisse Dini

P S Paolo
all'Orto

P della
Repubblica

Orto
Botanico

Via dei Mille

Via P Paoli

Via S Maria

Borgo Stretto

Piazza
delle
Vettovaglie

Via Palestro

P G Mazzini

Museo
Nazionale
di S Matteo

Via Santa Maria

Via Roma

Piazza
Dante Alighieri

Piazza
Garibaldi

Lungarno Medceo

Ponte
della Fortezza

Via Bonanno Pisano

S MARIA

Via Risorgimento

Piazza
F Carrara

Ponte
di Mezzo

Fiume Arno

Lungarno Bruno Buozzi

Via Trieste

San Nicola

Lungarno Pacinotti

Lungarno Gambacorti

Lungarno Galileo Galilei

Via San Martino

Ponte
Solferino

Santa Maria
della Spina

S MARTINO

Via Giovanni Bovio

Giardino
Scotto

Lungarno R Simonelli

Fiume Arno

Corso Italia

V Giordano Bruno

Ponte della
Vittoria

Cittadella

Lungarno Somnino Sidney

Via Francesco Crispi

Via S Antonio

Via Giuseppe Mazzini

Piazza
Guerrazzi

Bastione
S Gallo

Via Bonanno Pisano

Ponte della
Cittadella

S ANTONIO

Viale Benedetto Croce

Via Carlo Cattaneo

Via Nino Bixio

Via di Porta a Mare

Piazza
Vittorio
Emanuele II

Viale Bonaini

arno Cosimo I

Ponte della
Ferrovia

Via Cesare Battisti

Piazza
della Stazione

Via Filippo Corridoni

S Giovanni al Gatano

Railway
station

Leaning Tower of Pisa

The symbolic importance of the Leaning Tower of Pisa rivals that of the Eiffel Tower or the Statue of Liberty. But how much longer will it stand – or rather lean – for Italy? The 55m-high Tower of Pisa, after threatening to collapse for centuries, was a full 5m out of plumb in 1990; furthermore it was actually rotating in the soft subsoil.

Around the millennium, Italian engineers began the ambitious project of removing soil from beneath its foundations opposite the lean. By late 2001, the angle had been reduced by 10 per cent, and in 2008 engineers announced that it had stopped moving for the first time in its history. You can once again climb its 294 steps for the stunning view of the Arno, the Tyrrhenian Sea and the Apuan Alps, confirming that this is indeed the 'field of miracles'.

🍴 **Campanile €€**
Campo dei Miracoli. Book in advance via the website: *www.opapisa.it* or purchase tickets from the ticket office just behind the campanile. For further information contact the **Museo dell'Opera del Duomo**, *Piazza del Duomo 17; tel: 050 560547; fax: 050 560505.* Guided groups of 40 depart every 30 minutes *Apr–Sep daily 0830–2030 (mid-Jun–Aug until 2300), shorter hours in winter.* No children under eight.

the origin of the myth that it was built to tilt on purpose. Galileo put the tower's tilt to good use in 1589 by dropping assorted objects, comparing their speed, and formulating the theory of the constancy of gravity.

Camposanto Monumentale

During the Crusades, the Pisans imported 50 ships filled with earth from Golgotha for their cemetery, the Camposanto. The city's most prominent citizens were laid to rest in the holy earth until the 18th century. It is decorated with Roman tombs and sarcophagi.

Florentine artist Bonamico di Martino, nicknamed 'Buffalmacco', has been attributed as the creator of the alarming frescos that depict *Il Trionfo della Morte* (Triumph of Death), *Last Judgement* and *Inferno*. It is impossible to understand them fully without taking into account the plague epidemics that swept across Italy, beginning in 1348, and the sadistic visions of Hell that become a trademark of the Dominican order. A stray American bomb destroyed the other frescos during the Second World War (their ghostly remains can be seen in the Museo delle Sinopie). Beside the Camposanto, the old city wall forms an abrupt angle, leaving a rectangle free for the Cimitero Ebraico (Jewish Cemetery). Jews were allowed to bury their dead in the holy earth but not within the city walls.

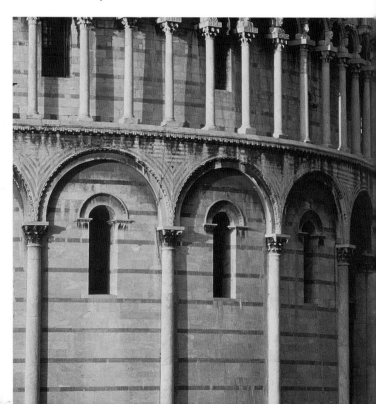

Duomo Santa Maria Assunta

The cathedral was begun in 1063 at the high point in Pisa's history after its defeat of the Saracens (about the same time that the Venetians were building San Marco). Perhaps it is only fitting that it was also the high point in Pisan-Romanesque architecture. It was the first church in Italy to use a Latin-cross floor plan with a dome over its intersection. The architect (according to Vasari) was a Greek named Buscheto. His models were the Byzantine basilica (perhaps the Hagia Sophia in Constantinople) and the Islamic mosque. The magnificent set of bronze doors was cast in 1180 by the architect of the Leaning Tower, Bonanno Pisano.

If possible, enter through the Portale di San Ranieri, opposite the Leaning Tower. The tomb of Emperor Henry VII is located to the right in the transept. The huge mosaic of Christ in the apse, by Cimabue, holds an open book with the words *Ego sum lux mundi* (I am the light of the world). The pulpit by Giovanni Pisano (1302–11) abbreviates the New Testament in stone, starting with the Annunciation and ending in the Last Judgement, adding enigmatic symbols like a lion goring a horse. Beneath the pedestal of Caritas is the figure of Venus covering her vagina with both hands. The two figures in medieval dress on the pedestal supported by Christ are self-portraits of Giovanni Pisano and his patron, Burgundio di Tado.

Below
Pisa's Campo dei Miracoli

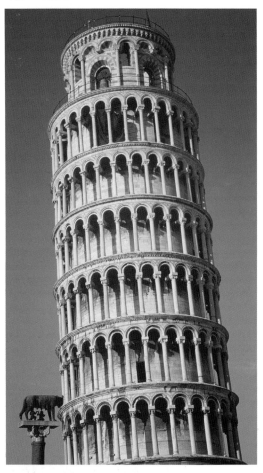

Museo dell'Opera del Duomo

The most striking thing in this museum is the dramatic view of the Leaning Tower from its courtyard and upper floors. Formerly a Dominican cloister, it forms a good setting for the original reliefs of the façade by Guglielmo and Rainaldo, sculpture by Nicola and Giovanni Pisano and Islamic objects that were brought back by Crusaders. Look for the ivory Madonna by Giovanni Pisano, carved around 1299, in the cathedral treasury (rooms 9–10).

Museo delle Sinopie

Despite the destruction of frescos that once decorated the Camposanto – by Gozzoli, Buffalmacco, Gaddi and Spinello Aretino – their *sinopie* survived. These are preliminary drawings made with a special kind of red chalk manufactured in the town of Sinope on the Black Sea. They have been brought here, to a former hospice of the Order of Santa Chiara. The drawings reveal the original intentions and the second-guessing of the artists. Etchings of the lost frescos are shown next to them for comparison, allowing you to push backwards through the creative process. However, it can leave your imagination aching for the real thing.

Museo delle Sinopie *Campo dei Miracoli. For opening times, see Campo dei Miracoli, p138.*

Museo Nazionale di San Matteo €€ *Piazza San Matteo 1 (Lungarno Mediceo); tel: 050 541865; fax: 050 500099. Open 0900–1900, shorter hours in winter.*

Above
Pisa's Leaning Tower

Museo Nazionale di San Matteo

Few tourists find their way from the Leaning Tower to this museum, located in a former Benedictine monastery on the bank of the Arno river, though it is one of the most important art collections in Tuscany. Look for the *Madonna del Latte* (*Madonna of the Milk*, or the nursing Madonna) with a breast shaped like a coke bottle. She was carved for the Santa Maria della Spina in 1345 by Andrea Pisano and his son Nino.

There are paintings by Francesco Traini, Pisa's most important medieval painter, and a polyptych by Simone Martini. The Apostle *Paulus* by the great Masaccio (room 6) is so vigorous and expressive that it stands out, even though it is only a fragment of the altar he painted for Pisa. The other 11 (!) pieces are scattered all over the world. There is an ineffable Madonna by Fra Angelico (1423) and one by Michelozzo (1430), too. Donatello's naturalistic bronze bust of San Rossore is here, as well as a crucifixion by Benozzo Gozzoli and the *Sacra Conversazione* by Domenico Ghirlandaio.

Piazza dei Cavalieri

The Roman forum was probably located on this square. It was the commercial nexus of medieval Pisa. Much to the humiliation and disgust of the Pisans, their Medici rulers built the massive Palazzo dei Cavalieri in 1560 and decorated it with coats of arms and busts of Florentine dukes. Napoleon would later turn it into a school (and so it remains). The Santo Stefano church, designed by Vasari, belonged to the armed Order of St Stephen, a special force created by Cosimo I to capture pirates. In practice, its members spent much of their time spying on Pisans and engaging in piracy themselves against Turks. The church has some of their Islamic booty on display.

The whimsical **Palazzo dell'Orologio** (designed by Vasari; *not open to the public*) tacks together an archway and a pair of ancient towers, one of which has a gruesome history. Count Ugolino della Gherardesca, the admiral of Pisa's fleet in their terrible defeat at Meloria, was made a scapegoat and allowed to die of hunger with sons and grandsons while locked up in the Torre della Fame. In an ultimate posthumous insult, Dante placed him in the lowest level of Hell where burning is too good for sinners and they are frozen instead.

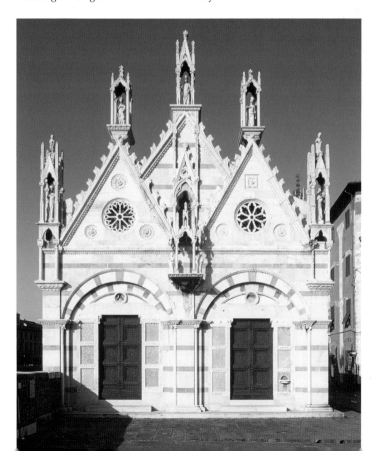

Right
The church of Santa Maria della Spina

Accommodation and food

Amalfitana € *Via Roma 44; tel: 050 29000; fax: 050 25218; www.hotelamalfitana.it.* Central yet quiet. The best rooms look out on the garden of a former convent. Booking recommended.

Trattoria La Mescita € *Via Cavalca 2 at the corner of Piazza delle Vettovoglie; tel: 050 957019. Closed Sat lunch and Sun.* Located near the market, this family restaurant serves savoury dishes such as *spaghettoni con lardo di Colonnata* (thick spaghetti with herbed lard), *baccalà bollito* (stewed cod) and *trippa alla Pisana* (tripe Pisan style).

Osteria dei Cavalieri €€ *Via San Frediano 16; tel: 050 580858; www.osteriacavalieri.pisa.it. Closed Sat lunch, Sun and Aug.* Extremely popular for simple, creative food. The short menu includes a couple of items each under *terra, mare, verdure* (earth, sea, greens) and wine by the glass.

Hotel Verdi €€€ *Piazza della Repubblica 5; tel: 050 598947; fax: 050 598944; www.verdihotel.it.* Comfortable, quiet, just a few steps from the river.

Royal Victoria Hotel €€€ *Lungarno Pacinotti 12; tel: 050 940111; fax: 050 940180; www.royalvictoriahotel.it.* Pisa's top hotel since 1839.

Villa di Corliano €€€ *San Giuliano Terme (Rigoli district); tel: 050 818193; fax: 050 818897; www.corliano.it.* The villa and its large park have been in the possession of the Count of Strido since the 15th century. In an annexe, Sergio Lorenzi, acclaimed Pisan chef and refugee from city life, runs a restaurant (*tel: 050 818858*).

Suggested tour

Total distance: 2km.

Time: Pisa is, for most visitors, a day trip. It would be easy to pass an entire day wandering around the buildings of the Field of Miracles where the masses of tourists seem to occupy a parallel universe apart from the actual city of Pisa. It is well worth saving a couple of hours to see the other side of Pisa. It is also better to eat there than in any of the restaurants in the immediate vicinity of the Leaning Tower.

Links: Lucca (*see page 108*) is only 22km from Pisa. Livorno (*see page 151*) is 18.5km to the south. The Garfagnana route (*see page 124*) comes within 33km, when it passes through Pietrasanta.

Route: Anyone is spoiled for choice in the Campo dei Miracoli (Field of Miracles) but precedence should be given to the **DUOMO SANTA MARIA ASSUNTA ❶** . You can climb up the **CAMPANILE ❷** to survey the surrounding landscape. There is more to the **BATTISTERO**

❸ than first meets the eye. To appreciate fully the size of the building, climb to its upper galleries. It is almost the same height as the Leaning Tower and the glimpses through its narrow windows offer fragments of a view. The **CAMPOSANTO** ❹, for all the wartime damage, holds its own among the monuments. The two museums on the Field, the **MUSEO DELL'OPERA DEL DUOMO** ❺ and the **MUSEO DELLE SINOPIE** ❻, are rewarding but not unmissable.

From the Campo dei Miracoli, go down Via Santa Maria and duck left into Via dei Mille brushing past the 11th-century church of San Sisto on the right before stepping into **PIAZZA DEI CAVALIERI** ❼. Take Via Ulisse Dini to broad Borgo Stretto – Pisa's main shopping street – to Piazza Garibaldi. Walk out to the middle of the **Ponte di Mezzo** ❽. This was/is the oldest bridge in Pisa with a fine view of river and city. It was destroyed in World War II but rebuilt using much of the original stone.

Detour: Continue across the bridge and turn right (west). Walk along the river (Lungarno Gambacorti) until the church of **Santa Maria della Spina** ❾ (thorn) comes into sight. It was a simple oratory for fisher folk and the odd traveller until it was transformed, in 1323, by a man who had acquired a true thorn from the crown of Jesus and the wealth to display it in style. The church was dismantled in 1871 and reassembled stone by stone at a point higher up the riverbank to save it from flooding. People interested in modern Italian history might be tempted to veer right, on the way back, into Via Mazzini. Giuseppe Mazzini, the man who did more than even Garibaldi to reunite Italy, died at No 29 on 8 March 1872. The house is now a museum of the Risorgimento (*see Setting the scene, page 34*).

Return to the Piazza Garibaldi, turn right (east) and stroll along the river going upstream. Like Florence, Pisa has erected magnificent palaces along the shore of the Arno over several centuries such as the 14th-century Palazzo Toscanelli, based on plans by Michelangelo, and the 13th-century Palazzo Medici. The church at Piazzetta San Matteo was built in 1027 and given the full baroque treatment six centuries later. Its former convent is now the **MUSEO NAZIONALE DI SAN MATTEO** ❿.

Rather than retracing your steps after the museum, walk back as far as the first square on the Arno, the Piazza G Mazzini. Cross it and take the first left into Via Buscheto, cross Piazza della Repubblica and press on in the same direction by way of Via Palestro and tiny Via Vernagalli. You will find yourself at Piazza Garibaldi again. Walk back under the arcades of Borgo Stretto and take the first left into the **Piazza delle Vettovaglie** ⓫. The square and its surroundings are a lively area of arcades, ancient lanes used for street markets and small shops and restaurants that cater to students and locals. The square itself has a market each weekday (*0930–1230; Sat 0930–2000*). Press on down Via di Cavalca, cross Via S Frediano and walk along Piazza

Dante Alighieri. Take the left-hand lane, the Coll Ricci, to Piazza F Carrara, coming face to face with **San Nicola ⑫**, then rounding the corner to the Via Santa Maria. The church's 13th-century campanile is Pisa's second Leaning Tower, consisting of a hexagon on top of a cylinder (had it been the other way round, it would have collapsed by now). Inside the tower is a brilliantly designed spiral staircase. According to the not always reliable Giorgio Vasari, it influenced Bramante when he was building his Belvedere staircase in the Vatican.

A short distance up the Via Santa Maria is the Domus Galilaena (No 26). At Piazza Cavalloti, turn left into the small lane of L Ghini. The **Orto Botanico ⑬** is the oldest botanical garden in Europe, planted in 1543 by a Luca Ghini on the shores of the Arno, and moved here in 1591. It has a corner full of 16th-century pots, arranged geometrically, and a delightful mini-*palazzo* decorated with seashells and mother-of-pearl. The star botanical attraction is a magnolia planted in 1787. This garden is only a few metres from the Campo dei Miracoli.

Also worth exploring

Five kilometres west of Pisa, the church of **San Pietro a Grado** seems to appear out of nowhere on a plain that was once full of water and ships entering the old port of Pisa. It marks the spot near the mouth of the Arno river where St Peter is said to have first set foot in Italy (in AD 44) during his journey from Antioch to Rome. The odd basilica has an embarrassment of apses – two at one end and three on the other. Inside its hoary sandstone walls are faded frescos of the life of St Peter and portraits of the popes. There are also recycled Roman columns from older buildings.

Nearby excavations have uncovered the oldest (4th century) Christian site in the region. The best way south from here is to follow the shore of the Arno river through a long alley of plane trees, the straight road to the sea and the coast towards Livorno. It is not all charming but still a lot more interesting than the ugly stretch of the *Via Aurelia autostrada*.

Gioco del Ponte

Residents of Pisa dress up in historical war costume. Opposing factions – north and south of the river – challenge each other to a number of tasks, such as heavy lifting. Preceded by a procession in costume. Last Sunday in June.

Above
Baptistry doors, Pisa

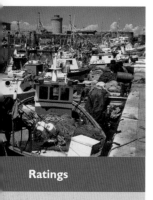

The Etruscan Riviera

Ratings

Archaeology	●●●●●
Seafood	●●●●●
Beaches	●●●●○
Scenery	●●●●○
Nature	●●●○○
Architecture	●●○○○
Museums	●○○○○
Shopping	●○○○○

Driving down the 'Etruscan Riviera', it is easy to wish that its reclaimed swampland had never been drained and the concrete of its holiday bunkers never poured – they clutter much of the northern coastline. However, the coastal road from Livorno has its moments and they become more frequent further south: there are still fishing villages, stretches of sand dune and *pineta* – coastal pine woods. The coast lives up to its name at Populonia, the remains of a vast Etruscan port city (most of it unexcavated) on one of the most beautiful bays in Italy. The coastal mountains are a welcome, neglected alternative to the seaside litter and throngs. They offer fascinating detours that could take you as far as the geothermal realm of the Colline Metallifere (*see page 156*). The vegetation of woods and *maquis* is broken by cultivation and a couple of famous wine estates.

CAMPIGLIA MARITTIMA

ⓘ APT office *Via Cavour-Palazzo Pretorio; tel/fax: 0565 837201; www.comune. campigliamarittima.li.it. Open in summer Tue–Sun 1000–1200 and 1800–2000; shorter hours in winter.*

Standing on the terrace beside the city gate of Campiglia Marittima, Porta a Mare, you can see a wide stretch of Tuscany's coast: the Golfo di Baratti, the bay of Follonica, the peninsula of Piombino and the high mountain ridges of Elba island. Inland the first thing the eye encounters is the Pieve di San Giovanni built in 1170 by Matteo 'the sinner' on the site of an earlier church. It is surrounded by a desolate cemetery with weathered medieval tombstones. Below it are the flatlands around Venturina. Campiglia was also built as a castle in 1000 by the counts of Gherardesca; Pisa controlled it from 1158 to 1406 before Florence took possession.

Porta a Mare leads to a narrow cluster of streets. One of them, the Via Roma, links it to the Piazza della Repubblica and its hoary Palazzo Pretorio (12th–15th century). Down the Via Curtatone and past another city gate stands the Teatro dei Concordi, a 19th-century theatre that is still in use. The 12th-century Rocca is in ruins.

Opposite
Coastal *pineta*

GOLFO DI BARATTI AND POPULONIA

Parco Archeologico di Baratti e Populonia €€€ *Tel: 0565 29002; fax: 0565 29107; www.parchivaldicornia.it. Open Jul and Aug daily 1000–1900; Jun and Sep Tue–Sun 1000–1900; Mar–May and Oct Tue–Sun 1000–1800; Nov and Jan–Feb Tue–Fri (by reservation only), Sat–Sun 1000–1600. Closed Dec.* The price of admission includes a tour of one complex of tombs (in Italian).

Populonia or *Fufluna*, as the Etruscans evocatively called it, was the only town on the sea that belonged to the legendary League of 12 cities. The Romans borrowed a lot from the League – magistrates' insignia, a cut of toga and a technique for interpreting sacrificial chicken livers.

The Golfo di Baratti, with its halo of parasol pines, is one of the most beautiful sights on the Tuscan coast. Divers continue to find important Roman and Etruscan objects in the bay. The beach itself is not great for swimming but is still crowded in the middle of summer.

In general, Etruscans preferred to live on the heights of inland hills. During the golden age (7th–6th centuries BC), Populonia had a flourishing trade with Volterra, Vetulonia and Chiusi; its population was perhaps 25,000. The inhabitants worked the iron ore from Elba as well as zinc, lead and copper from Campiglia Marittima and the Colline Metallifere. A period of relative decline began after a siege by the Roman general Sulla in the 1st century BC. However, Populonia became a bishopric 400 years later and managed to hang on until AD 835, when the spread of malaria drove the population inland to Massa Marittima.

During the Etruscan period, the city produced enormous quantities of iron and, in a surprising lapse of respect for their ancestors, the inhabitants used the necropolis as a dump for the slag. The tombs were discovered when Italy began to mine for iron ore in the area during the arms race that preceded World War I. In the **Parco Archeologico di Baratti e Populonia**, it is possible to study an entire catalogue of Etruscan tomb types and periods alongside the first complex of Populonia's predominantly Roman Acropolis, first opened to the public in 2007.

Above the Gulf of Baratti (180m) is an impressive castle (mostly for its location), built in the Middle Ages. An ambitious family, the Appiani, fortified it in the 14th century to defend their independence from Florence. Two of the towers still stand and offer sweeping views up the coast to Livorno. Nearby are the remains of an important Etruscan-Roman city – belonging, no doubt, to the port of Populonia – that is still being excavated. Most of it, and its impressive Cyclopean walls (you can see one section just before you enter town), are still underground.

Above
Etruscan tomb at Populonia

LIVORNO

ℹ APT office *Piazza Cavour 6; tel: 0586 898111; fax: 0586 896173; www.costadeglietruschi.it*

🐟 Acquario Comunale Diacinto Cestoni €€ *Piazza Mascagni 1; tel: 0586 805504; www. comune.livorno.it/acquario. Open daily (unless temporarily closed for cleaning) 1000–1200 and 1600–1900, shorter hours in winter.*

Livorno, or Leghorn as the English insisted on calling it for centuries, is Tuscany's largest port and third largest city. Although founded by Pisans, it was the Medici and their architect Buontalenti who created a new Livorno in 1571, with some help from an English knight named Sir Robert Dudley. The Medici, having achieved control of all Tuscany, needed a new outlet on the sea. Although it was built as a harbour and fortress, it nevertheless adhered to Renaissance principles, becoming a city of broad squares, arcaded passageways, fortresses and canals. World War II left gaping holes in the design but it is still possible to recognise some of the original scheme.

A set of 1593 laws known as the *Leggi Livornine* made the city a haven for Jews and Turks. Even Protestants gained refuge and Italy's first Protestant cemetery (*at Via Verdi 63*) is located here – the most famous grave is that of Tobias Smollett. However, this 'perfect' city was also used as the port of arrival for slaves who were bought and sold on its wharves. The city's most powerful work of art, in Piazza Micheli (by Pietro Tacca, 1615), is a statue of Medici ruler Ferdinand I who is completely upstaged by *quattro mori* – four black galley slaves – at his feet. The men in chains, straining every muscle in an unbearable posture, possess a massive dignity absent from the figure of Ferdinand.

Few tourists come to Livorno except to take a ferry to Elba, Sardinia or Corsica. However, the **Acquario Comunale Diacinto Cestoni** offers a fascinating look at life under water in the Mediterranean. If you would rather eat fish than watch it, Livorno has great seafood. As for atmosphere, it is a lively city with a large foreign population and baby-faced cadets from the Accademia Navale (Italy's largest military academy). The dock workers are well organised and, politically speaking, Livorno is the 'reddest of the red'.

Below
Livorno's New Venice quarter

PARCO ARCHEOMINERARIO DI SAN SILVESTRO

Parco Archeominerario di San Silvestro €€ *3km below Bampiglia on the road from Campiglia to San Vincenzo; tel: 0565 838680; fax: 0565 838703; www.parchivaldicornia.it. Open Jul–Aug daily 1000–1900; Jun and Sep Tue–Sun 1000–1900; Mar–May and Oct Sat–Sun 1000–1800; Nov and Jan–Feb Sat–Sun 1000–1600, Tue–Fri by reservation only; closed Dec. There is a discount on admission for people who have also visited the Parco Archeologico di Baratti. The price includes a tour (highly recommended) of the medieval mining town of San Silvestro. It is in Italian but an English-language audio commentary is available.*

A mining region whose origins go back to the Etruscans, San Silvestro first appears in a written record in 1004. The British were still mining the area at the beginning of the 20th century and called it – Etruscan Mines. From its ruined castle, the mining ghost town of Rocca San Silvestro, there are dramatic views of the Mediterranean. The castle changed its name many times: Castelnuovo, Castel Moncalvo, Rocca a Palmeto and Rocca di San Silvestro. It seems that the name Rocca is linked to the ancient owners: the Della Rocca from Pisa. San Silvestro was the name of its patron saint. The entire area is now part of the Parco Archeominerario di San Silvestro.

Right
Etruscan landscape

Opposite
Livorno's Monumento dei Quattro Mori

SAN VINCENZO

APT office *Via della Torre; tel: 0565 701533; e-mail: apt7sanvincenzo@ costadeglietruschi.it; www.costadeglietruschi.it & www.comune.san-vincenzo.li.it. Open Mon–Fri 0900–1300 and 1500–1700, Sat 0900–1300.*

The Pisans fortified the fishing village of San Vincenzo in 1304 and their tower still overlooks the marina. The 5km-long beach extends north and even further south of the centre of town. Via Vittorio Emanuele II is a classy seaside boulevard with cafés, boutiques and a couple of art nouveau buildings – the best place on the Etruscan Riviera for a self-absorbed *passeggiata*. The funny-looking cable car at the end of the beach is not part of the amusement park. It is used to transport chalk from the local hills to a factory, where it is crushed up and used in making fizzy carbonated drinks.

Accommodation and food

L'Antica Venezia € *Piazza dei Domenicani 15, Livorno; tel: 0586 887353. Closed Sun.* Right in the *Centro Storico* in the Venezia quarter (so-called for its many canals), this *trattoria* specialises in *cucina marinara* and the menu reflects what is fresh and available.

Il Canovaccio € *Via Vecchio Asilo 1, Campiglia Marittima; tel: 0565 838449. Closed Tue (except for summer).* A ledge just off a small square provides space for the outdoor tables with a view. *Zuppetta di frutti di mare* is a house speciality.

Paradiso Verde € *Via del Forte 9, Marina di Bibbona; tel and fax: 0586 600022; www.hotelparadisoverde.it.* Small, friendly beach hotel with garden.

Pensione Ristorante Alba € *Baratti; tel: 0565 29521.* Modest seaside hotel on the Bay of Baratti.

Vecchia Livorno € *Via Scali delle Cantine 34, Livorno; tel: 0586 884048. Closed Tue.* Skip the pizza at this small place, though it's good, and just go for the seafood starters and main courses: *linguine al baccalà* (with cod), *riso nero* (rice cooked in squid ink), *cacciucco* or grilled catch of the day.

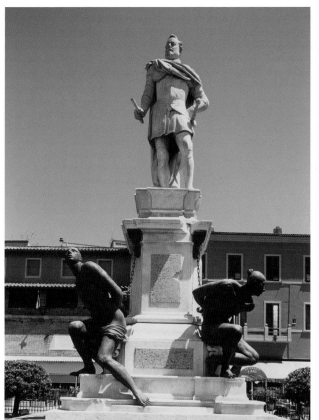

Ristorante Bar Pizzica €€ *Piazza della Vittoria 2, Campiglia Marittima; tel: 0565 838721.* Creative regional cuisine with specialities like *spigola al cartoccio* (baked sea bass) to be enjoyed from the spacious, elegant rear terrace offering panoramic views.

Gambero Rosso €€€ *Piazza della Vittoria 13, San Vincenzo; tel: 0565 701021. Closed Tue.* Widely regarded as the best fish restaurant on the Etruscan Riviera (by Michelin among others), with an unforgettable *menu degustazione*. It comes at a price but the wine list is surprisingly affordable.

Ferries from Livorno

There are regular ferries from Livorno to Capraia (3 hrs), Corsica (4 hrs), Elba (4 hrs), Sardinia (10 hrs) and Sicily (19 hrs).

Corsica Ferries *Porto Varco Donegani; tel: 0586 881830; fax: 0586 896103; www.corsicaferries.com.* Corsica and Sardinia.

Moby Lines *Porto Varco Galvani; tel: 0586 826847; www.moby.it.* Elba and Sardinia.

TOREMAR *in Porto Mediceo; tel: 0586 896113; fax: 0586 887263; www.toremar.it. Open 0800–1200.* Piombino, Elba and Capraia.

Below
Beach huts near
Forte dei Marmi

Suggested tour

Total distance: 82km; detour adds 10km (return).

Time: Purely from a driving perspective, this route is a day-trip. Add in quality time on the beach (but not, heaven forbid, in Jul–Aug), detours to the coastal hills and oenophilic reconnaissance in the vineyards and it quickly becomes more.

Links: The tour overlaps part of the one that takes in Volterra (*see page 162*). Drive further south, from Piombino, to join the route through the Maremma (*see page 171*).

Route: From **LIVORNO** ❶ drive south on the coastal road, trying to avoid the *Via Aurelia* as much as possible. The promontory of **Castiglioncello** ❷ was once the site of an Etruscan settlement. During the Middle Ages, pirates nearly put an end to its existence. In defence, Cosimo I de Medici added a fortified tower in 1560. By the 19th century, it was already a popular seaside resort and artists' colony. From **Vada** ❸, take the coastal road. There is a fine stretch of beach along the 8km between here and the Marina di Cecina. In places there are pine woods near the shore and peaceful enclaves. Ancient **Cecina** ❹ was an important city to the Etruscans and Romans, trading with Volterra, Pisa and Rome. Today's Cecina is a modern town created by draining the area in the 19th century and is entirely missable. The wide beach at **Marina di Bibbona** ❺ is 4km long with an 18th-century French fortress to admire in the middle, sand dunes and stands of pine. However, much of it is off limits and one of the best bits belongs to Club Med.

Detour: The mother of all cypress alleys – almost 5km long – was planted in 1801 by local aristocrat Camillo della Gherardesca. It forms a beeline for **Bolgheri** ❻. The fortified town is also famous for a red wine, Sassicaia, and another wine cultivated nearby – Ornellaia.

A wide road leads to the popular sea resort of **Marina di Castagneto-Donoratico** ❼, a white beach of fine sand with a ruined fort reduced to one tower. Walking south, you will find the beach less crowded. **SAN VINCENZO** ❽ is just 8km down the coast. From there, carry on to the **GOLFO DI BARATTI** and **POPULONIA** ❾.

Retrace the route going north a couple of kilometres and take the right fork down a country road that leads into **Venturina** ❿. There is no reason to linger unless you are in the mood for a sulphurous soak in baths in use here since Roman times. The ancient Terme Caldana is at the north end of town. A large *piscina* (pool) bubbles behind the nearby pizzeria with a constant water temperature of 32°C. The most picturesque spring is the Calidario at the east end of town, a walled basin of fresh water that flows out of the ground beneath a cliff at a temperature of 35°C (*Terme di Venturina, Via Aurelia Nord 8; tel: 0565 851066; www.termediventurina.it; open May–Oct Mon–Fri 0700–1200, 1600–1800, Sat 0700–1200*).

The road into the coastal mountains is clearly marked for **CAMPIGLIA MARITTIMA** ⓫. From there, it is a short drive down the valley to the **PARCO ARCHEO-MINERARIO DI SAN SILVESTRO** ⓬.

Also worth exploring

If you drive on to **Piombino**, it is probably for its ferry service to Elba. It is an industrial port with a less than poetic name – *Piombo* means lead – where noxious odours mingle with the sea air. However, it has its share of history, a fine old harbour and some streets with a morbid, turn-of-the-20th-century elegance. Its main street, Corso Italia, is excellent for shopping and ends in a 13th-century Pisan tower. From there, the Corso Vittorio Emanuele II coils its way through the *Centro Storico* past the Gothic Palazzo Comunale to the old harbour. The Via Panoramica justifies its name with views of Elba and the sea.

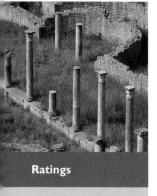

Volterra and the Colline Metallifere

Ratings

Geology	●●●●●
Scenery	●●●●●
Architecture	●●●●○
History	●●●●○
Nature	●●●●○
Art and craft	●●●○○
Children	●●●○○
Museums	●●●○○

Volterra is the most oddly self-contained hill-town in Tuscany. Once a massive Etruscan stronghold, it is set in the clouds on a ridge (550m) raked by howling winds. Over time, landslides have claimed pieces of the ancient city. By contrast, Devil's Valley – the hottest piece of the earth's crust on the European continent – is only a few kilometres to the south. The lava below the surface here is on the boil and generates violent jets of steam. Dante believed, like many medieval Tuscans, that it was the entrance to Hell. Devil's Valley is part of the Colline Metallifere (metal hills), a stretch of wild hills between Volterra and the medieval mining town of Massa Marittima. To the west, the coastal mountains above the Etruscan Riviera offer views of the sea and a roller-coaster ride through microclimes of chestnuts, pine trees, vines and cactus.

BOLGHERI

Count Ugolino, the ill-fated scion of the Gherardesca family, died with his sons and grandsons of starvation in Pisa's Hunger Tower in 1288.

From a point near the coast of the Etruscan Riviera, Italy's most famous avenue of cypresses leads almost 5km to Bolgheri. It was planted in 1801 by local aristocrat Camillo della Gherardesca and is the subject of a gloomy poem that is massaged into the memories of Italian schoolchildren. This was the seat of one of the most important families in Tuscan history, the Gherardesca. Most of the architecture dates from the 16th to 18th centuries.

CASTAGNETO CARDUCCI

A dense network of streets surrounds the 11th-century Castello of the Count della Gherardesca. There is a stunning view from the Piazzale Belvedere of the sea and the surrounding hills. The bust on the square is of Giosuè Carducci (1835–1907), the Nobel prize-winning poet who

Museo della Geotermia *Piazza Paolina, Larderello; tel: 0588 67724; e-mail: museogeotermia.larderello@ enel.it; www.enelgreenpower.enel.it/ en/green_tour/larderello. Open mid-Mar–mid-Sep Mon–Fri 0900–1200 and 1330–1730, Sun 0900–1200 and 1330–1830; shorter hours in winter. Free admission.* Information is available in English. If you call ahead, you can also rejoice in your first look at a *soffione* (a hole bored into the ground to let off the earth's steam) and a reconstructed *lagone coperto* from 1830 – a covered lake in which the steam is harnessed for heat and salt.

spent part of his childhood here and in Bolgheri. The village decided to honour the poet by adding his name to that of the village in the year that he died. Today Castagneto is equally renowned for its olive oil, which is among the best in Tuscany.

LARDERELLO

For people with an interest in modern architecture, Larderello boasts a church built in the 1950s by one of Italy's better modern architects, Michelucci (he also designed the train station in Florence).

The surreal town of Larderello rests at the foot of Aia del Diavolo (Devil's Wing) in the middle of Valli del Diavolo (Devil's Valley). It was named after a Frenchman, François de Larderel, who discovered a process in 1818 for producing large quantities of boric acid from the valley's *soffioni* (geysers). Adding to the infernal atmosphere is an odour of sulphur and rotten eggs. Still, it is nothing compared to the sewers of Paris, which people pay good money to visit.

The **Museo della Geotermia** is free and its exhibits will explain the ins and outs of geothermalism. Minerals first brought the Etruscans to the area, which was also heavily mined for mercury and iron in the

Middle Ages. The world's first and largest geothermal complex was constructed here in the 19th century. Shiny steel pipes snake through the landscape and converge on Larderello from all directions. They carry steam from beneath the earth, which generates enough energy for almost half the homes in Tuscany.

SASSETTA

At its October festivals, the entire village sits at long tables eating grilled thrush and other local specialities such as *sassetana* – wild boar stewed with olives – *pecorino* cheese and chestnut jam.

Sassetta (340m) is perched on a ridge that divides the Val di Cornia, an up-and-coming wine region, from the Sterza, a tributary river of the Cecina. The steep hills below it are dense with old-growth chestnuts. In the church of Sant'Andrea Apostolo, there is a Roman baptismal font decorated with the Orlandi coat of arms, a family that ruled here until the Medici took over. On the first three Sundays of October, the village holds the Festivals of Ottobre (October), Tordo (thrush) and Castagno (chestnut).

SUVERETO

Tua Rita *Notri 81 near Suvereto in Val di Cornia; tel: 0565 829237; www.tuarita.it.* The perfectionist winemakers of this small estate produce excellent reds – particularly the *perlato di bosco* from the Sangiovese grape – as well as *grappa* and olive oil.

Right on the border between the territories of Siena and Pisa, Suvereto is at least a millennium old. The ubiquitous Aldobrandeschi built a fortress here 1,000 years ago and a ruined fortress still looms over the city. Through the Porta alla Silici you reach the Piazza Gramsci and a cluster of Romanesque buildings, the Palazzo Comunale, the church of Sant'Agostino (1313) and the Torre del Ghibellino. The town walls were built by the Pisans in the 14th century.

VOLTERRA

Informazioni turistiche *Piazza dei Priori 20; tel/fax: 0588 87257; www.comune.volterra.pi.it & www.volterratur.it*

Museo Etrusco Guarnacci € *Via Don Minzoni 15; tel: 0588 86347. Open daily mid-Mar–Oct 0900–1900, Nov–mid-Mar 0830–1400.*

Opposite
Volterra church

The city of 'wind and stone' as D H Lawrence called it, Volterra is isolated and forbidding but not without charm. Etruscan walls and tombs are sliding into the abyss at one edge of town while its exquisite medieval town hall is still open for business in the centre. Volterra was one of the major Etruscan *lucumoni* or city-states, as demonstrated by vast archaeological finds. At its height, the town supported a much larger population than today. The city played an important part in the Roman civil war and was subjected to a two-year siege in AD 82 by Sulla. An impressive Roman theatre was unearthed in 1951 and its excavation was finally finished in 1997.

The **Museo Etrusco Guarnacci** houses one of the most important Etruscan collections in Italy. There are 600 funerary urns of carved sandstone, alabaster and terracotta, dating as far back as the Hellenistic era. It is best to begin at the top floor, which has many of

the best pieces and the best explanations as well as a view of the rooftops of Volterra. Work your way down one floor to *Gli Sposi*, a terracotta tomb cover that depicts an old married couple with astonishing realism; there are also bronzes such as the elongated figure *Ombra della Sera* (*Shadow of the Evening*), which greatly influenced the work of Swiss artist Giacometti (frankly, it is hard to see what he added that the original Etruscan artist hadn't already invented).

Museo Civico e Pinacoteca € *Via dei Sarti 1; tel: 0588 87580. Open daily mid-Mar–Oct 0900–1900, Nov–mid-Mar 0900–1400.*

Alabaster workshops

Fabula Etrusca *Via Lungo le Mura del Mandorlo 8–10; tel: 0588 87401; www.fabulaetrusca.it. Closed weekends. Reproductions of Etruscan jewellery.*

Paolo Sabatini *Via Matteotti 56/a; tel: 0588 81515; www.paolosabatini. com. Alabaster work.*

Auro Grandoli *Via di Sotto 4; tel: 0588 87107. Sculptor in alabaster who specialises in animals.*

Società Cooperativa Artieri dell'Alabastro *Piazza de Priori 5; tel: 0588 87590; www.artierialabastro.it. Alabaster work.*

Rossi Alabastri *Piazza della Pescheria; tel: 0588 86133; www.rossialabastri. com. Alabaster workshop open to visitors.*

In the Middle Ages, Volterra was a major stop on the road linking the Po river valley and Rome, the route taken by the pilgrims from Compostela to Jerusalem. This medieval prosperity created many superb artistic and architectural treasures. The Palazzo dei Priori (1208) is the oldest municipal palace still in use in Tuscany. The well-preserved façade has a lower part decorated by the enamelled coats of arms of the Florentine commissioners and by other marble or stone coats of arms. Near the Piazza dei Priori is the **Museo Civico e Pinacoteca** in a 15th-century building designed by Antonio da Sangallo. It displays art work from the church of San Giusto al Bostro (wrecked in a landslide). The art gallery exhibits notable works by Sienese painters such as Taddeo di Bartolo and Florentine artists including Ghirlandaio. Two star attractions are the masterful *Annunciation* by Luca Signorelli and the *Descent from the Cross* (1521), representing Mannerist genius Rosso Fiorentino at his most colourful and bizarre. The Duomo is a Romanesque-Pisan style basilica with unsubtle Renaissance additions such as a gaudy coffered ceiling and *trompe-l'oeil* marble pillars. The altar *Deposition*, carved in wood by an unknown Pisan artist, is an expressive and powerful work executed in the 12th century.

At the highest point of the hill of Volterra broods its Fortezza, really two castles in one: the trapezoidal 14th-century Old Fortress with an elliptic tower and the squat 15th-century New Fortress with five turrets. For connoisseurs of Renaissance military architecture, this is fortification at its finest – a fact that probably goes unappreciated by the men locked up inside (today, it is a maximum-security prison).

Gioco della Bandiera Contest between factions of the town competing for a flag. Last Sun in Sep.

Opposite
Volterra's rooftops

Below
The streets of Volterra

Accommodation and food

Da Badò € *Borgo San Lazzero 9, Volterra; tel: 0588 86477. Next to the Esso petrol station in the lower city. Dinner only. Closed Wed and a few weeks in summer.* A local restaurant with home-made pasta and dishes such as *coniglio in umido* (rabbit stew).

Seminario Vescovile € *Viale Vittorio Veneto 2, on the road leading out of Porta Marcoli, Volterra; tel: 0588 86028.* Old monks' cells with big brass beds rented for a song. On the edge of town but still within walking distance.

Trattoria del Sacco Fiorentino €€ *Piazza XX Settembre 18, Volterra (just a few steps from the Museo Etrusco); tel: 0588 88537. Closed Fri and Jan–Feb.* The restaurant's odd name recalls the brutal sacking of Volterra by the army of Lorenzo de Medici in 1472. But it is not the place to eat on the run. Everything is worth savouring: a plate of *gnocchi con le verdure novelle* (gnocchi with baby vegetables), *penne ai formaggi toscani piccanti* (pasta with spicy Tuscan cheese) or *coniglio in salsa di aglio e Vin Santo* (rabbit cooked in garlic and Vin Santo).

San Lino €€€ *Via San Lino 26, Volterra; tel: 0588 85250; fax: 0588 80620; www.hotelsanlino.com.* Volterra's top hotel is a converted monastery. It has its own pool and garden and is conveniently located near the Porta San Francesco.

Alabaster

A diaphanous gypsum stone, alabaster has been worked by craftspeople in Volterra for at least 2,500 years. It is easier to work than marble and ideal for portraying fine portraits and intricate detail. Etruscans used it to create a look-alike portrait of the deceased and scenes from his or her life on funerary urns and sarcophagi. Alabaster was a flourishing local industry until the 19th century, when the demand for it declined. The *alabatrai* (sculptors of alabaster) took long road trips, some as far as the Near East, to find customers, trading their wares for anything of value, including opium and spices. Today, alongside the bread-and-butter souvenir trade (such as copies of Michelangelo's *David*), many *alabatrai* continue to produce work of real artistic value.

Suggested tour

Total distance: 148km; the detour to Guardistallo adds 5km (return).

Time: Volterra really merits a day, which should include the Museo Etrusco and Le Balze (*see Detour below*). The rest of the route can also be covered in a day.

Links: The western part of this route runs parallel with the Etruscan Riviera (*see page 154*) and overlaps it at Bolgheri and Marina di Bibbona.

Route: Leave **VOLTERRA** ❶ on the road that is signposted to Cecina.

Detour: The Volterra experience is only complete with a visit to its northeast edge, where you can see massive fragments of the ancient city's embankment far out upon the now uninhabited plateau. Then you look down into the yawning void of eroded sandstone created by Le Balze (cliffs). These crevasses, up to 100m deep, seem to form spontaneously but are actually the result of a type of underground erosion caused by rain. In geological time, the phenomenon of Le Balze doesn't even merit the tick of the second hand. But for Volterra, a piece of its 3,000-year history (Etruscan walls and tombs, a monastery) is already lost forever. Despite the intervention of modern technology, Le Balze are still a threat to the future of Volterra. The abandoned monastery on the edge and the alabaster mines below, some of which date back to Etruscan times, add to the desolate scenery.

Drive through the broad, green valley that bears few traces of its long past as a highway for Etruscans, Romans, medieval Volterrans and Pisans, and modern travellers. Turn left (south) following signs for Montescudaio and Guardistallo, cross the valley and take the grandiose turns up to **Guardistallo** ❷.

Detour: A complicated web of narrow streets holds together the ancient town of **Montescudaio** ❸. From the broad piazza before the Abbadia Santa Maria Assunta, there are wide-ranging views of the woods and hills around Volterra and the coastal plains of Cecina.

Press on past Casale Marittima, another medieval village with views of the sea. The road drops for three lush kilometres before entering **Bibbona** ❹ where you can linger to walk along the ancient city wall, inspect the Pieve San Illario (11th–14th centuries) and the Renaissance Santa Maria della Pietà. Take the south fork in the road to Bolgheri. It also identifies itself as the Strada del Vino at regular intervals. When you reach the grand avenue of cypresses, turn left to enter **BOLGHERI** ❺.

Getting out of the car: At the opposite end of the alley of cypresses, beyond the *Via Aurelia*, stretches one of the best beaches on the

Opposite
Bolgheri's town gate

Etruscan Riviera at the **Marina di Bibbona**. If it is crowded, walk south from Forte di Bibbona. The further you go, the more white sand you'll have to yourself.

Drive just a few hundred metres beneath the cypresses in the direction of the coast and turn left, following the signs for Castagneto Carducci (and the Strada del Vino again). This is a blissfully empty stretch of road shaded in many places by *pineta* (umbrella pines). It ends in a T-junction. Turn left on the N329 and drive up to CASTAGNETO CARDUCCI ❻. The road climbs and plunges while views oscillate between the sea and steep, densely wooded hills. After the village of **SASSETTA** ❼, the vegetation changes and lush chestnut forest gives way to dusty hillsides, olive groves and even cactus at **SUVERETO** ❽. Turn left (east) on the N398 and drive along the Cornia and Secco rivers up to the spa town of Terme di Bagnolo and, shortly beyond, the clearly marked junction with the N439. Turn left (north) again to cruise this almost uninhabited stretch of the Colline Metallifere. The landscape begins to erupt at many points in *soffioni* (geysers) that form tall plumes of steam. Flowing lengths of silvery pipe crisscross the hillsides in patterns reminiscent of a Keith Haring poster.

The N439 skirts **LARDERELLO** ❾. If you want to enter the city centre (say to visit the Geothermal Museum) follow the bulls-eye sign down into the valley. Another lonely stretch brings you to **Pomarance** ❿, which was heavily bombed in World War II and doesn't offer much

La Strada del Vino

The Strada del Vino is aggressively signposted on the coastal cliffs between Cecina and Castagneto Carducci. The route leads through hilly expanses of olive groves, dense fragrant shrub, beneath gargantuan umbrella pines and down an elegant avenue of cypress. So where are the vines? In fact, they are mostly around Bolgheri although there are also promising, newer wine estates around Montescudaio and the Val di Cornia. The estates at Bolgheri produce Tuscany's most exclusive and expensive wines, eclipsing even Chianti or Brunello. During World War II, Bordeaux was unavailable so Marchesa Incisa, a local noblewoman, planted Cabernet grapes on her Tenuta San Guido estate. In 1968, it produced Italy's first pure Cabernet, Sassicaia, widely regarded as one of Italy's best reds ever and priced accordingly (see also www.stradavino.it).

Above
The Marina di Bibbona

atmosphere. However, east of the town still stands the ruined fortress, Rocca di Sillano. After that, you pass the Saline di Volterra, an old salt mine that was once the major supplier for the province of Tuscany, before returning uphill again to Volterra.

Also worth exploring

The **Rifugio Faunistico di Bolgheri** (L'Oasi di Bolgheri) contains many habitats: seashore, dunes, grassland, some of the oldest cypresses in Tuscany and marshes. Thousands of birds gather here – lapwings, cranes, grey herons, storks, the osprey and even eagles – to make it a birdwatcher's paradise. The only drawback is that this paradise requires advance reservations (*tel: 0586 224361; open Oct–May, Fri–Sat, 0900–1000, 1400–1630*). The entrance to the nature reserve is on the south end of the avenue of cypresses that runs to Bolgheri (the road that crosses the railway line and continues in the direction of the sea: *see page 154*).

Maremma

Ratings

Beaches	●●●●●
Nature	●●●●●
Scenery	●●●●●
Architecture	●●●●○
Children	●●●●○
Food and drink	●●○○○
Museums	●●○○○
Shopping	●○○○○

Maremma means 'by the sea' and Tuscany's largest province has many kilometres of sandy beaches. The plain around its capital, Grosseto, was actually under water in ancient times. The Etruscans made the waterlogged region one of the most fertile places on the Mediterranean: Vetulonia, Roselle and Sovana were all flourishing cities. However, by late Roman times, malaria (*mal aria*, or 'bad air', still the world's most common serious infectious disease) was spreading death. During the Middle Ages, castles, monasteries and entire cities were abandoned and most of the land fell into disuse except for winter cattle grazing. 'Siena made me, Maremma undid me,' sighs a noblewoman in Dante's *Purgatorio*. Malaria wasn't brought under control until the 1930s when Mussolini engaged in massive land reclamation. Spraying DDT in the 1950s finished the job.

CASTIGLIONE DELLA PESCAIA

ⓘ APT office *Piazza Garibaldi 6; tel: 0564 933678; fax: 0564 933954; www.comune. castiglionedellapescaia.gr.it and www.lamaremmafabene.it*

Castiglione is really two places: the fishing village and holiday resort at the mouth of the Bruna river and a severe old city above it enclosed by a fortified wall with 11 watchtowers and crowned by a partly ruined 14th-century Rocca. In between, the narrow streets are lined with bars and small restaurants – it's hard not to have a good time here, though the resort manages to remain quieter and less frenetic than some of the more popular seaside towns further north. A lagoon – the Romans called it the *Lacus Prilius* – once stretched from Castiglione to the area around Grosseto. The last remnant of it, the Padule di Castilgione to the southeast, is still one of the largest swamps in Italy, and as such is a haven for all kinds of wildlife, including rare birds, reptiles, mammals and bigger beasts, including wild boar. Wide sand beaches and stands of *pineta* (umbrella pines) stretch north and south of town.

GROSSETO

ⓘ APT office *Via Monterosa 206; tel: 0564 454510; fax: 0564 454606; www.gol.grosseto.it, www.lamaremmafabene.it and www.provincia.grosseto.it. Open Mon–Sat 0900–1300, Apr–Oct 1630–1830 (Aug until 1930).*

ⓜ Museo Archeologico e d'Arte della Maremma *€ Piazza Baccarini 3; tel: 0564 488750; e-mail: maam@gol.grosseto.it. Open daily May–Oct 1000–1300 and 1700–2000, Mar–Apr 0930–1300 and 1600–1800, shorter hours in winter.*

The capital of Tuscany's largest province is a mix of scruffiness and morbid charm. Unsurprisingly, the old city is the best part, encircled by fortifications that form a hexagon of six bulwarks. Its structure reflects the canons for fortified cities as put forth by architects between the 15th and 16th centuries, with the fortress representing 'reason' and the cathedral, 'heart'. Like Lucca, Grosseto converted its fortified walls into a public garden – hence its nickname *'piccola Lucca'*.

Sienese architect Sozzo di Rustichino built the Duomo between 1294 and 1302 on the ruins of a more ancient building. It was aggressively restored in the 19th century and the façade added. In the 20th century, Mussolini settled poor peasants from the Veneto region in the city and constructed new buildings for the town including the world's most pompous post office – the Palazzo delle Poste. The Corso Carducci, between the Piazza Nuova at the north end and the Porta Vecchia at the south end, is the main shopping street with the lively arcaded Piazza Dante in the middle. The **Museo Archeologico e d'Arte della Maremma** has a significant collection of Etruscan and Roman objects, as it should, given the wealth of finds from Vetulonia and Roselle.

MASSA MARITTIMA

APT office Via
Norma Parenti 22; tel:
0566 902756; fax: 0566
940095;
www.massamarittima.info
and www.lamaremma.info

Massa Marittima's
**Balestro del
Girifalco** (first Sun after
20 May and second Sun in
Aug) is one of the most
colourful festivals in
Tuscany, pitting three
terziere, or
neighbourhoods, against
one another.

Opposite
Massa Marittima's San
Cerbone church

Time and silt have made a mockery of the city's name – Massa 'on the
sea'. Now it feels like an inland island. It was the most important city
in the Maremma in the Middle Ages with 10,000 inhabitants. Plague
and malaria decimated the population to a few hundred for several
centuries and, today, the population has again reached its medieval
level.

The Piazza Garibaldi in Massa Marittima is one of the most
fascinating squares in Italy and frequently shows up on slides in
courses on urban planning. It is an ellipse with five-pointed stellar
projections and a commanding fountain. The square is dominated by
the Pisan-style Romanesque-Gothic cathedral dedicated to San
Cerbone, Bishop of Populonia (570–3) and patron saint of Massa. Its
construction goes back to the beginning of the 12th century, but it
has been radically restored and added to over the centuries. The whole
structure is decorated with lots of blind arches and enigmatic figures –
man, beast and things in-between. The Latin-cross interior divides
three naves with majestic travertine columns surmounted by
sculptured capitals – no two are alike. The 13th-century Palazzo
Pretorio houses the Museo Archeologico. After conquering the city in
1335, the Sienese built the Fortezza dei Senesi, now a ruin, in the
upper city – Città Nuova.

However much Massa is admired today for its art and architecture,
its historical reason for being was mining. Massa Marittima lies
embedded between two hills that were once rich in iron (Colline
Metallifere) – it was a major 'industrial' town in the Middle Ages. It
was here that the first European mining code was drawn up. The
Museo della Miniera is a reconstruction of a mine with displays about
the long evolution of mining methods and technology.

ROCCASTRADA

On the hilltop in
Sticciano (an
unspoilt village off the N73
south of Roccastrada) is a
fine 13th-century
Romanesque church, San
Mustiola, that can be
visited after obtaining the
priest's permission.

Driving up to Roccastrada is like approaching an island of brown rock,
floating between the sky and the wheat-covered plain around
Grosseto, stretching southwest to the sea. It belonged to those lovers
of heights, the Etruscans, became part of the territory of Siena in 1317,
and fell to the Medici in 1559. The Castello di Montemassi dates back
to the 10th–11th centuries and belonged to the Aldobrandeschi. The
fortress is composed of two square blocks, a large walled yard and an
octagonal-shaped tower on the western escarpment. There is also a
lower set of walls. This is essentially the same rock monster portrayed
in a fresco by Simone Martini in the Palazzo Pubblico in Siena. He
shows how the Sienese won the day with the battifolle, a siege engine
that looks like a portable wooden fortress.

Cucina in the Maremma

Maremma's gastronomy can't decide between turf and surf. Will it be wild boar or *cacciucco* (fish stew)? Grilled fish or grilled goat? A dish of snails seems to occupy middle ground. Massa Marittima has an interesting *rosé* called Monte Regio.

Accommodation and food

Massa Marittima and Castiglione della Pescaia both make a good base for the Maremma; however, there are not many hotels in either place so make reservations in advance. The tourist offices keep lists of country pensions and *agriturismi*.

Corallo € *Via Sauro 1, Castiglione della Pescaia; tel: 0566 933668; www.residence-corallo.it. Closed Tue (except in summer and Nov). A pensione,* with the town's best home-made pasta. Booking recommended.

Vecchio Borgo € *Via Parenti 12 (just behind Piazza Garibaldi), Massa Marittima; tel: 0566 903950.* One of the best cheap eats in the entire Maremma.

Il Canto del Gallo €€ *Via Giuseppe Mazzini 29, Grosseto; tel: 0564 414589. Closed Sun, no lunch. No credit cards.* Located in the old Medici quarter near the *Centro Storico*, the 'cock's crow' has the best quality-price ratio in town. Chef Nadia Svetoni never misses a beat, from vegetable lasagne to grilled meats and game dishes such as *cinghiale alla cacciatora*. She even makes her own sorbet.

Il Sole €€ *Corso della Libertà 43, Massa Marittima; tel: 0566 901971; fax: 0566 901959.* The city's top hotel (out of only four), occupying a converted *palazzo*; it has parking. All rooms are comfortable but those at the back are quieter.

Suggested tour

Total distance: 146km; detours to Vetulonia add 10km (return), to Le Rocchette 14km (return), to Torre Civette 38km (return) and to Roselle 12km (return).

Time: The route can be done in a day, with time for a short swim, if you skip Grosseto and the detours. Massa Marittima and Castiglione della Pescaia both have a lively evening *passeggiata*.

Links: For a more complete tour of the Maremma, this route should be combined with the other Maremma route (*see page 180*).

Route: Drive south of **MASSA MARITTIMA** ❶ on the N439 for 6km and follow the signs for Grosseto. After another 13km, follow the signs for Castiglione della Pescaia.

Detour: The ruins of **Vetulonia** ❷ are on the way (signposted Necropoli Etrusca), an uphill deviation of 5km. This was the site of another one of the Etruscan League of 12 cities. Vetulonia prospered as a mining town near the shore of the ancient lagoon, the *Lacus Prilius*. Unlike the other cities in the League of 12, Vetulonia was never settled by the Romans. It was destroyed at an unknown date and lost until its discovery at the end of the 19th century underneath the hilltop village named Colonne di Buriano. All that is left are piles of stones from its original 5km wall, a couple of tombs and a small museum that is rarely open. However, it is a romantic setting and can have a strong effect on people with the imagination to conjure up life from rubble. Among the tombs, look for the site of the Tomba della Pietrera, one of the largest ever found. It once contained life-size statues of gods and goddesses that are regarded as among the earliest examples of Etruscan plastic art (they are now in Grosseto).

Continue along the plain, skirting wheat fields, canals and the Bruna river to **CASTIGLIONE DELLA PESCAIA** ❸.

Detour: Castiglione has acceptable beaches but the best ones are a short drive northwest, on the N322 then forking left along the narrow coastal road to **Le Rocchette** – excellent for swimming, swish beachside hotels and well-appointed camping sites. For a wilder beach, drive further north on the N322 (15km) and take the road to **Torre Civette**.

Getting out of the car: There are fine walks to be had along one of the most unspoilt stretches of Tuscany's coast between Torre Civette and Follonica, or around Castiglione della Pescaia, further south. Whichever you choose, you can be sure of enjoying a fabulous panorama of the island of Elba and of the Mare Tirreno.

The N322 going south out of Castiglione della Pescaia crosses the harbour and follows a ruler-straight road through a 9km stand of coastal pines, the Pineta del Tombolo. There are a number of picnic places beneath the trees and a couple of trails to the beach. At San Carlo, take the road northeast to **GROSSETO** ❹ that skirts the flat riverbed of the Ombrone river. Exit the town on the N1 *autostrada* going north.

Detour: To visit the ruined city of **Roselle** ❺ (Zona Archeologica di Roselle – **Rusellae** € *Via dei Ruderi; tel: 0564 403043; open daily 0830–sunset*), take the road to Siena, N223, and follow the signs (avoiding the exit for modern Roselle, which you will see first). It is a fascinating but confusing pair of hills and a vale covered with early Etruscan to medieval ruins that are still being excavated. There is a polygonal ring of Etruscan walls that is almost completely preserved – as high as 7m in places – and, most rare, an intact Etruscan home.

Roselle also belonged to the Etruscan League of 12 cities, having been founded in the 7th century BC. After fierce resistance, it fell to the Romans in the 3rd century BC. Like Vetulonia, it was on the shore of *Lacus Prilius*, a lagoon that began to silt up late in the Roman period. The town became a diocese seat in 499 and, at the end of the 6th century, was one of the last Byzantine strongholds in Tuscany. Invading Saracens destroyed it in 935.

To return to the route, drive 2km back in the direction of Grosseto and turn north on to the *Via Aurelia autostrada* (N1).

Turn off the *autostrada* at Braccagni. The road north to Roccastrada is clearly marked. It begins as a peaceful country lane lined with cork trees then banks smoothly upwards through uninhabited hills. You will come to an abrupt T-junction near the top of a ridge. Turn north (left) for Roccastrada (not right to Strada di Roccastrada). **ROCCASTRADA** ❻ is at the top of the ridge.

Carry on 5km north and watch for signs marked Sassofortino, where you will turn west (left). A peaceful, leafy mountain road zigzags to **Roccatederighi** ❼ , which overlooks a valley of dense *maquis* and chestnuts. It was first mentioned in the 13th century as the Rocca Filiorum Guaschi (the name of the ruling family) and as Filiorum Tederigi or Tederigoli. It warred against Volterra and Massa Marittima before becoming the property of the Republic of Siena at the end of 1200. The original fortress has been incorporated into later stone buildings. None of that really lessens the impact of this strange place, hewed directly out of the cliff with an amazing, bird's-eye view of the Maremma and the Ligurian and Tyrrhenian seas. The effect is bizarrely organic – like a human coral reef.

After the town is a Y-junction. Take the right fork 8km to the hamlet of Gabellino and turn southwest (left) to reach Massa Marittima. The road winds through more green shrub and stands of forest that survived the axes of woodcutters who migrated here from the Apennines.

Also worth exploring

San Galgano is the oldest Gothic church in Italy and Tuscany's most haunting ruin. Cistercian monks, master builders who translated the theological principle *God is light* into architecture, built it in the 13th century (they worked on the cathedral in Siena during the same period). In the 16th century, a greedy abbot sold off the lead from the roof. Two centuries later, the campanile collapsed. Today, it is open to heaven and paved with a meadow. On top of a nearby hill, the lonely **Oratorio di San Galgano al Montesiepi** is a rare Romanesque church for its shape – it is perfectly round. Inside are faded 14th-century frescos by Ambrogio Lorenzetti, and a sword embedded in a stone by St Galgano who renounced military life to become a hermit – a pacifist contrast to the Arthurian myth of the Sword in the Stone.

Maremma: Monti dell' Uccellina to Pitigliano

Ratings

Beaches	●●●●●
National Parks	●●●●●
Nature	●●●●●
Scenery	●●●●●
Wildlife	●●●●●
Children	●●●●○
History	●●●○○
Museums	●○○○○

The nature reserve of Uccellina is the wildest corner of Tuscany. *Pineta* – sparse forests of umbrella pine – alternates with moorland and *macchia*, fragrant and almost impenetrable masses of brush and scrub, bristling myrtle, rosemary and broom. Thousands of birds use the park as a place to rest on their journey between Europe and North Africa (its name means 'of the little birds'). Wild boar, foxes and deer cross paths here with Italy's only wild horses. Uccellina even has cowboys – *butteri* – who tend livestock in the marshy areas that cannot be reached by any other means. Just 15km further down the coast, the circular peninsula of Monte Argentario offers Tuscany's most dramatic piece of coastline. Inland, the Maremma is a chequerboard of olive groves, fields of grain and surpassingly lush, heavily wooded hills, particularly around the ancient Etruscan cities of Pitigliano and Sorano.

MONTE ARGENTARIO

ⓘ **Informazioni turistiche** *Piazzale S. Andrea, Porto Santo Stefano; tel: 0564 814208; fax: 0564 814052; www. lamaremma.info and www. comunemonteargentario.it*

Ⓟ Porto Santo Stefano has ferries €€ to the island of Giglio, and (in summer) to the privately owned island of Giannutri (day trips only). Ferry information is available at the **TOREMAR** office, *Piazzale Candi 1; tel: 0564 810803; fax: 0564 818455; www.toremar.it* or the tourist office.

For all its long history of human settlement, much of this former island, particularly the interior, remains uninhabited and almost wild. Il Telegrafo (635m) is its highest point. Monte Argentario was in Spanish hands for many centuries, which accounts for the Spanish architecture and forts. It was an island until the 18th century when silting caused two sandy fingers of land to appear – the Tombolo di Gianella and Tombolo di Feniglia – gradually connecting it to the mainland and creating the Laguna di Orbetello. In 1842, a dyke was built to connect the town of Orbetello to the mainland.

ORBETELLO

ℹ **Pro Loco** *Piazza della Repubblica 1; tel/fax: 0564 860447; www.proloco-orbetello.it and www.lamaremma.info. Open daily Jun–Aug 0930–1300 and 1630–2000, Sep–May 0900–1230 and 1600–1900.*

Orbetello was an Etruscan harbour and still preserves a piece of its Etruscan walls. But what you see today dates mostly from a period of Spanish occupation that lasted almost 300 years. It was the capital of Presidio, a small Spanish principality, between 1557 and 1808. The city gate of the Porte del Soccorso still bears the arms of the Spanish king on it.

The **Duomo Santa Maria Assunta** was built in 1376 by the Sienese during the time of Niccolò Orsini, though often remodelled by the Spanish. Its sloping, weathered façade has a rose window and a quatrefoil frieze with eccentric figures; for example, the rampant lion

ⓘ Museo Archeologico Guzman € *Via Mura di Levante; tel: 0564 860447. Open Jun–Sep Fri–Sun 1800–2300, Oct–May 0900–1200.*

Nature Reserve € *Tel: 0564 820297. Guided tours only Sep–Apr Sat & Sun 0930–1500.*

Below
Maremma beach

spearing a fish – the coat of arms given to the city by Siena. Inside, perhaps the most interesting object is the *antependium* that decorates the altar. It reflects the early Christian fixation with certain animals: lions, horses, snakes and doves.

Across from the Duomo, in a former convent, the **Museo Archeologico Guzman** displays the *Frontone di Talamone*, an Etruscan temple frieze of terracotta excavated at Talamone and meticulously reconstructed. It tells the mythic story of the 'Seven against Thebes', with blind Oedipus in the centre.

Orbetello is bordered on both sides by lagoons: the one to the north is a **Nature Reserve** (Riserva Naturale Provinciale Laguna di Orbetello) under the protection of the World Wide Fund for Nature (WWF) and of special appeal to birdwatchers, who have sighted almost half of Italy's bird species within the boundaries of its eight square kilometres.

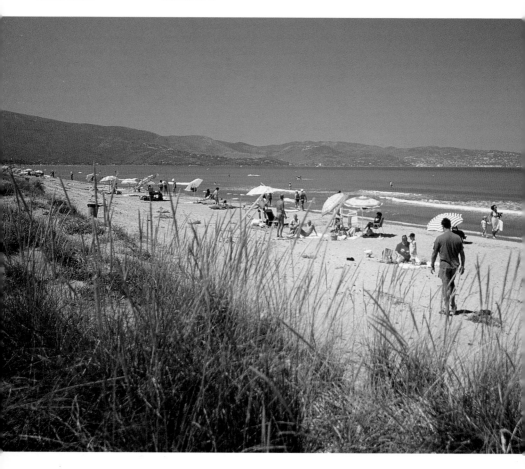

PARCO NATURALE DELLA MAREMMA

Parco Naturale della Maremma €€
Centro Visite del Parco in Alberese; tel: 0564 407292; fax: 0564 407278; www.parco-maremma.it. Contact the Azienda Agricola Alberese (*tel: 0564 407180; www.alberese.com*) if you are interested in riding with the *butteri* (cowboys). Every year in August there is a rodeo in the park.

Maquis and forest, impenetrable in places, cover the slopes of a coastal range – Monti dell' Uccellina – that looms 400m above a shore of grottoes and small bays. The 100-sq km park stretches from Principina a Mare in the north to Talamone in the south. The north part includes the mouth of the Ombrone river, sand dunes, swamps, reeds and pine groves. Wild horses and white, sharp-horned cattle roam free when they are not being herded by cowboys on horseback – welcome to the Italian Wild West. Wildfowl and flamingos live in its swamps. The ruined abbey of San Rabano, located deep in the coastal bush, is a reminder of the fact that the park has a long history of human settlement. The park has a series of trails 4–12km long.

PITIGLIANO

Pro Loco *Via Roma 6; tel/fax: 0564 614433; www.pitigliano-toscana.com*

Il Laboratorio dell'Erborista *La Rotta 122/a; tel/fax: 0564 619417; www.laborerbe.it.* A herbalist shop with herbal cosmetics, infusions, honey and marmalade.

Few towns have quite the same impact on first sight as Pitigliano. The city seems to have been grafted by time rather than built on to stone cliffs rising above the deep river valleys of the Lente and Meleta. The base of the town is honeycombed with Etruscan tombs – some now used as wine cellars or garages. The Orsini family controlled the region in 1293 and left behind palaces, a fortress designed by Antonio Sangallo and an amazing aqueduct. The baroque Duomo Santi Pietro e Paolo is worth a look but it is essentially the whole medieval ensemble and its atmosphere that are unforgettable. The Via Zuccarelli and obscure lanes running out of it such as Vicolo Goito and Vicolo di Riforme – the former Jewish Quarter – give way to terraces that have dramatic views of the Meleta valley.

Tuscany's Little Jerusalem

For almost 400 years, Pitigliano had such a thriving Jewish community that it came to be known as *piccola Gerusalemme* – Little Jerusalem. Today, there are three families left, a reconstructed synagogue used as a museum and the Jewish cemetery. In the 18th and 19th centuries, more than 20 per cent of Pitigliano's inhabitants were Jews. A 1938 census lists Jewish bus drivers, doctors, factory workers, bankers, farmers, merchants and teachers. By the end of the war, they were all gone. Edda Servi-Machlin, the daughter of Pitigliano's last rabbi, published a book in 1981, *The Classic Cuisine of the Italian Jews* (Giro Press, NY). In it, she points out that the local dialect uses Hebrew words such as *Adonai* (God) and *Zona* (whore) and that Pitiglianese cuisine offers *billo*, a kind of 'ham' that is made of turkey.

PORTO ERCOLE

ⓘ Pro Loco *Piazza
della Repubblica 3,*
Orbetello; tel: 0564 860447;
www.portoercole.org

Below
Porto Ercole

The town is wedged higgledy-piggledy between the bay and a pair of grim Spanish forts, Stella and Filippo, now condominiums for yuppies from Rome. On 18 July 1610, Michelangelo Merisi, better known as Caravaggio, was found dead here on the beach. Depending on whom you read, he died of malaria, pneumonia, sunstroke or from the clinical knife-thrust of a baroque-era hit man. He had been in hiding, having killed one of his lovers in a duel four years earlier. Ironically, Caravaggio did much of his best work while on the run. Three days after his death, a document arrived from Rome granting him clemency.

Cucina in the Maremma

Anguille (eel) is a local delicacy that comes from the Orbetello lagoon and is smoked, grilled or marinated. Bianco di Pitigliano is a white wine that has much in common with Orvieto Classico. Far and away the best-known wine in the Maremma is the red Morellino di Scansano. It contains at least 85 per cent Sangiovese and tastes somewhat like Chianti.

Above
Parasol pine

Accommodation and food

La Conchiglia € *Via della Marina 22, Porto Ercole; tel: 0564 833134.* Small and surprisingly quiet *pensione* near the harbour.

La Lampara € *Lungomare Andrea Doria 68, Porto Ercole; tel: 0564 833024.* Friendly *trattoria* with pizza, a seafood menu and the best prices on the harbour.

Il Tufo Allegro € *Vicolo della Costituzione 2, Pitigliano; tel: 0564 616192. Closed Tue, and Jan and Aug.* Home-made soups and pasta such as superb *pappardelle gialle al sugo di agnello* (broad noodles with lamb sauce); there are also some *piatto ebraico* (Jewish dishes) based on traditional recipes.

Il Pellicano €€€ *4km west of Porto Ercole; tel: 0564 833111; fax: 0564 833418; www.pellicanohotel.com.* One of Tuscány's most expensive hotels, occupying its own piece of the coastline.

Terme di Saturnia €€€ *Off the side of the road, Via delle Terme 1; tel: 0564 600800; fax: 0564 600111; www.termedisaturnia.it.* Guests have free access to the baths. The hotel has a good restaurant, beauty salon and other comforts – enough to satisfy the most demanding hedonist.

Above
Orbetello beach

Suggested tour

Total distance: 131km. The detour on Monte Argentario adds a lot of time but almost no distance; detours to Talamone and Sovana both 8km (return); detour to Terme di Saturnia is 25km (return).

Time: Three days would probably be the minimum for an exploration of Monti dell'Uccellina, Monte Argentario and the hinterland around Pitigliano, assuming a couple of walks, a soak in Saturnia's hot springs and a visit to an Etruscan tomb or two. The driving can be done in a day.

Links: This route begins at a point near the circuit that includes Grosseto (*see page 171*). The two routes taken together provide an extended tour of the Maremma.

Route: Turn off the *Via Aurelia autostrada* (N1) at the exit for **PARCO NATURALE DELLA MAREMMA** ❶ and carry on to Marina di Alberese.

Getting out of the car: An easy 4km trail begins at the car park. Walk back up the road 100m and turn left into the path marked 'A7'. The trail leads to the mouth of the Ombrone river and returns to the car park along a trail through sand dunes.

The coastal mountains in the park are only accessible by foot. First of all, you have to drive further south to the town of **Alberese**. The price of admission includes a bus ride (*it runs every hour*) to the hamlet of Pratini (*no private cars allowed*), which is the point of departure for trekking in the park. There are trails to San Rabano (6km); the guard tower of Castel Marino and Torre Lungo (both 5km); and to the bay of Cala di Forno (12km).

Detour: Just 4km off the N1, **Talamone** ❷ is the stuff of legends. It seems that Talamone, the father of Ajax, died here and the high hill that juts out into the sea and which the town rests on, is his tomb. Of Etruscan origin and inhabited by the Romans, it is now a fishing village gradually being taken over by tourism. The almost windowless castle that overlooks it was designed by Vecchietta in the 15th century. Talamone's modern claim to fame is that Garibaldi landed on its shores in 1860 with his 3,000 followers.

Getting out of the car: Three hiking trails lead out of Talamone into the southern part of the Parco.

Get off the N1 at Albinia and follow the finger of land that joins the mainland to **MONTE ARGENTARIO** ❸; the view of the bay on both sides is mostly blocked by umbrella pines.

Arriving on the island, turn right and follow the signs around the bay for **Porto Santo Stefano** ❹. Once in town, avoid the Porto to the right (unless you want a ferry to the island of Giglio) and turn left up the steep main street following signs for the Strada Panoramica. Prepare yourself for some of the most beautiful coastal scenery in Tuscany and some of the hairiest driving, particularly in the afternoon. The people of Santo Stefano use this narrow road for the ritual of *passeggiata*. For the first few kilometres, you will have to manoeuvre between couples in various stages of courtship, families pushing prams, and old men and women with canes. After a few kilometres, there are turn-offs for a bread, salami and wine picnic. You will catch, out of the corner of your eye, the tantalising gleam of diminutive beaches nestled among the cliffs below; sadly, most of them are inaccessible or privately owned. The Strada Panoramica advances to a Y-junction.

Detour: Turn right to continue on the Strada Panoramica. The road circles the entire peninsula and more than lives up to its name. There are fantastic views of the Giglio and Giannutri islands. The landscape is so inspiring you might be tempted to go for it. The beginning is solid enough despite the potholes. Warning signs appear thick and fast including one that warns of a lack of warning signs. Roman yuppies who live on the island cruise along with an *autostrada* nonchalance. However, the further you go, the more it feels like a place for paragliding rather than motoring.

Go left (north). Carry on along the lagoon side of Monte Argentario to the picturesque **PORTO ERCOLE ❺**. From there, retrace the route 4km and turn right on the N440. **ORBETELLO ❻** is in the middle of the lagoon. If there is time, take a walk beneath the palm trees along Viale Mura di Levante. Exit the city through the triple-corniced gate with matching obelisks built by the Spanish in the 17th century. Turn left on the *Via Aurelia* (N1) and then right on the N74 at Albinia. The road is a straight shot through a plain beneath endless alleys of birch and plane trees. After the hamlet of Marsiliana it curves in sync with the Elsa river before mounting a ridge and circling around **Manciano ❼**. The town is little visited by tourists, though it has an authentic medieval core, a Sienese castle (1350) and a museum with prehistoric finds from the Fiora valley.

Detour: Drive north on the N322 and take the right fork at Montemerano, another fortified town. Depending on the season and time of day, you can see the steam from a distance, rising up from the **Terme di Saturnia ❽**, to say nothing of a lot of parked cars. Legend would have you believe that the spring was founded by Saturn, the Roman god of sowing. More than two million litres of 37.5°C carbon-sulphur-boric water flows out of it each hour. The water is said to be an effective treatment for rheumatism, bronchitis and constipation.

The **Cascate del Mulino**, a set of cascades near a ruined mill that form pools in the travertine rock below, is an ideal place to soak. On weekends and in summer, you will share it with a horde of people –

Above
Pitigliano

big extended families, luvvies, picnickers, flower children – it's all like the crowded finale of a Fellini movie. The source of the water is a little further upstream and is monopolised by a luxury spa and resort where you can soak for a day (with optional mudbath or massage) or stay overnight in its hotel for a price (*see page 179*).

Arriving on the road from Manciano, the first look at **PITIGLIANO** ❾ is one of the most impressive sights in Tuscany.

Detour: Drive north and follow the signs to **Sovana** ❿. The town rotted away for centuries and barely clawed its way back to life in the 20th century. It is utterly quaint and, for people who don't mind their history in a dustbin, fascinating. Sovana sits on top of a vast Etruscan City of the Dead that stretches further than the eye can see or, thus far, the archaeologist can dig. It belonged to Etruscan Suana and straggles along for 3km outside of the city. Most of the tombs are from the 3rd to 2nd century BC and many of them are linked by a mysterious network of ancient roads that were either hewed through rock or built as deep ditches. The number of tombs on view is small but at least they are easy to find – just follow the yellow road signs.

In the Middle Ages, the town's fortunes were closely linked with the Aldobrandeschi family. Pope Gregory VII, its most successful son, was born here in 1021. Gregory was the Pope who forced Henry IV to come to Canossa on his knees. The building where he was supposedly born survives and, oddly enough, now houses a 'museum' full of giant snails that ooze up and down the walls of their aquariums. The wonky cathedral at the end of the diminutive town dates from the 12th to 14th centuries with a portal and capitals decorated with strange medieval symbols.

A number of fine craftspeople, some of them escaped townies, now have shops in Sovana. One of them, an artisan named Francesco di Pinto, makes handmade paper and stationery of a quality you would normally only find in places such as Florence or Venice (**Il Leone Dipinto** *Via del Duomo 12; tel/fax: 0564 615552*). There is also a terracotta workshop near the car park, which turns out magnificent Etruscan reproductions.

Also worth exploring

North of Pitigliano (9 or 18km depending on the road), **Sorano** (*www.comune.sorano.gr.it*) is as fascinating as Pitigliano and perhaps even more dramatic for its position at the edge of a green-gold gorge formed by the River Lente. Sorano rests on a sandstone cliff riddled with caves and tombs and was also part of the Orsini empire. Many of its buildings are stamped with the family heraldic symbols – the bear, the lion, the rose and the stripes. The Orsini built its proudest monument, the perfectly preserved Renaissance Fortezza. If for no other reason, Sorano is unmissable because it might not be there next time. Landslides have already claimed some streets and houses. Still, it is no ghost town. The core remains inhabited and an energetic community of local craftspeople is fighting to save it.

Florence to Arezzo via Casentino

Ratings

Castles	●●●●○
Food and drink	●●●●○
Monasteries	●●●●○
Nature	●●●●○
Outdoor activities	●●●●○
Scenery	●●●●○
Shopping	●●●●○
Museums	●●○○○

The Casentino is the name given to the wild reaches of the upper Arno. The landscape, formed during the last Ice Age, oscillates between sharp ridges, dense forest, high pastures and flat valley bottoms (that were once ancient lakes). The Arno river tumbles and loops through the valley. It flows from sources high on the slopes of Mount Falterona beneath the village of Stia and past the towns of Poppi and Bibbiena, before curving just north of Arezzo on its way to Florence. The region was settled by Etruscans and became an all-important north–south passage in the Middle Ages, guarded by numerous castles. The heights of the Casentino have been a place of spiritual retreat for almost a millennium, since St Romuald founded a hermitage at Camaldoli, and St Francis is said to have found peace where the monastery of La Verna now stands.

AREZZO

ⓘ Informazioni turistiche *Piazza della Repubblica 28, by the train station; tel: 0575 377678; fax: 0575 20839; e-mail: info@arezzo.turismo. toscana.it; www.provincia.arezzo.it & www.apt.arezzo.it. Open Apr–Sep Mon–Sat 0900–1300 and 1500–1900, Sun 0900–1300, Oct–Mar Mon–Sat 0900–1300 and 1500–1830, first Sun of the month 0900–1300.*

Although Arezzo is not very popular with tourists, Italians recently voted it as one of Italy's best places to live. The Etruscans thought so too – it was part of the League of 12 cities. One of the two most famous Etruscan bronzes was found here – the Chimera (Florence has the original). It became Roman *Arretium* in 294 BC and still has a well-preserved amphitheatre. The poet Petrarch (1304–37) would recognise much of the *Centro Storico* today, and native son and Renaissance man Giorgio Vasari (1511–74) even more, since he designed a lot of it.

The nexus of the old, hilly part of town is the Piazza Grande, framed by Vasari's Palazzo delle Logge, the Palazzo della Fraternità dei Laici and the Romanesque Pieve di Santa Maria. This splendid Romanesque church is a massive, almost geometrical collection of porticos, columns, blind arcades and loggias, all crowned by an ambitious bell tower (1330), known as 'the tower of a hundred holes'. The sombre interior feels empty and its big arches are said to be a prelude to Gothic style. The oldest part is the presbytery and five-naved crypt.

The star artistic attraction is the *Madonna and Saints* on the main altar, a polyptych by Pietro Lorenzetti (1320).

However, the jewel in Arezzo's art history crown is in the main choir chapel of the church of San Francesco. This fresco cycle – the ***Legend of the True Cross*** (1452–66) by Piero della Francesca – is one of the most important works of art created in the Renaissance. Part of it is on view again after years of restoration. It has been suggested that the frescos were commissioned to boost interest in the Crusades, which were beginning to lose popularity. One panel, the first night scene in Western painting, depicts the Emperor Constantine's prophetic dream of victory over Maxentius, aided by the cross that he will carry the following day into battle.

The **Casa di Giorgio Vasari** was the home of the artist and consultant to the Medici Duke Cosimo I. Vasari decorated the rooms

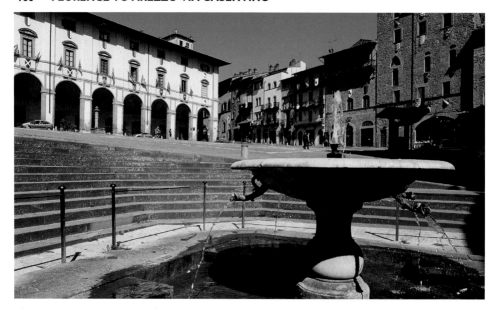

Duomo San Donato € *Piazza del Duomo; tel: 0575 23991. Open 0630–1230 and 1500–1900.*

There is a vast **antique fair** in the *Centro Storico, around the Piazza Grande, on the first weekend of each month (information, tel: 0575 377678).*

Busatti Arezzo *Corso Italia 48; tel: 0575 355295; www.busatti.com. Open Tue–Sat 0900–1300 and 1600–2000. Fabrics of great quality at affordable prices in a tradition that goes back many centuries. They are created in a small Tuscan workshop in the town of Anghiari, founded in the 19th century.*

Pitti Casa *Via San Lorentino 15; tel. 0575 299779. Handles for doors, drawers and so on, made from glass, porcelain, steel, wood, bone and stone.*

himself with frescos and paintings in Mannerist style. The Camera della Fama (hall of fame) has Vasari assuming a heroic pose in a group of famous artists whose lives he described as a biographer.

Arezzo's cathedral, the **Duomo San Donato**, occupies the highest point in the city. Begun in 1277, it was not finished for several hundred years – the 'Gothic' campanile and façade were actually completed in the 19th and 20th centuries. Guillaume de Marcillat, a Domenican monk from Chartres, created the rare 16th-century stained-glass windows, including the *Miracle of Whitsun, Raising of Lazarus* and *Expulsion of Moneychangers from the Temple*. In the left aisle, the tomb of Bishop Guido Tarlati impresses with marble reliefs of miracles and battles; just to the right is a fresco of Maria Maddalena by Piero della Francesca.

Above
Arezzo's Piazza Grande

Giostra del Saracino

The Joust of the Saracen takes place on the penultimate Saturday in June at night and the first Sunday in September in the afternoon. Two hundred and fifty participants – soldiers, musicians, valets, flag-jugglers and knights – parade to the Piazza Grande. Eight knights in heavy armour, two from each of Arezzo's four quarters, take turns charging a huge effigy of a Saracen. They score by striking his shield with their lances and avoiding the effigy's counter-attack when it rotates and strikes back with a whip. The winner receives a golden lance.

CASTELLO AND PIEVE SAN PIETRO DI ROMENA

Castello di Romena
€ *Via Romena 12/A; tel:*
0335 1220930. Closed for
restoration. (The modest
Museo Archeologico e delle
Armi € is open by
appointment.)

Pieve di San Pietro *Via*
Romena; tel: 0575 583725.
Open by appointment only.
Free.

Originally built by the counts of Guidi to defend the upper Arno valley, the Castello was, in its glory days, the most famous castle in the Casentino and mentioned with great respect by Dante. Only one of its original 14 towers has survived but the weed-covered castle ruins are still impressive. The austere 13th-century **Pieve di San Pietro di Romena** is an imposing Romanesque church resting squat in a broad field of sunflowers below the castle. (If it is locked, there is a guardian across the road. She will sometimes open it, depending on the time of day; that is, not during the lunch and siesta period.)

PIEVE A SOCANA

Pieve di Sant'Antonio
Tel: 0575 592561. Open
summer 0800–1300 and
1530–1900, winter
0830–1230 and 1500–1730.

The site of the Romanesque parish church of **Sant'Antonio** has seen some form of worship for 2,500 years: an Etruscan temple once stood here. Behind the apse of the church, in a cornfield, is an altar used by the Etruscans to perform sacrifices – of what or whom we don't know – but the blood grooves are clearly visible.

Below
Arezzo's Chimera fountain

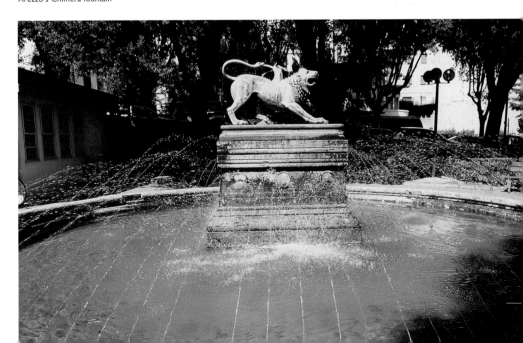

POPPI

Castello dei Conti Guidi € *Piazza Repubblica 1; tel: 0575 520516; www.castellodipoppi.it. Open daily Jul–Aug 1000–1900, mid-Mar–Jun and Sep–Oct 1000–1800, Nov–mid-Mar Thu–Sun 1000–1700.*

About 15km from Poppi, La Verna is the spot where St Francis fasted and prayed and, on the night of 16 September 1224, on a *crudo sasso* (bare rock), received the stigmata.

Poppi is visible for miles around thanks to the extraordinary **Castello dei Conti Guidi**, a fairy-tale fortress that leaps out at you from its deep moat. The castle was built in 1260–72 with additions in 1291 by Arnolfo di Cambio (of Palazzo Vecchio fame). The courtyard seems to have gone untouched for some 700-odd years. The balustrade of its freestanding staircase has a hundred miniature stone columns and is decorated with coats of arms from the entire region. The Knight's Hall impresses, as does the bedroom of the counts of Guidi, with remarkable medieval mod cons. The library possesses 20,000 volumes and 600 illuminated manuscripts.

From the ramparts of the castle you can look north up the valley towards Campaldino where Dante fought in a battle between Arezzo Ghibellines and Florentine Guelphs on a hot summer day in 1289; or east across the Apennines towards Camaldoli; or southeast towards La Verna. After the castle, the centre of historic Poppi is well worth a visit – you can stroll through most of it beneath ancient arcades. The central 'piazza' is scarcely bigger than one of the Mercedes Benz that occasionally park there.

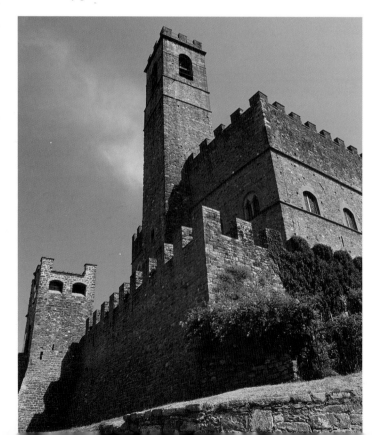

Right
Poppi's Castello dei Conti Guidi

STIA

ⓘ In the immediate vicinity of Stia are two medieval castles built by the counts of Guidi: the **Castello di Palagio Fiorentino**, now a small contemporary art museum, lies in an enchanting garden (**Museo d'Arte Contemporanea** € *Via Vittorio Veneto 35; tel: 0575 583706; www.comune.stia.ar.it. Open Jun–Sep Sat 1600–1900, Sun 1030–1230 and 1600–1900; or during exhibitions or by appointment*); the **Castello di Porciano** € *Porciano; tel: 0575 582635; www.castellodiporciano.com. Open daily May–Oct 1000–1200 and 1600–1900, or by appointment* has the best view, from its imposing tower above the narrow valley of the upper Arno. Today, it contains an agricultural museum.

Right
Stia's Piazza Tanucci

One of the most beautiful villages in the Arno valley, Stia is a starting point for excursions into the area around Monte Falterona. The parish of Santa Maria Assunta dates back to 1150 when it was built on a pre-existing religious building referred to around the year AD 1000. Little remains of the exterior of the 12th-century building. The apse and façade were demolished and given baroque replacements. The interior, with a nave and two aisles separated by monolithic columns in sandstone, preserves the Romanesque forms. The capitals bear distinctive decorations of animals, floral plants and alien-seeming humans. There is an ineffable *Madonna and Child* by Andrea della Robbia on which he used the long-lost secret of his glaze to strikingly radiant effect.

Accommodation and food

Cucina in the Casentino

The Casentino makes use of some of Italy's best olive oil and lots of game, *charcuterie*, mushrooms and mountain-stream trout. As a first course, locals relish *maccheroni*, also known as *pappardelle* (broad noodles). *Scottiglia* is a spicy stew of several meats – chicken, rabbit, lamb and sometimes game. Another local speciality is chicken, duck or rabbit *in porchetta* (stuffed with herbs).

Two of the most memorable places to stay in the region are the monasteries of La Verna and Camaldoli. Both have guest rooms with en-suite bathrooms (cold stone cells are not on offer). There are family rooms, too – just don't ask for a double bed. Guests are in no way required to follow the monastic routine. Reserve far in advance.

Foresteria del Santuario della Verna € *Monastery of La Verna; tel: 0575 534210; fax: 0575 599320; www.santuariodellaverna.com.* Saint Francis slept here (before the monastery was established) and received the signs of the stigmata.

La Foresteria € *Monastery of Camaldoli; tel: 0575 556012; fax: 0575 556001; e-mail: monastero@camaldoli.it; www.camaldoli.it.* Bunk with the monks here.

La Torre di Gnicche € *Piaggia San Martino 6, Arezzo; tel: 0575 352035. Closed Wed, and for two weeks in Jan, one week in Aug.* In a 13th-century palace with a view of Piazza Vasari. Excellent soup, pasta and traditional dishes such as *grifi all'aretina* served with local wine.

Buca di San Francesco €€ *Piazza San Francesco 1, Arezzo; tel: 0575 23271; www.bucadisanfrancesco.it. Closed Mon eve and Tue.* One of Arezzo's best. The dining room is a sumptuously decorated cellar of a medieval palace.

Below and above
Arezzo restaurants

Hotel Continentale €€ *Piazza Guido Monaco 7, Arezzo; tel: 0575 20251; fax: 0575 350485; www.hotelcontinentale.com.* Excellent mostly for its location and roof terrace.

La Lancia d'Oro €€ *Loggie del Vasari, Piazza Grande 18/19, Arezzo; tel: 0575 21033. Closed Sun eve and Mon.* Overpriced, but located on one of the most beautiful squares in Italy.

La Tana degli Orsi €€ *Via Roma 1, Pratovecchio; tel: 0575 583377. Eves only, closed Wed and Apr, Nov.* This *trattoria* renders homage to local ingredients with tremendous flair and enthusiasm, particularly in game dishes such as hare with bilberries and forest mushrooms.

Suggested tour

Total distance: 92km; detours: the loop to Vallombrosa, 14km; La Verna, 46km (return).

Time: It is possible to enjoy the Casentino on the way from Florence to Arezzo and do it in one day of driving. However, that will leave little time for getting out of the car.

Links: The route ends in Arezzo, which is the beginning of the Upper Tiber Valley route (*see page 199*).

Route: Leave **Florence** ❶ on the N67 in the direction (east) of **Pontassieve** ❷ and continue east on the N70, lurching in abrupt turns above the valley.

Detour: After only 5.5km, you come to a fork and the beginning of a panoramic road (signposted Vallombrosa). The rural scenery and silvery-grey olives give way, after much toing and froing, to a vast forest of spruce and pine as well as elm, maple, chestnut and beech trees; beneath them are ferns, broom and, in spring, alpine violets. The road takes a wide curve through the resort town of Saltino that became fashionable at the turn of the 20th century and still boasts palatial hotels such as the Grand and Croce di Savoia. At the heart of the forest lies the **Abbazia di Vallombrosa** ❸. Giovanni Gualberto Visdomini, having persuaded warring knights to retire from the world and live in solitude, founded the Order in 1051. However, today's fortress-like abbey dates from the 16th to 17th centuries, when Vallombrosans were rich and wallowing in baroque conspicuous consumption. Twenty monks still live there and work the garden. John Milton visited the abbey in 1638 and found the surroundings worthy of mention in *Paradise Lost*. The abbey's Antica Farmacia (old pharmacy) offers all kinds of interesting souvenirs including an elixir that 'makes life healthier, more delicious and desirable'. Right in front of the abbey grounds is an old stone bridge that leads back to the N70 (signposted San Miniato in Alpe) via a narrow, leafy tunnel of a road. In the autumn, chestnuts rain down on the road and the forest is full of mushroom-hunters in rubber boots poking in the ground and ignoring the rusty signs telling them to leave the *funghi* alone.

Continue to the highest point in the range, **Passo della Consuma** ❹. The road gently descends through the magnificent countryside of the Casentino along a ridge reaching a fork after 10km. Drive left (north) in the direction of Stia/Pratovecchio. Three kilometres further downhill, a narrow lane on the right leads off to **CASTELLO DI ROMENA** ❺. The main road executes a few delightful turns through lush scenery and levels out just in time for an old stone bridge over the Arno. **STIA** ❻ is at the opposite end.

Getting out of the car: From Stia, take the road towards the Passo La Calla for 2km and take a left turn in the village of Papiano to reach the tiny church of Madonna di Montalto (856m). From here, a trail leads to Lago degli Idoli through a forest of ancient chestnuts and fir trees. It is advisable to take a detailed topographic map (*available in Stia and Pratovecchio*).

Paolo Uccello, the artist whose obsession with perspective virtually drove him mad, was born in **Pratovecchio** ❼ though he didn't leave any work there. It is a pleasant town with arcaded squares – a typical feature in this region. The most interesting town in the whole valley is **POPPI** ❽, living like many Tuscan towns on two levels – uphill is history and downhill is work.

Further down the valley is **Bibbiena** ❾. One of the oldest cities in the region, it was on the frontline of the medieval struggle between Arezzo and Florence for domination of the Casentino. Today it is the industrial centre of the valley. In the town centre, the Pieve di Santi Hippolito e Donato (12th century) has some beautiful Sienese school paintings and an altar by Bicci di Lorenzo (1373–1452). From Bibbiena's Piazza Tarlati, you can see far up the valley to Poppi and beyond.

Detour: Turn off at Bibbiena to take the road to the monastery of **La Verna** ❿, which is at 1,129m in a forest of pine and beech. During the tourist/pilgrim season, La Verna offers more people-watching than solitude.

A few kilometres south of Bibbiena, **PIEVE A SOCANA** ⓫ is clearly marked. However, if you drive too fast, you might blow through the little town where it is located. After looking at the church and the Etruscan altar in the cornfield behind it, get back on the route by returning to the entrance of the village and cruising the peaceful country road that wanders south along the Arno for 10km (avoid the turn towards Tulliano) as far as **Subbiano** ⓬, *Sub Janum* to the Romans, a riverside village built on the remains of an ancient castle.

Above
Poppi

Carry on another kilometre and you will find yourself on the main road again with a fleeting left look at the Castelnuovo, a massive 15th-century tower. Crossing back over the Arno, the road shoots past a couple of modest suburbs and then, suddenly, the splendid cathedral of **AREZZO** ⓭ appears on a hilltop. The N71 deposits you at the gates of its historic centre.

Also worth exploring

St Romuald established the monastery at **Camaldoli** in 1024 and set in motion a movement of reform within Benedictine monasticism, which left important traces in Umbria and the Marches. St Romuald lived to be 120 years old (like Moses), having spent 20 years in the world, three years in the monastery and 97 as a hermit.

Upper Tiber Valley

Ratings

Architecture	●●●●○
Art	●●●●○
Food and drink	●●●●○
Shopping	●●●●○
Children	●●●○○
Nature	●●●○○
Scenery	●●●○○
Museums	●●○○○

The Upper Tiber Valley, or Valtiberina, begins in Tuscany at its easternmost edge and continues deep into Umbria, alternating between narrow ridges, hilly farmland and canals used to drain swampland. In ancient times, the River Tiber formed the line between the Umbrians (east) and the Etruscans (west). It remained a borderland through the centuries, divided between Byzantines and Lombards and fought over by the bishops of Arezzo, Roman popes and Florence. Culturally, it is an eccentric place. Wealthy Romans such as Pliny erected villas here, feudal lords built castles and abbots constructed monasteries. There is a strong local craft tradition, based on lacemaking. It is also an important agricultural centre, particularly for tobacco. The spirit of Piero della Francesca, the most enigmatic Renaissance artist, pervades this itinerary. His greatest masterpieces are found in his birthplace Sansepolcro, in Arezzo, and the village of Monterchi.

BADIA DI SAN SALVATORE DI MONTE CORONA

At the foot of the hill of Monte Corona stands this beautiful abbey (*open daily*) with one of the finest crypts in Umbria. It was founded shortly after the year 1000, perhaps by St Romuald (*see page 193*). In the elevated presbytery there is an ancient (8th-century) *ciborium*. On the top of the hill is a hermitage where a reformed Camaldolese community called 'montecoronese' was founded in the 16th century by the Venetian Paolo Giustiniani, the author of the authoritative *Rules of the Hermitic Life*. The abbey is linked to the hermitage (700m) by an idyllic path.

Left
Badia di San Salvatore di Monte Corona

Bibbiena
Chiusi della Verna
Chitignano
stel gnano
Talla
Subbiano
Capolona
Pieve Santo Stefano
Monte dei Frati △ 1454
Sestino
Badia Tedalda
Borgo Pace
Piandimeleto
Urbino
Sant'Angelo in Vado
Urbania
Metauro
Mercatello sul Metauro
Sansepolcro
San Giustino
Apecchio
Piobbico
Anghiari
Citerna
Le Ville
Monterchi
Monte Santa Maria Tiberina
Città di Castello
Pietralunga
Cantiano
Appennino Umbro-Marchigiano
Arezzo
Monte Favalto △ 1082
Nestore
Castiglione Fiorentino
Promano
Montone
Gubbio
Carpina
Cortona
Umbertide
Badia di San Salvatore di Monte Corona
Mercatale
Lisciano Niccone
Riccio
Castel Rigone
Tavernacce
Marciano della Chiana
Folano della Chiana
Tuoro sul Trasimeno
Isola Maggiore
Passignano sul Trasimeno
Le Pulci
Piccione
Valfabbrica
Bosco
di Siena
Lago Trasimeno
Magione
Corciano
Città di Domenica
Perugia
Castiglione del Lago
Isola Polvese
Montepulciano
Lago di Montepulciano
Lago di Chiusi
Casalini
Torgiano
Assisi
Bastia
Chianciano Terme
Chiusi
Paciano
Tavernelle
Cannara
Nestore
Sarteano
Cetona
Città della Pieve
Piegaro
Deruta
Bevagna
Radicofani
M Cetona △ 1148
Monteleone d'Orvieto
Tevere
Gualdo Cattaneo
Fabro
Ficulle
Marsciano
San Venanzo
Fratta Todina
Monte Castello di Vibio
Collazzone
Bastardo
Giano dell'Umbria
Chiani

0 10km
0 5 miles

Città di Castello

ⓘ Informazioni turistiche *Piazza Matteotti; tel: 0758 554922; fax: 0758 552100; e-mail: info@iat.citta-di-castello.pg.it; www.cdcnet.net*

Ⓣ Torre Civico €
Open Tue–Sun 1000–1230 and 1500–1830, shorter hours in winter.

Pinacoteca Comunale
€€ Via della Pendinella 22/a; tel: 0758 520656. Open Tue–Sat 1000–1300 and 1430–1830, Sun 1000–1830.

Palazzo Albizzini (Collezione Burri) €€
*Via Albizzini 1; tel: 0758 559848; www.fondazioneburri.org and the former **Seccatoi del Tabacchi** €€ 1.5km on the old Perugia road. Both open Mar–Nov Tue–Sat 0900–1230 and 1430–1800, Sun 1030–1230 and 1500–1800, shorter hours in winter.*

Centro Tradizioni Popolari *€ Villa Cappelletti; tel: 0758 552119 (2km in the direction of Umbertide). Open Nov–Mar Tue–Sun 0930–1230 and 1430–1730, Apr–Oct 0830–1230 and 1500–1900.*

⌂ There is a clothing and shoe market on **Piazza Gabriotti** every Thursday and Saturday.

In the Middle Ages, the valley was as famous for lace as Flanders. **Bussati Telerie**, *Via del Popolo*, sells traditional textiles, curtains and lace.

In Roman times, Città di Castello was known alliteratively as *Tifernum Tiberinum* and residents still refer to themselves as Tiferni. The Lombards dubbed it *Castrum Felicitatis* (Castle of Happiness). Cesare Borgia seized it for the Church in 1500. It is a working town that doesn't attract too many tourists within its 16th-century walls. Growing and curing tobacco are more important to the local economy than souvenirs.

Architecturally, the influence of early Renaissance Florence is ubiquitous in its *Centro Storico*, from the Palazzo Comunale to the **Duomo Florido e Amanzio** (minus the unfinished baroque façade) on the triangular Piazza Gabriotti. The most remarkable work of art in the Duomo (*open daily*) is a Mannerist painting by the Florentine artist Rosso Fiorentino in which Christ appears as an afterthought while pride of place is given to peddlers and a Moor. From the **Torre Civico**, you can see as far north as Monte La Verna in Tuscany.

In the Via della Pendinella, you will pass the Palazzo Vitelli alla Cannoniera (1521–32) designed by Antonio da Sangallo the younger with a sgraffito façade by Giorgio Vasari and Cristoforo Gherardi. Inside is the **Pinacoteca Comunale**, the second most important art gallery in Umbria (after the one in Perugia). Its highlights include works by Raphael and Luca Signorelli.

The work of modern conceptual artist Alberto Burri can be admired in two places – the Renaissance palace of **Albizzini**, and the **Seccatoi del Tabacchi** (a former drying hall for tobacco) just outside the city walls in the direction of Umbertide. Also outside town, the **Centro Tradizioni Popolari** offers a break from monuments and churches, providing a glimpse into the vastly humbler world of Umbrian farmers and artisans.

MONTERCHI (MUSEO DELLA MADONNA)

Museo della Madonna € *Via della Reglia; tel: 0575 70713; www.comunemonterchi.it. Open Nov–Mar Mon–Fri 0900–1300 and 1400–1700, Sat, Sun & holidays 0900–1700, Apr–Oct Mon–Fri 0900–1300 and 1400–1900, Sat, Sun & holidays 0900–1900.*

The high hill of Monterchi was dedicated to the cult of Hercules in Etrusco-Roman times. Today, visitors come here to pay homage to a woman: a heavily pregnant Madonna painted by Piero della Francesca. She is as rare as she is beautiful – there are very few representations of pregnant women in Western art. The *Madonna del Parto* is located in a climatically controlled chamber behind glass, in a school building next to a cemetery. She appears to be an ordinary middle-class woman of her time getting over a bout of morning sickness. But symmetrical angels flank her, a reminder that it is the Saviour moving in her womb. The banal and divine are serenely juxtaposed here. Pregnant women from the region used to come to pray in her presence until the local authorities decided to turn her into a one-woman museum (moving her from the cemetery chapel), and to charge admission.

MONTE SANTA MARIA TIBERINA

This extraordinary hill-town (population 150), Etruscan in origin, has sweeping views as far as the eye can see of golden fields interrupted by dark-green copses, and the humid Tiber valley.

The town actually became the capital of an independent mini-state in 1355 with a little help from the Holy Roman Emperor, Charles IV. The rulers, the Del Monte family, proudly called themselves 'Bourbons' from then on. They minted their own money and built an official duelling ground next to the church of Sant'Agostino, where citizens were allowed to fight to the death in public. Somehow the family held its own for many centuries while the rest of Umbria was swallowed up through force or strong-armed persuasion by the Papal State. Ironically, it was the arrival of Napoleon's troops in 1798 that brought down these hilltop 'Bourbons'.

The Del Monte castle, a weathered medieval-Renaissance amalgam, is worth a look. The parish church of Santa Maria has a very early Romanesque altar (to the right in the choir) with a St George and the Dragon that look as though they were carved by aliens.

Opposite
Città di Castello's Palazzo Comunale

Alberto Burri (1915–95)

A native of Città di Castello, Alberto Burri began his artistic career as a prisoner of war in Texas, USA, after serving as a military doctor in Tunisia. His first works of art were executed on burlap potato sacks (the only form of canvas he could get as a POW). After the war, he spent his entire artistic career exploring the properties of simple materials in works such as *Sacchi* (Sacks), *Legni* (Wood) and *Ferri* (Iron). He also experimented with fire to 'transform' his works in a series entitled *Combustioni*. Burri was a major influence on American pop artists Robert Rauschenberg and Jasper Johns. By the 1970s, he had entered a phase of extreme minimalism, creating simple geometric forms with *cellotex*.

UMBERTIDE

ℹ Informazioni turistiche *Via Cibo;* tel: 075 9417099; *www.umbertide.it and www.umbria2000.it*

Umbertide was a place where Umbrians and Etruscans met to trade along the Tiber river. The Romans called it *Pitulum*. Destroyed by Totila, it was rebuilt in the Middle Ages and renamed Fratta. Finally, in the 19th century, it acquired its present name, in honour of the king who united Italy.

The square tower of the Rocca (1374–90) is the town landmark. The *condottiere* Braccio Fortebraccio was captured and shut up in the fortress in 1393. His ransom was his own castle in Montone. Twenty years later he returned to sack the town. The city suffered under heavy bombing during World War II when Allied forces were fighting for the Tiber valley. King George VI reviewed the Allied troops here in July 1944.

Piazza Matteotti is a perfect little square framed by *palazzi* and the 13th-century church of San Francesco. The city's artistic pride and joy is the magnificent (and beautifully restored) *Deposition* (1516) by Luca Signorelli in the 17th-century church of Santa Croce.

Cucina in the Valtiberina

Porchetta, oven-roasted pig stuffed with herbs, is especially popular. Other local ingredients that contribute to the good life are the precious white truffle, well-aged *pecorino* cheese and local watermelon.

Accommodation and food

Oscari € *Via Roma 25, Monte Santa Maria Tiberina; tel: 0758 571023.* This place functions as the village-everything: bar, café, *trattoria* and grocery shop. There is a small patio for an alfresco meal of pasta with *funghi* and truffles.

Trattoria Lea € *Via S Florido 38, Citta' di Castello; tel: 0758 521678.* Savoury, traditional regional Umbrian specialities including *cappelletti in brodo* (meat-filled pasta in broth), roast lamb and pasta in mushroom sauce, all served up in a rustic ambience. Don't miss 'fish day' on Tuesdays and Fridays.

Valuberti € *Valuberti 16.17.18.19 Montanina 52043 Castiglion Fiorentino; tel: 0575 650234; e-mail: aldafa@tin.it.* Valuberti (25 minutes from Città di Castello) is a hamlet with just eight buildings. Of the seven inhabiting families, Alda Fantina and companion Claudio rent out rustic stone cottages. For the gourmand, they supply vegetables (in season), olive oil, wine, eggs, cheese, rabbit, *prosciutto* – you name it.

La Locanda del Capitano €€ *Via Roma 7, Montone; tel: 075 9306521; fax: 075 9306455; www.ilcapitano.com.* A castle conversion in the home town of Fortebraccio.

Relais San Pietro €€ *Polvano 3, Castiglion Fiorentino; tel: 0575 650100; fax: 0575 650255; www.polvano.com.* A small family-owned inn situated in an 18th-century hamlet overlooking the Chio valley. Amenities include swimming pool and restaurant specialising in traditional regional recipes.

Tiferno €€ *Piazza R Sanzio 13, Città di Castello; tel: 0758 550331; fax: 0758 521196; www.hoteltiferno.it*. Well-appointed rooms in a 17th-century *palazzo*.

Il Postale di Mario e Barbara €€€ *Via de Raffaele Cesare 8, Città di Castello; tel: 0758 521356; www.ristoranteilpostale.it*. Savour truffle-enhanced dishes here. Prices are very reasonable for the quality.

Suggested tour

Total distance: 116km; detour add 20km.

Time: One to two days.

Links: The Upper Tiber Valley meets the Arno Valley and Casentino region at Arezzo (*see pages 184–6*). It is traversed in its entire length by the N3bis and the *Superstrada* E45, which connects Rome with northern Italy.

Route: From **Arezzo ❶**, drive southeast (from the Piazza San Giusto) along Via Mino da Poppi, which soon enters Via Trento e Trieste and Via Anconetana. Keep right at the first T-intersection and stay on the main road as it passes through a village called La Pace (ignoring the right to Loce de Stoppe). You now wind through olive groves and umbrella pines up to the village of San Firenze. Idyllic scenery – you would hardly believe you just left the city. A reminder is at the top of the road where prostitutes in miniskirts and hot pants loiter by the roadside in the middle of the fragrant pine forest. Turn left here to get on the N73 and follow the signs for Sansepolcro. The curvy road moves in sync with a tributary of the Tiber, the Cerfone. The scenery is lovely, but the new E78 now cuts through the valley, drawing away much of the traffic but missing the beauty found on the slower route. After 17km, take the right fork in the direction of Città di Castello. **MONTERCHI ❷** is signposted after just a couple of kilometres.

Leave Monterchi on the road going south to **MONTE SANTA MARIA TIBERINA ❸**. This is a country road, the worse for wear but idyllic and solitary. Keep to the left (ignoring roads to Ripoli and Fonaco). After visiting the town, retrace the route 100m. The road to Città di Castello is just below the town. Follow the bends of a plunging road that drops into the Tiber valley and forces the occasional sharp turn between the oaks and shrub. It finally lands you in the rich vegetation of the river valley floor brushing past tobacco and sunflowers. The road crosses the Tiber and hugs the old city walls. There is a dusty, free car park along the Tiber outside the walls of **CITTÀ DI CASTELLO ❹**.

Continue down the east side of the Tiber, on the country road rather than the *autostrada*.

Detour: Just after the village of Promano, the road leads under the *autostrada*. At the next fork, turn left (east) and drive up to **Montone ❺**. The fortified village once belonged to one of Italy's most famous

Above
Rolling hills

medieval *condottieri*, Andrea Braccio, nicknamed 'Fortebraccio' (strong arm). From the remains of his fortress you can see yet another old castle, the Rocca d'Aria – Rock of Air. The former convent of San Francesco has a serene cloister and a terrace with amazing views of the Tiber valley. Inside is the **Museo Comunale e Museo Etnografico** (€ *Via San Francesco 4, Montone; tel: 075 9306535; www.sistemamuseo.it. Open Apr–Sep Fri–Sun 1030–1300, 1530–1800; Oct–Mar Sat–Sun 1030–1300, 1500–1730*) with original frescos and paintings by Bartolomeo Caporali.

Leaving the town, follow the signs for Corlo. **UMBERTIDE** ❻ spreads out in the flat part of the Tiber valley below. Upon leaving, return the way you came, curving past a round church and the castle and crossing the Tiber over the same rusty iron bridge. Take the first left under a trestle, signposted **BADIA DI SAN SALVATORE DI MONTE CORONA** ❼. You will all but collide with its polygonal tower that stands on the roadside, at the end of a lane of cypresses. A mysterious, five-naved crypt leads into the chapel which has undergone extensive restoration.

Getting out of the car: From the Badia di Monte Corona, there is a path, flanked by old beeches and chestnut trees, leading up to the Eremo di Monte Corona. The path is now officially a nature trail. The Eremo is an ancient hermitage built by the Camaldolensians during the 16th century.

Leave the abbey, following the Tiber further south along a shelf-like road that squeezes between fields of tobacco and corn on one side and oaks on the other. Eventually, it hits a T-junction at Pieve San Quirico. Turn left to cross over to the east side of the Tiber and carry on south, skirting the villages of **Le Pulci** and **Bosco**. From there, drive into **Perugia** ❽, following the bull's-eye symbol for the *Centro Storico*.

Also worth exploring

ⓘ **Museo Civico** € *Via Aggiunti 65, Sansepolcro; tel: 0575 732218; www.musei.provincia.ar.it. Open Jun–Sep 0930–1330 and 1430–1900, Oct–May 0930–1300 and 1430–1800.*

Situated 39km northeast of Arezzo, at the foot of the last tract of the Tuscan Apennines, is the birthplace of Piero della Francesca. **Borgo Sansepolcro** dominates the Upper Tiber Valley as it opens out in a vast amphitheatre of hills. The heart of the town forms a quadrangle of medieval walls, four towers and a Medici fortress. The cathedral and the Loggia delle Laudi are certainly of interest and, on the second Sunday in September, a *Palio della Balestra* (crossbow tournament) takes place. But the main reason to come is a painting in the **Museo Civico** – *Resurrezione* (1459), regarded in Piero's lifetime as his greatest work. In modern times, it rendered Kenneth Clark speechless though he later wrote an entire book about it, observing apologetically that the painting expresses 'values for which no rational statement is adequate'. Aldous Huxley went one better and called it 'the greatest painting in the world'.

Poppi

Bibbiena

Chiusi della
Verna

3bis

Castel
ocognano

Chitignano

Talla

Subbiano

Capolona

71

19

Pieve Santo
Stefano

258

Badia
Tedalda

Monte dei Frati
1454

Sestino

Piandimeleto

Urbin

E78

Borgo
Pace

Sant'Angelo
in Vado

Mercatello
sul Metauro

70

Urbania

Urbania

Piobbico

73bis

Sansepolcro

Apecchio

San Giustino

A p p e n n i n o   U m b r o - M a r c h i g i a n

Anghiari

12

73

14

Le Ville

Citerna

E78

Monterchi

2

14

221

Pietralunga

Cantiar

14

Arezzo

1

7

73

13

12

Monte
Favalto
1082

Monte Santa
Maria Tiberina

3

Città di
Castello

4

26

Promano

Museo Comunale
Museo Etnografico

Montone

5

25

219

452

298

Gubbio

19

Castiglione Fiorentino

71

3bis

27

219

Marciano
della Chiana

17

327

10

Umbertide

6

416

38

7

Badia di San Salvatore
di Monte Corona

E45

32

Tavernacce

298

A1

Lucignano

Foiano
della Chiana

Cortona

S

Riccio

9

Mercatale

Lisciano
Niccone

19

44

Piccione

Le Pulci

alunga

5

E35

24

Tuoro sul Trasimeno

29

Castel Rigone

75bis

Valfabbrica

318

rita di Siena

326

S

Isola Maggiore

Lago
Trasimeno

6

Passignano
sul Trasimeno

Magione

Corciano

Città di
Domenica

2

Bosco

Castiglione
del Lago

Isola
Polvese

20

599

20

Perugia

8

10

3

Assisi

Bastia

Montepulciano

21

17

Casalini

38

220

Torgiano

28

75

Chianciano
Terme

16

326

146

Chiusi

71

11

Paciano

Tavernelle

Cannara

Sarteano

Cetona

15

Città
della Pieve

Piegaro

220

E45

Deruta

34

Bevagna

478

M Cetona
1148

A1

Monteleone
d'Orvieto

Gualdo
Cattaneo

Radicofani

41

71

3bis

Marsciano

Collazzone

Bastardo

0   10km
0   5 miles

Fabro

S

Ficull

San
Venanzo

Fratta
Todina

Monte Castello

Giano
dell'Umbria

Perugia

Ratings

Architecture	●●●●●
Art	●●●●●
Entertainment	●●●●○
Museums	●●●●○
Shopping	●●●●○
Children	●●●○○
Food and drink	●●●○○
Nature	●●○○○

Time travel is easy in Perugia. All it takes is an escalator ride from the underground car park, which sweeps you past the foundations of an entire medieval district. The city sits on a mountaintop that has been inhabited for at least 3,000 years and still bears traces of an Etruscan Golden Age (3rd–1st centuries BC). There is much to see here: Umbria's most important art gallery with masterpieces by Fra Angelico, Piero della Francesca and Perugino; a palace, square and fountain that rival any in Italy; and a monumental Etruscan arch. And if that is not enough, the cathedral claims to have the Virgin's wedding ring. In the Middle Ages, Perugia had a reputation for blood feuds and the practice of self-flagellation. Today, it is better known for *baci* – 'kisses' (chocolates with nougat cream), its university and one of Europe's best jazz festivals.

Sights

APT office *Via Mazzini 21; tel: 075 57591; fax: 075 5736828; www.umbria-turismo.it & www.perugiaonline.com*

Informazioni turistiche *Piazza IV Novembre 3 (Palazzo dei Priori); tel: 075 5736458; fax: 075 5739386.*

P Cars are virtually excluded from the city centre and parking spaces around the periphery are full by 0900.

Arco Etrusco

Perugia's best surviving city gate is indeed Etruscan in its lower reaches. The massive blocks of stone forming the two towers belonged to 3rd-century BC Etruscan defences. This was the main gate of seven that pierced a vast wall encircling the city for nearly 3km. The upper level of the gate, with its Ionic columns, arches and frieze of shields, was added to by the Romans. Crowning the whole structure is a 16th-century loggia, its delicacy forming a lyrical contrast with the Cyclopean foundation beneath.

0   200m

0   150 yards

⇧
North

Parco
S Angelo

Porta
Bulagaio

Strada Comunale del Bulagaio

Porta
S Antonio

ZONA UNIVERSITARIA

Viale Orazio Antinori

Porta
Conca

Via Alessandro Pascoli

Via Fabretti

Via dell'Acquedotto

Piazza
Braccio
Fortebraccio

Viale S Antonio

Arco
Etrusco

Via Pinturicchio

Muro Urbico Etrusco

Via Cesare Battisti

Via U Rocchi

S Francesco
al Prato

Oratorio di
San Bernardino

Via dell'Aquilone

Acquedotto
Duecentesco

Via Bartolo

Capella di
San Severo

Via Brunacci Brunamonti

Torre
degli Sciri

Piazza
Morlacchi

Duomo
S Lorenzo

Piazza
Michelotti

Piazza
Piccinino

Pozzo Etrusco

Viale Orazio Antinori

Via dei Priori

Piazza
Ferri

Piazza
della Stella

Piazza
Danti

Fontana
Maggiore

Via G Alessi

Giardini
della
Canapina

Porta
S Susanna

Via dei Priori

Piazza
IV Novembre

Palazzo dei Priori

Mercato
Coperto

Via XIV Settembre

Viale Pompeo Pellini

Via della Cupa

Corso Vannucci

Galleria
Nazionale
dell'Umbria

Porta
S Margherita

Piaggia Colombata

Scala
Mobile

Collegio
del Cambio

Piazza
Matteotti

Palazzo Capitano
del Popolo

Giardini
del Campaccio

Via Arturo Cecchi

Via della Cupa

Piazza
della
Repubblica

Via San Prospero

Via Bonazzi

Corso Vannucci

Via Baglioni

Via XIV Settembre

Viale Pompeo Pellini

Porta
S Giacomo

Rocca
Paolina

Corso Cavour

Via Tancredi Ripa di Meana

Via Indipendenza

Giardini
Carducci

Porta
Eburnea

Piazza
del
Circo

Palazzo Penna

Basilica di
S Domenico

Via del Bucaccio

Via del Parione

Via Masi

Viale Roma

Railway
station

Museo
Archeologico

Corso Cavour

Scala Mobile
Rocca Paolina

Via Masi

Via Fiorenzo di Lorenzo

Largo
Cacciatori
delle Alpi

Porta
S Pietro

Porta
S Girolamo

Via XX Settembre

Giardini
di
S Giuliana

Piazza
Partigiani

Via Cacciatori delle Alpi

Via Fratelli Pellas

Piazzale
Europa

Via XX Settembre

Stadio di
Atletica
Leggera

Viale Roma

Borgo XX Giugno

Via Fratelli Pellas

SAN PIETRO

**Collegio del
Cambio** € *Corso
Vannucci 25; tel: 075
5728599. Open Mar–Oct
daily 0900–1230 and
1430–1730, Nov–Feb
Tue–Sun 0900–1400.*

Duomo di San Lorenzo
*€ Piazza Danti; tel: 075 572
3832. Open daily.*

Collegio del Cambio

The rooms of the medieval Exchange Guild are one of Perugia's unmissable sights. In 1496 the members of the Guild commissioned the local artist Pietro Vannucci – known to posterity as Perugino – to paint the walls. The result is one of the masterpieces of the Italian Renaissance.

In the spirit of Renaissance humanism, the frescos unite pagan and Christian imagery. On the left wall are the allegorical figures of *Prudence* and *Justice* above the historical figures whose life and works were filled with such qualities – *Socrates* and the *Emperor Trajan*; then *Strength* and *Temperance* exemplified by *Pericles* and *Leonidas*, amongst others. Between the two, Perugino painted his own unflattering self-portrait. The great artist is … a fat man with a double chin. One of his lyrical landscapes, suffused with the dawn sunlight, forms the background to the Nativity scene on the end wall. Perugino was a master of three-dimensional perspective, and the Nativity demonstrates that particular gift. We glimpse the landscape of wooded hills and winding streams through a series of arches, under which shepherds kneel. The arches are supported on classical columns – another reference to a fusion of classical and Christian values.

Duomo di San Lorenzo

The main façade (unfinished) of the cathedral is in the Piazza Danti. The stone pulpit outside was built for San Bernardino, a medieval preacher who attracted crowds too large for the cathedral. The baroque portal was added in 1729. From the 15th to the 18th centuries many important artists contributed their works of art to San Lorenzo; among them Agostino di Duccio, Perugino, Luca Signorelli and Federico Barocci (his magnificent Deposition of 1569 is to the right of the entrance). The Cappella del Sant'Anello contains what is said to be the Virgin's wedding ring.

Fontana Maggiore

The great medieval sculptors Nicola Pisano and son Giovanni seem to have had a head start on the Renaissance with this fountain, such is its realism and balance. The themes are an eclectic mixture of Christian and pagan, secular and religious, fabulous and mythical subjects – an encyclopaedic hodgepodge that made perfect sense to the medieval mind. The labours of the months, signs of the zodiac, the Garden of Eden, Samson and Delilah and Aesop's Fables are all here, and a Vestal Virgin for good measure. Twenty-four statues personify Perugia, nearby Lake Trasimeno (the woman with the fish), saints, monks, evangelists, prophets and a long since forgotten governor of Perugia, sceptre in hand. The three bronze water-carriers are the Three Graces or the Three Theological Virtues, depending on whom you ask.

The fountain was a hydraulic as well as artistic achievement: it was completed in 1277 with the help of Friar Bevignate, a hydraulic genius who pumped water into Perugia from Monte Pacciano nearly 3km away.

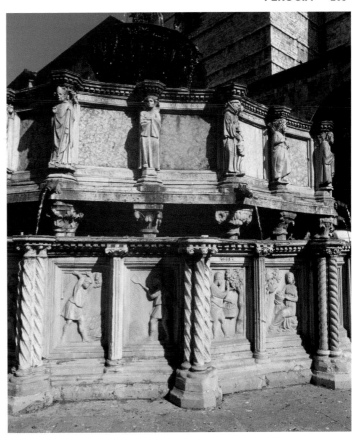

Right
The Fontana Maggiore

Galleria Nazionale dell'Umbria €€

Palazzo dei Priori, Corso Vannucci 19; tel: 075 5741410; www. gallerianazionaleumbria.it. Open daily 0930–1930. Closed 1st Mon of each month.

Galleria Nazionale dell'Umbria

This is the richest artistic collection in Umbria, filling 33 rooms with state-of-the-art lighting and multimedia exhibits in English and Italian. Unsurprisingly, Umbrians are well represented. The former palace chapel is still decorated with magnificent frescos by Benedetto Bonfigli (1450), some of which are damaged. There are a dozen works by Umbria's greatest painter, Perugino, including his early masterpiece the *Adoration of the Magi* (1475–7), his *Madonna della Consolazione* (1496–8) and a mature work, *Christ Entombed*, a stark and expressive painting of the dead Christ. Major works by Perugino's followers, Lo Spagna and L'Alunno, are given pride of place as well as Fiorenzo di Lorenzo's lovely *Adoration of the Shepherds* (1490). However, there is only one huge painting by Pinturicchio, the *Pala di Santa Maria dei Fossi*; otherwise, his best work is to be seen in Spello and Siena (*see pages 240 and 76–87*). There are many masterpieces from beyond Umbria's borders, including two of the gallery's most sublime works of art: Fra Angelico's luminous *Madonna and Child with Angels and Saints* and a legendary polyptych by Piero della Francesca painted at about the same time as the cycle of frescos in Arezzo (*see page 185*).

Palazzo dei Priori

Perugians call their palace, which has been polished by 600 years of sunshine and rain, the most beautiful public building in Italy. Since the Middle Ages, the palace has been the heart of political life in town. It was built intermittently between the 13th and 15th centuries but a sense of unity somehow prevails, provided in part by the two tiers of 14th-century windows that traverse the walls of pink and white stone. The windows of the lower tier have Gothic lancets contained within rectangles, while those above are surmounted by triangular frames. The battlement on top was a 19th-century addition.

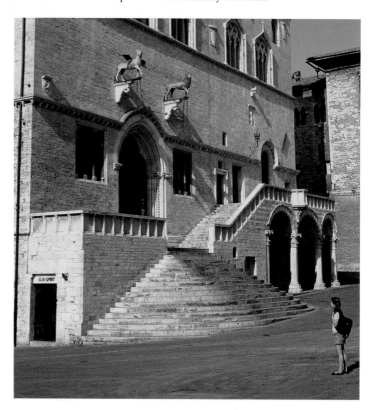

Right
The Palazzo dei Priori

Pozzo Etrusco €
Piazza Piccinino 1; tel: 075 5725778. Open daily Apr–Sep 1000–1330 and 1430–1830.

Pozzo Etrusco

The Etruscan Well is located beneath the Palazzo Ranieri di Sorbello. One of the most important and well-preserved Etruscan hydraulic works, it dates back to the second half of the 3rd century BC. The well, 35m deep, has a diameter of 5.6m at the top and decreases to 3m at the bottom. A small passageway leads down the shaft to a gangway suspended above the water. The top of the well is in the middle of Piazza Piccinino (to the right when you exit).

Accommodation and food

Entertainment and festivals

Perugia is full of students, Italian and foreign, who come to study at its ancient University, the Academy of Fine Arts or the University for Foreigners. Nightlife in Perugia is never dull, especially during Rockin' Umbria (first half of June), Umbria Jazz Festival (first half of July) and *Sagra Musicale Umbra* (second half of September).

Perugia is by far the liveliest city in Umbria and well worth a stopover. However, because of the traffic and modern suburbs, it makes no sense to use Perugia as a base for touring the surrounding region.

Cesarino € *Piazza IV Novembre 5; tel: 075 5736277. Closed Wed.* Excellent *trattoria-pizzeria* set in a 13th-century palace with a view of the Fontana Maggiore. It serves delicious pizza and home-made *tagliatelle*. Main courses might be *agnello a scottadito* (lamb chops) or roast *piccione* (pigeon). It is often very crowded.

Hotel Fortuna €€ *Via Luigi Bonazzi 19; tel: 075 5722845; fax: 075 5735040.* Central, with a garage.

Hotel La Rosetta €€ *Piazza Italia 19; tel and fax: 075 5720841; www.perugiaonline.com/larosetta. Facing Piazza Matteotti.* The *camera da letto matrimoniale* (No 55) has vaulted, *trompe-l'oeil* ceilings and Venetian glass chandeliers. There is parking, too.

Locanda degli Artisti €€ *Via Campo Battaglia 10; tel: 075 5735851; www.perugiaonline.com/locandadegliartisti. Closed Tue.* Located in the historic town centre, the restaurant's ancient walls display work from well-known and aspiring artists. Regional Umbrian and national cuisine rules the kitchen with a lot of creative variations like ravioli with nettles, pork chops with radicchio and capelletti with walnuts.

Castello dell'Oscano €€€ *Strada della Forcella 37, Cenerente, 5km north of Perugia; tel: 075 584371; fax: 075 690244; e-mail: info@oscano.com; www.oscano.com.* A castle fit for a king, cardinal, aristocrat or anyone with a bit of plastic. All the history and luxury still costs less than the top hotels in Perugia. Suite 402 has the best view.

Locanda della Posta €€€ *Corso Vannucci 97; tel: 075 5728925; fax: 075 5732562.* Ornate façade outside, period interiors and mod cons inside; and parking.

Shopping

Casa del Parmigiano *Via Sant'Ercolano 36; tel: 075 5731233.* Owner Mario Corradi sells cheese and salami from all over Umbria. Ask for *pecorino di botte* – sheep's cheese packed in a bottle in such a way that it continues to age; or the rare *il roccaccio*, a cheese made near Todi, that is aged for 10 to 18 months.

Ceccarani di Santino Panettaria *Piazza Matteotti 16; tel: 075 5721960.* The best baker in Perugia – 30 kinds of bread, festive and seasonal sweets, and pastries such as *torciglioni* and *torte al formaggio e biscotti*.

Majolica

The town of Deruta, 17km south of Perugia off the N3, is given over almost entirely to majolica. Its long main street is lined with workshops and showrooms. You can choose between reproductions (*reproduzione* or *tradizione*) and contemporary designs (*artistiche* or *moderne*). Many shops will offer a discount of 20 per cent for payment in cash.

If you want to see the complete range of ceramics under one roof, visit the **Museo Regionale della Ceramica** in the former Convento di San Francesco € *tel and fax: 075 9711000; www.sistemamuseo.it.* Open *Jul–Sep daily 1000–1300, 1530–1900; Apr–Jun daily 1030–1300, 1500–1800; Oct–Mar Wed–Mon 1030–1300, 1430–1700.* The earliest records of pottery production here date to 1387 and the earliest surviving pieces, from the end of the 15th century, show the influence of Faenza in their colours and designs. The Derutans came to specialise in monumental plates and vases with heavy relief moulding. Grotesque ornament, fruit and foliage scrolls are typical and the predominant colours are rich yellow and midnight blue.

Guiditta Brozzetti *Via T Berardi 7; tel: 075 40236; www.brozzetti.com. Open 0900–1300 and 1400–1800; weekends by appointment only.* Fabrics are woven on 18th- and 19th-century looms in a converted Franciscan convent.

Pasticceria Sandri *Corso Pietro Vannucci 32; tel: 075 5724112.* Pastry heaven behind a turn-of-the-20th-century façade.

La Salumeria dei Fratelli Temperini *Corso Cavour 30; tel: 075 5721606.* Umbrian salami comes in many forms here, some unpronounceable, and all delicious: *coppa, mazzafegati, salsicce* and, of course, *prosciutto*.

Suggested tour

Total distance: 2km.

Time: Two days should be the minimum for Perugia.

Links: The tour of the Upper Tiber Valley ends here (*see page 199*), and Perugia is the starting point for the Umbrian Apennines (*see page 225*). Lake Trasimeno (*see page 212*) and Assisi (*see page 228*) are just a few kilometres away.

Route: From the car park at Piazza Partigiani, the escalators that lead up to Perugia pass through an eerie underground city, the remains of 25 towers and 3 churches that were used as a foundation for the Rocca Paolina, a papal fortress that stood here for 300 years. It was torn down in the 19th century after Perugia regained its independence. At the top are the 19th-century Piazza Italia and the **Giardini Carducci** ❶, a terrace with a sheer drop of 300m and a view that takes in Assisi and the Umbria valley.

The **Corso Vannucci** ❷ is the main street of Perugia (named after the famous painter, better known to the world as Perugino) and perhaps the best place in all of Umbria for people-watching. The *passeggiata* here is endlessly fascinating. There are hundreds of young men and women strolling, gossiping, flirting, pairing off – Botticelli or Raphael could easily have recruited nymphs and pageboys here – as well as couples with children, schoolchildren and grandparents. After just 200m, the Corso ends in the Piazza IV Novembre, an extraordinary medieval ensemble, framed by the **PALAZZO DEI PRIORI** ❸ and the **DUOMO DI SAN LORENZO** ❹, with the **FONTANA MAGGIORE** ❺ in the middle (*note: the tourist office in the Palazzo dei Priori has excellent city maps*).

After walking in a circle around the fountain, turn into Via Maestà delle Volte and pass under the strange medley of arches into Piazza Cavalotti, bear right into Via Baldeschi then duck under the first arch to the left – this is Via Appia, really just a set of stairs. The steps deposit you on the **Via dell'Acquedotto** ❻. A 13th-century aqueduct that brought water to the Fontana Maggiore, it is now a street and

Museo Archeologico Nazionale dell'Umbria
€ *Former Convento di San Domenico; Piazza Giordano Bruno 10; tel: 075 5727141; fax: 075 5728200; www. archeopg.arti.beniculturali.it. Open Mon 1430–1930, Tue–Sun 0830–1930. Houses a rich collection of Etruscan finds.*

surely one of the most original in Umbria. This improbable byway practically leads through the living rooms of several Perugian residents and affords a bird's-eye view of lush, secret gardens. At the bottom, make a sharp right into Via Fabretti and continue to the end of the street and round the corner. Stepping into Piazza Braccio Fortebraccio, you will come face to face with the monumental **ARCO ETRUSCO ❼**. To its right is **Palazzo Capitano del Popolo ❽**, a 15th-century Renaissance palace.

Detour: The street that leads under the arch – Via Ulisses Rocchi – has a vaulted wine bar, **Bocca Mia**, at No 32 and the city's best wine shop, **Enoteca Provinciale**, at No 16.

Facing the arch, walk left up a series of steps (the Via Bartolo) past the city wall (the lower stones are also Etruscan). Keep hugging the stone parapet and you will soon find yourself marching up a zigzag of steps, the Via delle Prome. Catch your breath at the narrow square at the top, the Piazza delle Prome, while studying the city rooftops and the surrounding hills. There are usually young Italian couples here, snogging passionately and oblivious to tourists.

Walk to the end of the square and turn right at the university building into Piazza Michelotti, technically the highest part of town, where you have a choice of two lefts. Take the second one into the murky Via dell'Aquila. After a few metres, a couple of curves and some steps, an arch appears to the right. Duck underneath it, climbing up to the Piazza Raffaello. The small church to the left, the **Capella di San Severo ❾**, contains the city's only painting by Raphael (1505), which depicts the Holy Trinity and a brace of saints. The saints were actually painted by Perugino in 1521 when he was 70 and no doubt he thought of his former pupil Raphael – already dead at 37 – whose fame had so greatly surpassed his own. You can spy on it through the crevice in the wooden door or pay a small fee to enter and see it.

Cross the square and veer under the arch to your left, walking up another set of stairs through a no-name piazza and descending through a narrow passage between the Chiesa della Compagnia della Morte and a wall. In the middle of the Piazza Piccinino is the well-head of the **POZZO ETRUSCO ❿**. A staircase follows the shaft of the well some distance underground. The entrance is at the end of the square on the left. Continue on to Piazza Danti (in front of the cathedral) and walk up the steps into the Duomo. On exiting, walk into the now familiar Piazza IV Novembre.

Walk back through the throng of people on the Corso Vannucci and duck under the archway – the Priori Arch – below the bell tower that interrupts the Palazzo dei Priori, and let gravity do the rest. The steep Via dei Priori is one of the most remarkable streets in Umbria. The name of the first cross street, the Via della Gabbia (cage), recalls the days when prisoners were hung out for the public to abuse in an open-air cage. To the left is Sant'Agata church. Downhill a bit further is the Piazza Ferri, and just before it on your right is the baroque San Filippo Neri (1626–34). At the end of Via Priori is the green and the salmon-pink façade of the church of San Francesco al Prato, which has been threatening to collapse for 500 years and nearly did during the 1997 earthquake (*not presently open to the public*); right next to it is the **Oratorio di San Bernardino** ⓫ with a striking façade of dancing girls, cherubs and musicians playing viols, sackbuts and trumpets in an orgy of celebration. It's an odd way to honour the pulpit-thumping St Bernard, one of the greatest orators of the Middle Ages, who specialised in sermons on vanity, usury and greed. Ironically, he has been declared the patron saint of advertising. It is hard to imagine him plugging *haute couture*. The dresses of 14th-century rich women were, in his words, ' … the fruit of robbery and usury, of peasants' sweat and widows' blood, of the very marrow of unprotected orphans. If you were to take one of these gowns and press it and wring it out, you would see, gushing out of it, a human being's blood'.

Retrace your steps along Via dei Priori to Corso Vannucci. Follow Corso Vannucci right until you reach Galleria Kennedy. A short walk left along here will bring you to **Piazza Matteotti** ⓬. Just to the left is the entrance to a market, the **Mercato Coperto** ⓭, with stunning views from its terrace.

Also worth exploring

The most interesting church in Perugia is one of the least visited. Built in the second half of the 10th century over an Etruscan-Roman graveyard, **San Pietro** received a Mannerist face-lift in the 16th century that only partly covered its primitive medieval design. There are no less than three cloisters. A 17th-century porch leads to the first one (1614) which hides the old façade: here a 16th-century portal gives access to the church. Worth noting are the ceiling by Benedetto da Montepulciano (1553) and the superb choir (1525–35) carved and engraved by Stefano Zambelli di Bergamo. Outside the church, a corridor leads to a second cloister (also early 16th century) and yet another corridor leads to the 'Cloister of the Stars' designed by Perugian architect Galeazzo Alessi in 1571. Across the street, the 18th-century Giardini del Frontone (Frontone Gardens) have a fine view of the plain of Assisi.

Right
Perugia's Via Ritorta

Lake Trasimeno

Ratings

Scenery	●●●●●
Art	●●●●○
Children	●●●●○
Food and drink	●●●●○
Nature	●●●●○
Architecture	●●●○○
Museums	●●○○○
Shopping	●●○○○

Lago Trasimeno is the largest lake on the peninsula of Italy. A vast sheet of blue-green water with 45km of shoreline, it is shut in by gentle hills on three sides covered in oak and olive trees. The lake and its shore have been all things to men: Etruscan gardens and graveyards; the stage for Hannibal's greatest victory over Rome; the region's most important source of protein (fish) in the Middle Ages; an underwater Duchy for Napoleon (he meant to have it drained); and, today, a rare natural reserve attracting migratory birds. For the painter Perugino, the lake was a prelude to infinite space, a golden, tranquil landscape that shimmers behind his saints and virgins.

CASTIGLIONE DEL LAGO

ℹ Informazioni turistiche *Piazza Mazzini 10; tel: 075 9652484; fax: 075 9652763; e-mail: info@iat.castiglione-del-lago.pg.it; www.lagotrasimeno.net*

🏛 Palazzo della Corgna € *Tel: 075 9658210; www. castiglionedellago.it. Open mid-Mar–Apr 0930–1300 and 1530–1900, May–Jun 1000–1330 and 1600–1930, Jul–Aug 1000–1330 and 1630–2000, Sep–Oct 1000–1330 and 1530–1900; Nov–mid-Mar 0930–1630.*

The Etruscans living in Chiusi used the territory of Castiglione for farming. The headland was a formidable defence of the Byzantine Duchy of Perugia in the 7th century against the neighbouring territories of Lombardic Tuscany. Castiglione was then fought over by Arezzo, Cortona and Perugia; the latter emerged the victor. In 1247 Frederick II of Swabia conquered and destroyed the town and rebuilt it in the form it is today, with the help of Elias, a monk with a knack for fortification from Cortona. His symmetrical plan – three roads, three squares and three city gates – is still in place. The monk's masterpiece was the nearly impregnable Rocca del Leone (1247) – a pentagon with four towers; it remains one of the finest examples of medieval military architecture in Umbria and still dominates the lake from the tip of its promontory.

By the 16th century, the town was in Perugian hands again. It became a part of the Papal State in 1648. The **Palazzo della Corgna** may not look like much but behind the unfinished façade are lifelike frescos begun by Niccolò Circignani (known as Il Pomarancio) in 1574. The best are in the Room of the Exploits of Asciano della Corgna with scenes from the battle of Lepanto. A 300m corridor through the city wall joins the *palazzo* to the castle.

CITTÀ DELLA PIEVE

ⓘ **APT office** *Piazza Matteotti 4; tel: 075 298031; www.cittadellapieve.org*

The dramatic hill-town above Lake Trasimeno was Perugino's birthplace and possesses several interesting works by him. In pre-Christian times, it was called Monte di Apollo, and successively Castelforte di Chiuscio and Salpio or Castrum Salapinum. With the coming of Christianity and the parish worship of San Gervasio, it assumed the name *Castrum Plebis*, which has been perfected in today's Città della Pieve. One of the striking things about the town is that it is made almost entirely of deep red brick. Città was a major producer of

Right
Fishing nets, Lake Trasimeno

Oratorio di Santa Maria dei Bianchi €
Via Pietro Vannucci; tel: 075 9652484; www.perugino.it.
Open daily 0930–1300 and 1600–1930. If the door is locked during these hours, ask for the custodian at No 42 or enquire at the tourist office.

brick in the Middle Ages. Chief among Perugino's works here is the *Adoration of the Magi* in the **Oratorio di Santa Maria dei Bianchi**. If you have nothing better to do, seek out the evocatively named Via della Baciadonna (of the woman's kiss) and decide for yourself if it is, as the townspeople claim, the narrowest street in Italy.

ISOLA MAGGIORE

For sailing times of ferries to the island €, *tel: 075 506781* or view the website *www.apmperugia.it*

Second in size of the three Trasimeno islands, Isola Maggiore is said to have been visited by St Francis one stormy night in 1211. The hamlet on the shore has not changed that much since it was a 15th-century fishing village. Even native son and medieval Umbrian poet Matteo dell'Isola might recognise it. On the south side of the island is an 18th-century villa (residence of the Marquesses Guglielmi), built on the former site of the Franciscan convent founded in 1328.

A trail from the village leads up through olive groves to San Michelle Arangelo (309m), the highest point on the island with sweeping views in all directions. From there, you descend to the opposite (east) side of the island to the Cappella di San Francesco and a second chapel, where St Francis is said to have disembarked. The trail continues around the island and passes the Romanesque church of San Salvatore. Isola Maggiore has a centuries-old tradition of lacemaking and exquisite pieces are still produced by hand using a simple crochet hook.

ISOLA POLVESE

Isola Polvese € The island is open to visitors from Easter to end Sep, and year round to groups (*tel: 075 9659547; fax: 075 9659546; www. polvese.provincia.perugia.it*).

Ten minutes by boat from the village of San Feliciano, Polvese is a heavily forested and uninhabited island. There is a ruined Franciscan monastery to explore, with thousands of olive trees planted by its former residents, as well as alleys of oleander and a good beach for swimming.

Oasi La Valle San Savino

Oasi La Valle San Savino € Tel: 075 8476007; e-mail: oasilavalle@libero.it. Open Jun–Sep daily 0900–1300 and 1600–2000, Oct–May Tue–Sun 0900–1300 and 1500–1800.

Lake Trasimeno is on an important route used by birds migrating to the tropics. This part of the lake is strictly protected and far and away the best for birdwatching. Red herons arrive from Africa to breed here in spring. Cormorants come in winter. There are watchtowers to view them from and, on weekends, visitors are allowed to circle noiselessly in electric boats.

Panicale

Pro Loco Piazza Umberto 1; tel: 075 8378017.

San Sebastiano € Tel: 075 837183. Frescos on view May–Sep 1030–1230 and 1600–1900, Oct 1000–1230 and 1500–1800, Nov–Apr 0930–1230 and 1500–1700.

Below
Lake Trasimeno fisherman

This town has a helical plan – fairly typical in medieval Umbria. The name has multiple meanings: 'holy hill', 'everything is beautiful', 'Pan got angry' and 'millet is cultivated here'. Although its origins are probably Etruscan, Panicale came into its own as a Roman fortress. In the Middle Ages, it was witness to countless sieges and wars, particularly between Perugia and Chiusi. Its officially impregnable castle was surrendered in 1643 to Mathias, leader of the Florentine army.

The walled town has two legendary frescos – the *Coronation of the Virgin* and the *Martyrdom of St Sebastian*, both by Perugino, in the church of **San Sebastiano**.

Passignano sul Trasimeno

Pro Loco Via Roma 25; tel: 075 827635.

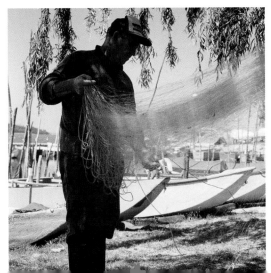

Historically, Passignano, built on the shores of the lake with houses rising above one another, was the easiest way to get from point 'A' (Umbria) to points 'B' (Florence and Siena), without going across or around the lake. Thanks to this strategic position, it was constantly attacked throughout its history. That explains the two medieval towers with ogival gates. The town was once home to Società Aeronautica Italiana, a company that manufactured seaplanes in the 1920s and 1930s. As a result, it was heavily bombed during World War II. They still train pilots here. However, the lakeshore is given over to cafés, bars and souvenir shops. Passignano has regular ferry services to the other lakeside towns and the Isola Polvese and Isola Maggiore.

Accommodation and food

⊙ **Azienda Agricola F.lli Palombaro** *Via della Strage 8, Monte del Lago; tel: 075 8400122. Open 0700–0900 and 1600–1800.* You can buy excellent local olive oil here (some of it is classified *denominazione d'origine Umbria*), for example, Il Castel di Zocco.

The tourist office in Castiglione del Lago has printed the wild boast that, from Lake Trasimeno '20% of the world's artistic heritage' is 'at hand'. Rome is only a couple of hours' drive on the A1 *autostrada* and much of Tuscany and Umbria is within easy driving range.

Da Sauro € *Via Guglielmi 1, on Isola Maggiore in Lake Trasimeno; tel: 075 826168.* The only place to stay overnight on the lake islands, run by a fisherman and his family. Their restaurant serves outstanding starters such as *linguine alla tinca* or *risotto al pesce di lago*.

Locanda del Galluzzo € *Trecine, 2km west of Castel Rigone; tel: 075 845352; fax: 075 845312; www.locandadelgalluzzo.it.* Welcoming *agriturismo* that accepts overnight guests.

Rosso di Sera € *Via Fratelli Papini 81, Magione; tel: 075 8476277. Dinner only. Closed Tue and half Nov.* Earthy lakeside *trattoria* with an emphasis on regional cuisine as well as fish – stuffed pigeon and veal tongue, for example.

L'Acquario €€ *Via Vittorio Emanuele II 69, Castiglione del Lago; tel: 075 9652432; www.castiglionedellago.it/acquario. Closed Fri; in winter Tue and mid-Jan–mid-Feb.* Elegant hole-in-the-wall restaurant on the main street with a terrific *menu degustazione*. The house speciality is *filetti di anguilla* – skewers of lightly smoked eel. They also serve other typical Trasimeno fish dishes such as *carpa regiona in porchetta* (stuffed carp). Home-made desserts.

Relais La Fattoria €€ *Via Rigone 6, Castel Rigone; tel: 075 845322; fax: 075 845197.* A medieval building in an idyllic hilltop location with a kidney-shaped swimming pool and managed with a friendly, personal touch.

The landscape of Perugino

During Perugino's lifetime (1450–1523), central Italy experienced over 30 years of bloodshed, beginning with the invasion of Charles VIII in 1494. Every available army in Europe made its way to Italy to get its share of plunder. The countryside was burnt and devastated; there was hunger, disease and despair. There is, however, no famine, rape or murder in the artistic universe of Perugino. 'He had a feeling for beauty in women, charm in young men and dignity in the old, seldom surpassed before or since', observed art critic Bernard Berenson. His beautiful people inhabit a fantastic topography almost as enigmatic as the scenery in the *Mona Lisa*. The background of many paintings is the same: a rarefied ring of low hills hovers around a misty lake that is and isn't Lake Trasimeno. While driving around Lake Trasimeno, you can contemplate its mystic counterpart in Perugino frescos and paintings in Città della Pieve and Panicale. He died of the plague while at work in the hamlet of Fontignano, in view of the lake.

Suggested tour

Total distance: 160km; detour adds 4km.

Time: One long day.

Links: This route begins 31km from Perugia (*see page 202*); it is just an 11km downhill drive from Città di Castello to Chiusi, which is on the Crete and Val d'Órcia tour (*see page 105*).

Route: The best way to begin a tour of Lake Trasimeno is with a boat ride. Boats leave from **PASSIGNANO SUL TRASIMENO ❶** several times a day. On your way, look left (southeast) at the abstract sculpture of a jet plane. After a visit to **ISOLA MAGGIORE ❷**, retrieve the car and follow the lakeside road towards Tuoro. An international team of artists created the Campo del Sole (Field of the Sun) at Punta Navaccia on the Lido di Tuoro (another point of embarkation for island ferries). The works form a large spiral (comet-shaped) marked by 27 sculpted columns leading to a central table surmounted by a symbol of the sun.

Turn north to drive to **Tuoro ❸**. A natural amphitheatre of low hills surrounds it with farmland in between. Not much at first glance but this was the scene of one of the greatest battles in European history. Sixteen thousand Romans lost their lives, massacred by Hannibal's Carthaginian army in 217 BC. The names of villages in the neighbourhood record the battle's aftermath: Sanguineto (bloody) and Ossaia (bones).

Detour: In the hilly part of Tuoro (it was on the lakeshore during the Middle Ages), the Centro di Documentazione sulla Battaglia del Trasimeno has an exhibition that looks at the various theories about what happened. You can then follow a history trail, the Percorso Storico-Archeologico della Battaglia, on the actual site of the battle. There is also a pit where Hannibal burned the Roman bodies. It takes imagination to visualise the battle, something the Roman historian Livy had no shortage of: 'So great was the fury of the struggle', according to him, 'so totally absorbed was every man in its grim immediacy, that no one even noticed the earthquake which ruined large parts of many Italian towns, altered the course of rivers, brought the sea flooding into estuaries and started avalanches in the mountains'.

Follow the signs for Castiglione del Lago. Be sure to take the left fork into Borghetto or you will be sucked on to the *autostrada* and deported to Tuscany. A blind turn through the village leads past the cemetery and alongside the lakeshore. The fortified peninsula of **CASTIGLIONE DEL LAGO ❹** rises up in the distance looking very much like an island in the lake. There is usually free parking outside the walls. From

Above
Lake Trasimeno carp

there, it is more or less a straight shot to Moiano, following the N71. On the way, the landscape in the rear-view window widens to include all of Lake Trasimeno, framed by the gentle hills of Paciano and Chiusi. The glowing redbrick city of **CITTÀ DELLA PIEVE ❺** has paid parking just outside the walls.

Upon leaving, drive back to the north entrance to town and steer west around the city along a smart belvedere that ends beneath a row of parasol pines. The road now cruises through a dreamy piece of 'mystic Umbria'. The visibility is breathtaking and the smooth curves down to Tavernelle will make even a cheap hire car feel like a Porsche. The hills are covered with pines, spruce, oak and orderly rows of cypresses.

You must leave this road and veer steeply left to reach **PANICALE ❻**, constructed of the same red brick as Città della Pieve. Here are spectacular views of Lake Trasimeno that take in most of the places described in this chapter: the shoreline that seems to come and go like an optical illusion, the peninsula of Castiglione del Lago to the left, Polvese island on the right, and the Maggiore and Minore islands in the lake's centre. The scene is encircled by an undulating crown of hills that gently roll away into the flats of Valdichiana. On the way down, the lake approaches slowly, as the road wheels around olive groves and sloping fields of wheat. Carry on through the village of Casalini and keep right (in the direction of Perugia).

Turn right again on the lakeside road and follow the shore, then go uphill away from the lake as it rounds a swampy point. Watch for signs to the left leading to **San Feliciano ❼**. You will pass the Castello San Savino before actually reaching this small fishing village. Its **Museo della Pesca** (Museum of Fishing, € *Lungolago Alicata 1; tel: 075 8479261. Open Jul–Aug daily 1000–1300, 1600–1900; Apr–May and Jun–Sep Tue–Sun 1000–1230, 1500–1800, shorter winter hours*) has much to tell about the daily lives of lake fisher folk through the centuries. Twenty types of lake fish swim in aquariums and wooden models show traditional boats and palisades used to catch them. This is also the point where you can catch a ferry to the **ISOLA POLVESE ❽**, the largest island on the lake and the best one for walking and birdwatching.

The road now follows the shore closely, along the **OASI LA VALLE SAN SAVINO** ❾ and past the ruined Castello di Zocco before narrowing in on **Magione** ❿, a town of Etruscan origin at a strategic point between Perugia and Chiusi. To assist medieval pilgrims, the Jerusalem Knights Hospitallers founded a hospice here. From Magione, either return to Passignano sul Trasimeno or take the *autostrada* to Perugia.

Also worth exploring

Castel Rigone is one of Umbria's most charming villages in an area of almost empty hills northeast of Lake Trasimeno. You can see half of Tuscany from it – Montepulciano, Monte Cetona and the extinct volcano of Monte Amiata – before you even begin to look at Umbria. On a clear day, even Monte Vettore (2,476m) and the Apennines reveal themselves. Its church, the Santuario della Madonna dei Miracoli, is a Renaissance masterpiece. The solitary road that leads from here to Umbertide offers pastoral, off-the-beaten-track bliss.

Gubbio and the Umbrian Apennines

Ratings

Mountains	●●●●●
Outdoor activities	●●●●●
Architecture	●●●●○
Nature	●●●●○
Scenery	●●●●○
Walking	●●●●○
Shopping	●●●○○
Museums	●●○○○

G ubbio claims to have been one of the first five towns founded after the biblical Flood. That would at least explain why it is built so high up a mountain. To the southeast, the stretch of Apennines beneath Monte Cucco (1,566m) is sometimes called the 'womb of the Apennines' because of its vast system of caves. The springs from these mountains provide much of the water that makes Umbria 'the green heart of Italy'; some of the best mountain hiking in the region is to be had here. The Parco Regionale del Subasio could be called the park of St Francis. In it lies the mountain where he felt moved to compose his great spiritual poem, *The Canticle of Creatures*.

GUALDO TADINO

🛈 **Pro Loco** *Via Calai 39; tel: 075 912172; www.protadino.it & www.gualdo.tadino.it*

🐗 Gualdo Tadino is famous for a type of ceramic with red and gold glazing; there are workshops along the Via Flaminia. The small town is the centre for a lot of *caccia* (hunting) with many shops selling guns and accessories that no self-respecting Italian huntsman would be seen without.

Time has been cruel to the people living here: invaders pushed them to build their houses ever higher up a steep hill and earthquakes brought them tumbling down, the most recent being the 1997 quake that hit Umbria. The Roman *Tadinum*, a city on the plain and a staging post along the *Via Flaminia*, survived the depredations of Hannibal and an attack by Caesar during the Roman civil war but Totila the Goth annihilated it when his forces swept down through Italy towards Rome. The Byzantine commander Narses avenged the town in AD 442 by killing Totila beneath its ruined walls. The new city – Gualdo Tadino, meaning 'wooded Tadino', from the Lombardic *wald* (wood) – was built in relative safety higher up the side of Monte Penna.

The modest main square, the Piazza dei Martiri della Libertà, recalls the partisans who fought the Nazis during World War II. The Duomo, closing the eastern side of the square, has a delicate rose window and

Museo Civico €€
Via della Rocca;
tel: 075 916078;
www.sistemamuseo.it. Open
Jun–Sep Mon–Sun
1030–1300 and 1530–1900,
Apr–May Thu–Sun
1030–1300 and 1500–1800,
Oct–Mar Sat–Sun
1030–1300 and 1430–1700.

Romanesque portal (1256). There is also the former church of San Francesco, now an art space, devoted to temporary exhibitions. It has frescos by native son Matteo da Gualdo as well as a Roman sarcophagus. It is a stiff but rewarding climb from the car park outside the city walls up to the Rocca Flea, the 13th-century fortress built under the rule of the Holy Roman Emperor Frederick II. It houses the **Museo Civico** with works by Alunno and Matteo da Gualdo.

GUBBIO

Informazioni
turistiche *Via della*
Repubblica 15; tel: 075
9220693; fax: 075
9273409; e-mail:
info@iat.gubbio.pg.it;
www.comune.gubbio.pg.it.
Open Mon–Fri 0830–1345
and 1530–1830, Sat
0900–1300 and 1530–1830,
Sun 0930–1230.

Pinacoteca e
Museo
Archeologico
Comunale € *Palazzo dei*
Console, Piazza della
Signoria; tel: 075 9274298.
Open Tue–Sun 0830–1930,
Mon 1430–1930.

Palazzo Ducale € *Via*
Federico da Montefeltro; tel:
075 9275872. Open
Tue–Sun 0900–1930.

Local Gubbio craftspeople make black burnished *bucchera* vases, modelled on graceful Etruscan prototypes.

In many respects, Gubbio is the perfect medieval hill-town. The population in the Middle Ages was actually twice what it is today. The tall austere buildings seem as ancient as time. Many have been rebuilt so many times that they are now a patchwork of centuries. The Roman part of the town is mostly in the plain, with remnants of a rectilinear street pattern, walls, town gates and the well-preserved 1st-century Roman theatre (off the Viale dei Teatro Romano); it is still used for summer theatrical performances.

When Gubbio was partly destroyed by Totila the Goth, the Gubbians shifted higher up the side of Monte Ingino. They constructed two narrow terraces shored up by cliff-like walls over 20m high. The scale of this achievement can best be appreciated from the Giardini Pensili, a small garden in front of the Palazzo Ducale, which offers dizzying views down over the cascading rooftops of the medieval town.

The town's focal point, the Piazza dei Consoli, has a similar view and the **Palazzo dei Consoli**, one of the most magnificent town halls in Umbria with tripartite windows, battlements and a finger-like campanile. High on the buttress to the right of the façade is an iron cage in which the civil authorities used to dangle criminals, exposing them to the sun and the ridicule of all Gubbio. Inside, the barrel-vaulted 14th-century hall seems untouched since it functioned as council chamber. The **Pinacoteca e Museo Archeologico Comunale** occupies the upper floors and is worth seeing for its medieval interiors alone and the extraordinary loggia that overlooks the rooftops of Gubbio. The star exhibits are the seven massive bronze Eugubine Tablets (*see box on page 225*). Otherwise, the art collection is modest (the best work, Fiorentino's *Madonna of the Pomegranate*, was stolen in 1979).

The Duomo is just a few streets uphill from the Piazza dei Consoli. The interior has fine and rare stained-glass windows and an unusual vaulted ceiling. The 13th-century Palazzo dei Canonici, an integral part of the cathedral itself, houses the Museo Diocesano which displays, among other works, the *Madonna in Majesty* by Mello da Gubbio, one of the most important Gubbian painters from the 14th century. However, architecturally speaking, the 15th-century **Palazzo Ducale**, just

Funicular € *Porta Romana, Via San Girolamo; tel: 075 9273881. Open daily Jun and Sep 1000–1315 and 1430–1700, Jul–Aug 0830–1930, Oct–May Thu–Tue 1000–1315 and 1430–1700. Also at the Porta Romana is a medieval tower open daily 0900–1300 and 1530–1930.*

opposite, is more interesting for its period Renaissance interiors. It was built for the Duke of Urbino, probably by the same architect who designed the Duke's palace in Urbino. From here, it is a steep 2km walk to the Basilica Sant'Ubaldo (827), the church dedicated to the city's patron saint – 300m higher than the city (note: there is an old **funicular** from the Porta Romana). The most interesting thing in the church is the *ceri*, or candles, that are carried in the annual, uphill race from the cathedral to commemorate the saint's feast day (his 'incorrupt' body is sealed inside a glass coffin on display). The view from the top is superb – you see the peaks of the Apennines, the Scheggia and, of course, the profile of medieval Gubbio.

Back in the town centre, the 13th-century Palazzo del Bargello in the Via dei Consoli is also worth seeking out. It was a 13th-century prison. The Fontana dei Matti (Fountain of the Mad) stands in front of the Bargello and is so-named because it was once believed that you would go mad if you waded round the basin three times. Today, on holidays, young men wade around the fountain to qualify as 'honorary madmen of Gubbio'. South of the Bargello, the River Camignano flows down the side of the street of the same name, and emerges in the wide, oval-shaped Piazza Quaranta Martiri (Square of the Forty Martyrs). On 22 June 1944, retreating Nazis shot 40 Gubbian women and children here in retaliation for an attack by the Italian resistance on local German troops.

PARCO REGIONALE DEL MONTE CUCCO

ℹ Centro Nazionale di Speleologia *Corso Mazzini 9, Costacciaro; tel: 075 917271; fax: 075 9170647; www.parks.it. This centre organises excursions into the region's cave system. It also sells detailed maps for walking and hires out hang-gliding equipment.*

The stretch of Apennines on which the Monte Cucco (1,566m) rises up has a vast system of caves and its mineral springs fill up the region's aqueducts with water before flowing into the Sentino river. It is heavily wooded and abundant in fossils. Hiking, cross-country skiing, hang-gliding and spelunking are popular (the Parco Regionale has some 30-odd trails). There are even wolves here, though you are not likely to see one; you might see deer, wild boar and porcupine as well as hawks, golden eagles, eagle owls and kingfishers.

On the more northern part of the territory there are several Benedictine and Camaldolensian abbeys, of which the most important are Sant'Emiliano at Isola Fossara and the hermitage of San Girolamo at Pascelupo.

PARCO REGIONALE DEL SUBASIO

The park of Subasio takes its name from the most famous mountain in Umbria. Monte Subasio (1,290m) rises at the southern end of the chain, looking out over a landscape of valleys and hills that includes ℹ Maps and guides to the park are available from the Tourist Information Centre in Assisi (*see page 228*), *or contact the Ente Parco tel: 075 815181; www.parks.it. Open daily 0900–1300.*

the Umbria valley. The mountain provided the pink stone for the churches of the town of Assisi. Indeed, the historic centre of Assisi is included in the park.

Right
Gubbio rooftops of Siena-brown tiles

Accommodation and food

Campeggio Valsorda € *In Valsorda, 8km northeast of Gualdo Tadino; tel: 075 913261. Open May–Sep.* Camping in the Apennines and a point of departure for walkers.

Dei Consoli € *Via dei Consoli 59, Gubbio; tel: 075 9220639; fax: 075 9273335.* The best budget option in the best possible location but no parking. Ask for a room off the street.

Hotel Bosone Palace €€ *Via XX Settembre 22, Gubbio; tel: 075 9220688; fax: 075 9220552. Closed Jan–Feb.* Near the cathedral with great views. It even has parking.

Taverna del Lupo €€€ *Via Ansidei 21, Gubbio; tel: 075 9274368; www.mencarelligroup.com.* Creative variations on Umbrian tradition.

Shopping

Medio Evo (Acacia Giuseppe) *Zona Industriale Ponte D'Assi, Gubbio; tel: 075 9272596; fax: 075 9228455; www.medioevo.com.* 'Middle Ages' is a company specialising in the reproduction of ancient weapons. This is the place to get value for money if your idea of a souvenir is a crossbow, pike or double hatchet. Mallets come with 1–3 spiked balls and there are iron chastity belts for both sexes. The delivery of a suit of armour or full-size guillotine takes two months. Owner Giuseppe Acacia insists that an ancient weapons fetish doesn't reflect a love of war and violence but simply an appreciation of the region's history (he is certainly right about the history bit).

Suggested tour

Total distance: 140km; add 6km for the detour to Abbazia di Santa Maria di Sitria, 18km for Monte Cucco and 16km for Conca di Valsorda (all return).

Time: Gubbio is the highlight on this itinerary for the culture vulture (not counting Perugia or Assisi) and it can be explored in half a day. For nature lovers, with or without a spiritual bent, or spelunkers, this stretch of Apennines is almost too good to be true and could absorb many days.

Links: This route departs from Perugia (*see page 202*) and ends in Assisi (*page 228*); it is readily combined with the route through the Upper Tiber Valley (*page 199*).

Route: Leaving **Perugia** ❶ on the N298, take the road to Gubbio, one of the most beautiful in Umbria. After passing through a zone of creeping industrialisation and a town called Piccione, it begins a long climb, bringing into view the steeples of Perugia, the rounded summit of Monte Subasio and, on a clear day, Lake Trasimeno. The road follows a ridge for some distance. On the right, the Castello di Petróia appears and, a little further uphill, the Abbazia di Vallingegno. The first sight of **GUBBIO** ❷, stranded so high up on the side of Monte Ingino, is memorable. To get there you have to drive across the wide plain below and past some light industry. There is a large, free car park between the Roman theatre and the *Centro Storico*. Upon leaving Gubbio, take the N298 northeast through the gorge of the Camignano river that seems to slice through Monte Ingino. Turn south on the N3 at **Scheggia** ❸, which still has a tower from the time when it was *Shisa*, a Roman city.

Detour: The N360, at Scheggia, climbs up the Sentino valley to Isola Fossara. From this village, a winding byroad leads through beautiful wooded countryside until, after about 3km, you reach the semi-ruinous **Abbazia di Santa Maria di Sitria**, with its restored 11th-century church sitting on the top of a 6th-century crypt. St Romuald built the small monastery in 1014. He stayed in one of the cells, maintaining a seven-year vow of silence (1014–21), in which he nevertheless converted many men to Christianity.

Continue on for another 10km and you will reach an even more remote abbey just across the Umbrian border – **Eremo di Fonte Avellana**. This hermitage, surrounded by oak woods and mountain pasture, was founded in AD 980. Off the graceful Romanesque cloister, you can visit the original monastic cells. Dante stayed in one in 1310 while in exile from his native Florence. Perhaps it was here that he had his vision of Hell, wrote out the list of the damned (including many of his enemies), assigned them to seven levels and refined their

---

Who were the first Umbrians?

Although the Umbri gave their name to the Umbria, we know next to nothing about them. This mysterious people lived a thousand years before Christ. They did not leave much behind except for the foundations of some massive walls and seven bronze tablets, which were discovered in Gubbio. These Eugubine Tablets were found in 1444 in a field close to Gubbio's Roman amphitheatre and the text, written in a mixture of Etruscan and Latin characters, describes religious rites, forms of prayer and liturgical regulations practised by the Atiedii, a local college of priests. There is a list of enemies and precise instruction on how to sacrifice them ritually if captured, as well as the rule 'exterminatio' requiring all foreigners to be sent out of town before the purification rites began, and then describing the places and methods for animal sacrifices.

Via Flaminia

The *Via Flaminia* is named after the ill-fated Gaius Flaminius who lost a brilliant political career and an entire army, to say nothing of his life, in the Battle of Lake Trasimeno (*see page 217*). The road crossed Umbria from Narni, passing through the towns of Terni, Spoleto, Foligno, Spello and Gualdo Tadino, and on up the Chiascio valley through the *coloniae* (towns built by retired Roman army veterans) such as Sigillo, Scirca, and Costacciaro and finally to Scheggia. From there, it linked Rome to the town of *Arminium* (now Ravenna) on the Adriatic Sea. As the Roman empire grew, the road carried goods from all over the Mediterranean. In later centuries, the road traffic included invading armies of Goths and Lombards heading for Rome.

eternal tortures in *terza rima*. The hermitage was an important medieval centre of learning: the Dante Alighieri library, named in honour of the poet's visit, occupies the former scriptorium where manuscripts were laboriously copied by hand. It is one of the very few examples in Europe to have survived in perfect condition.

Continue through a fertile plain with the flat-topped mountains rising in a row on the left. Just a couple of hundred metres before **Sigillo ❹**, there are impressive remains of a Roman bridge to the right. Beyond it, fields and meadows spread out to the west in the direction of Chiascio. You are now in the middle of the **PARCO REGIONALE DEL MONTE CUCCO ❺**.

Detour: The mountains can be explored by taking the left turn in Sigillo. After 9km this scenic road comes out near the summit of Umbria's highest peak, **Monte Cucco ❻** (1,566m). The mountain meadows here make a popular picnic spot for local people in the summer. A short walk back down the same track, at Ranco di Sigillo, gains the entrance to a vast cave system that penetrates deep into the mountain reaching to a depth of almost 1km. During the summer one of the more accessible caves, the **Grotta del Monte Cucco**, is open to the public (*for a more extensive tour, enquire at the Centre for Speleology: see page 223*). Ranco is also the starting point for numerous hikes.

GUALDO TADINO ❼ seems to hang from the edge of Serra Santa mountain. It suffered major damage in the earthquake and the town is still struggling. Huge metal braces buttress many buildings and no one knows when they will come down.

Detour: The road up to Conca di Valsorda (1,000m) leads to a vast mountain meadow between the peaks of Monte Maggio and Serra Santa. Depending on the time of year, it is bright with the sky-blue of chicory, the yellow of broom, the pink of perennial sweet peas and campion and the white of ox-eye daisies. An easy-to-follow track leads to the summit of the Serra Santa (1,421m) with a tiny pilgrim church and sweeping views of the Apennines.

From Gualdo, follows the signs west for the N444. The road leads directly into the **PARCO REGIONALE DEL SUBASIO ❽** and a 34km roller-coaster ride through scenery so dear to the heart of St Francis. The road slips into **Assisi ❾** through the Porta Perlici.

Also worth exploring

The N219, which follows the Assino river from Gubbio to Umbertide in the Tiber valley (*see page 198*), could easily be nicknamed 'castle row'. There is the Castello di Carbonara, near Mocaiana, followed by the ruins of Castello di Monte Cavallo looming above the abbey of Camporeggiano. Further down the road are the Castello di Serra Partucci and the Castello di Poggio at the junction of N219 and N3bis.

Piobbico

Apecchio

Pergola

Cagli

Appennino

33

Pietralunga

Cantiano

Eremo di
Fonte Avellana

Monte
Catria
△
1701

Città di
Castello

Abbazia di Santa
Maria di Sitria

Sassoferrato

14

Scheggia e
Pascelupo

Isola Fossara

20

452

Umbro-Marchigiano

360

Mocaiana

298

25

219

13

PARCO
REGIONALE
DEL
MONTE CUCCO

Montone

3

Monte
Cucco
1566
△

Gubbio

Costacciaro

5

Ranco

6

Camporeggiano

16

3bis

Serra Partucci

Sigillo

4

Fabriano

219

14

76

22

Umbertide

Fossato di Vico

8

Monte
Maggio
△
1351

Abbazia di
Vallingegno

8

10

Conca di
Valsorda

32

Gualdo
Tadino

7

△
1421
Serra
Santa

Castel Rigone

19

24

E45

298

Petroia

3

Piccione

35

14

361

38

Bosco

Valfabbrica

444

ione

318

Città di
Domenica

2

Corciano

10

Perugia

1

5

20

Nocera
Umbra

220

3

Bastia

Assisi

9

8

Monte
Subasio
1290 △

38

Torgiano

75

28

PARCO
REGIONALE
DEL SUBASIO

19

Valtopina

43

Cannara

Spello

E45

77

Deruta

Foligno

34

Marsciano

3bis

Bevagna

0   10km

Gualdo
Cattaneo

0   5 miles

Collazzone

Montefalco

Sellano

Trevi

27

Assisi

Ratings

Architecture	●●●●●
Art	●●●●●
Scenery	●●●●○
Food and drink	●●●○○
Children	●●○○○
Museums	●●○○○
Nature	●●○○○
Shopping	●○○○○

Assisi, the birthplace of St Francis, is one of the world's most important pilgrimage destinations – as sacred in the minds and hearts of Christians as St Peter's in Rome. The two-storeyed Basilica where St Francis is buried attracts tourists in almost equal numbers (in other words, millions), eager to gaze on frescos by Giotto, Cimabue, Simone Martini and Pietro Lorenzetti. The entire city is of pinkish travertine hewn from Monte Subasio, the mountain it rests on, and its 'stones speak infinitely of virtue and sanctity', according to Pope John Paul II. They also change colour at sunset, glowing several shades redder. The town's position on a spur above the valleys of the Topino and Chiascio rivers attracted Umbrian and Etruscan inhabitants and the Romans left an impressive temple of Minerva. However, the Assisi that survives is almost entirely medieval.

Sights

ⓘ Informazioni turistiche *Piazza del Comune 12; tel: 075 812534; fax: 075 813727; e-mail: info@iat.assisi.pg.it; www.assisi.umbria2000.it, www.assisi.com & www.assisiaccessibile.it. Open Easter–Oct Mon–Sat 0800–1400 and 1500–1800, Sun 1000–1300 and 1400–1700, Nov–Easter mornings only.*

Basilica di San Francesco

The saint who led a life of absolute simplicity and poverty is buried in one of the most monumental churches in Christendom. The two-storeyed edifice, combining earthy Romanesque features with limitless engineering ambition, rests on a series of arcaded buttresses that looks like an aqueduct. The German poet Goethe called it a 'dreary pile' and compared it to the tower of Babel – two centuries before the installation of multilingual tourist tapes. The first stone was laid the day after Francis's canonisation only two years after his death in 1226. The saint was buried in secret in 1230 by Brother Elias, one of his original disciples, to prevent someone (namely, the Perugians) from stealing the body. His remains were discovered in 1818 and re-interred in the crypt. It is best to begin here and make your way up, symbolically, from darkness to light.

The ceilings and walls of the lower basilica are covered in some of the most important medieval frescos in Europe (bring a powerful hand

Basilica di San Francesco € *Piazza San Francesco; tel: 075 819001; e-mail: assisisanfrancesco@libero.it; www.sanfrancescoassisi.org. Open daily Easter–Nov lower church 0600–1915, upper church 0830–1845; Nov–Easter lower church 0600–1845, upper church 0830–1845. Closed depending on the services, usually Sun morning and holidays.*

torch or a pocket full of change to feed the coin-operated spotlights). The *Scenes from the Life of St Martin* in the Cappella di San Martino, the last of the frescos to be executed in the lower basilica, are arguably the best. The artist, Simone Martini, worked on the chapel from 1322 to 1326 and was responsible for all the decorations, including the stained-glass windows depicting 18 saints and the marble decoration of the floor.

The earthquake of September 1997 caused considerable damage to some of the frescos in the upper basilica. However, it has been painstakingly restored. Modern technology played an important role: restorers recorded 120,000 fragments of a Cimabue fresco in a database and reassembled it with the help of a virtual model.

The luminous upper basilica is still the artistic highlight of a visit to Assisi. The plan of the basilica is simple and has remained untouched since completion in 1253: just a nave, choir, transepts and apse. The apse and transepts, which you enter first, are covered in frescos by Cimabue and his assistants. Look hard at Cimabue's *Crucifixion*,

San Damiano € *Tel: 075 812273; www.assisiofm.it. Open 1000–1200 and 1400–1800 (1630 in winter).*

Palazzo dei Priori *Piazza del Comune; reception office open Mon–Sat 0800–1400. See local events calendar for exhibitions.*

Below
The cloister of San Damiano

considered to be his finest work. However, the glory of the basilica is the fresco cycle illustrating the *Life of St Francis* on the lower walls of the nave, a work that transformed the emphasis of Western art. Giotto 'was always going to nature itself for new ideas' according to Vasari. He found inspiration in the life of St Francis.

Palazzo dei Priori

Still a Town Hall after all these centuries, this palace is not one but four linked buildings, pierced by tunnels, one of which is painted with colourful grotesque ornament. This haphazard group is not exactly beautiful but the 14th-century façades are decorated with massive wrought-iron lamps. After the 1997 earthquake it was completely restored and continues to function as a municipal seat, with space for public exhibitions and concerts.

San Damiano

A humble building of rough, unadorned stone, San Damiano could be mistaken for a farmhouse were it not for the simple arcade in front of the church and the cloisters, added in the 16th century. Inside the church, on the right, 14th-century frescos recall the decisive incident in the life of St Francis when Christ spoke to him from the Cross saying 'Go, Francis, and repair my house.' Another scene shows St Francis offering money for the restoration of San Damiano and then being pursued by his angry father. The church contains a remarkable crucifix. It is said that the artist Innocenzo carved the body and left the work unfinished overnight. When he returned the next day, he found the head miraculously completed. Moreover, the head of Christ has three different expressions – anguish, death and tranquillity – depending on whether you view if from the left, right or centre.

San Rufino € *Tel:*
075 816016; www.
assisimuseodiocesano.com.
Open in summer daily
0700–1300 and 1500–1900,
in winter 1430–1800.

San Rufino

San Rufino has perhaps the most outstanding Romanesque façade in Umbria, a sculptural masterpiece, partnered by the massive and stately Romanesque campanile. This site was chosen for the cathedral because, before the canonisation of St Francis, the town's principal saint was the early Christian martyr, San Rufino (d AD 238).

The façade is divided into three parts, both vertically and horizontally, with a rare symmetry to the whole. The middle tier, horizontally, is separated from the lower one by a running arcade carved with eccentric humans, animals and birds. Above, three caryatids – comical figures straining under the supposed weight of the structure – support the central rose window. Symbols of the Evangelists are carved at the corners of an imaginary square frame enclosing the whole window. Christ is seated between the sun and the moon below the lunette of the central portal.

Below
Romanesque Madonna
and Child on the façade
of San Rufino

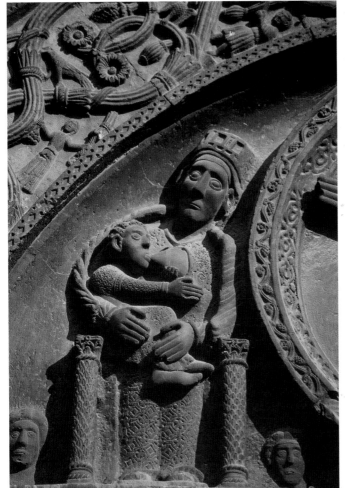

The crypt is entered through the door on the right side of the piazza (signposted *Accesso al sotteraneo*) and San Rufino's 3rd-century sarcophagus tomb lies there. However, his bones are now beneath the cathedral's main altar not far from the ironbound marble font used to baptise three future saints – Francis, Clare and Agnes – and the future Holy Roman Emperor, Frederick II (born in 1194). The Museo Capitolare, entered from the right of the apse, contains a fine triptych by Nicolò Alunno, one of the best of the early Umbrian painters, depicting the martyrdom of San Rufino.

On leaving the cathedral look for the small door in the right-hand aisle near the exit; this leads down to the 1st-century BC Roman water storage cistern that now forms the foundation for the campanile.

Santa Chiara *Piazza Santa Chiara; tel: 075 812282. Open daily 0630–1200 and 1400–1900 (1800 in winter).*

Foro Romano e Collezione Archeologica € *Via Portica 2; tel: 075 813053. Open Jun–Aug 1000–1300 and 1430–1900, Mar–May and Sep–Oct 1000–1300 and 1430–1800, shorter hours in winter.*

Santa Chiara

Huge flying buttresses anchor this church to the ground making it look like some great pink and white insect – the buttresses were added in the late 14th century to prevent the whole structure from collapsing. In plan, the basilica is a copy of the upper church of the Basilica di San Francesco. Begun in 1257, it was built alongside the little 12th-century church of San Giorgio – the place in which St Clare first set eyes on St Francis at the age of 18. The speed with which the basilica was built might explain its penchant for falling over. As for its plainness, the church was once covered in colourful frescos, but these were whitewashed over by a disapproving mother superior because they were attracting too many admiring visitors who were distracting the nuns from their prayers. The decorative bands of alternating rose and white limestone and the delicate rose window form the principal elements of the west front next to the campanile – all essentially Romanesque in style.

Inside, the great aisle-less, groin-vaulted nave is Gothic. The best of the surviving frescos are found in the transepts. On the end of the wall on the left (north) transept there is a touching Nativity scene painted in the 14th century and a 13th-century Virgin and Child, a pure and powerful work in Byzantine style. The remains of St Clare herself are displayed in the crypt beneath a rather ugly neoclassical high altar. Clare's body was rediscovered in 1850 and, as you would expect of a saint's body, it was perfectly preserved inside the coffin. She did not long survive exposure to the open air and deteriorated rapidly until human hands intervened to produce the saintly sleeping figure that lies in the crypt today.

Santa Maria sopra Minerva (Temple of Minerva)

The former temple still possesses six elegant fluted Corinthian columns that form the classical porch (*pronaos*). The garden-variety baroque interior was added in 1634 when the church was dedicated to San Filippo Neri.

The lower steps of the Temple are underground in the **Foro Romano**. This is located in the crypt (all that survives) of the 11th-century church San Nicolo – now full of Roman coffins and Etruscan funerary urns. A passage from the crypt leads beneath the Piazza del Comune to the subterranean remains of what was once regarded as the city's *Foro Romano* (Roman forum). However, some scholars now believe they belonged to the sanctuary of the Minerva Temple and that the forum was located beneath San Rufino. In any case, walking down the chilly lane of the former Roman town of *Assisium* under the medieval piazza of Assisi is an eerie experience. The massive blocks of travertine are worn by chariot wheels and equipped with gutters that collected rain almost 2,000 years ago.

Accommodation and food

The tourist office keeps a list of 20 monasteries in the region that accept guests. Many convents in Assisi board guests; they are a homely alternative to budget hotels, albeit one with a curfew.

Castel San Gregorio € *Via San Gregorio 16, Frazione San Gregorio di Assisi – 10km north of Assisi off the N318; tel: 075 8038009; fax: 075 8038904. Closed three weeks Jan.* Atmospheric castle complex that goes back 700 years. There are only 12 rooms, with views of the plain below Assisi or the beautiful Italian-style garden.

La Piazzetta dell'Erba € *Via San Gabriele dell'Addolorata 15b; tel: 075 815352. Closed Mon and two weeks Jan.* A dedicated young couple runs this small *trattoria* (their parents work the kitchen). Choices are few but all good. Choose one course or many, starting with Umbrian soup or a sandwich made with a traditional bread called *torta al testo*.

Buca di San Francesco €€ *Via Brizi 1; tel: 075 812204. Closed Mon.* Perhaps the best in Assisi for regional cuisine and wines, though it is a little self-conscious about it and usually full of well-heeled tourists. Choose between the medieval cellars and the well-planted garden.

Umbra €€ *Via degli Archi 6; tel: 075 812240; fax: 075 813653; www.hotelumbra.it. Closed mid-Jan–mid-Mar.* A well-equipped hotel and family-run restaurant just off the main square. Room 34 has a view of the Umbria valley.

Hotel Subasio €€€ *Via Frate Elia 2; tel: 075 812206; fax: 075 816691; www.hotelsubasio.com.* Right next to the Basilica, with wonderful views from many rooms. A hotel with a lot of tradition – Marlene Dietrich lounged on a bed here – that still sets itself high standards.

Above
The Eremo delle Carceri, St Francis's hermitage in the hills above Assisi

Suggested tour

Total distance: 2km.

Time: There is a great deal to see in Assisi and it is convenient for visiting other towns in Umbria but the atmosphere is often monopolised by the relentless flow of tourists and pilgrims. Two days is enough.

Links: Assisi is the destination of the Umbrian Apennines tour (*see page 225*) and the beginning of the route to Todi (*see page 244*). It is only 20km from Perugia (*see page 202*).

Route: The best time of day to begin a tour of Assisi is when it opens at 0630. You can be sure of a parking space and serenity in the **BASILICA DI SAN FRANCESCO ❶** before tour groups storm the place (if early is not an option, try late in the afternoon). After the Basilica, walk down Via San Francesco, lined with shops selling overpriced majolica plates, made-in-China embroidered blouses, wooden crucifixes and leather sandals. You can also buy a plastic friar in an Inter Milan T-shirt.

P Cars can be left in one
of the car parks at
Porta San Pietro (tel: 075
815311), Porta Moiano (tel:
075 813707), Piazza
Matteotti (tel: 075 815164),
Porta San Giacomo, Piazzale
Ufficio or Piazza del
Mercato.

**Pinacoteca
Comunale €€** Via
San Francesco 10; tel: 075
812033;
www.sistemamuseo.it. Open
daily Mar–Oct 1000–1300
and 1430–1800 (1900
Jun–Aug). Shorter hours in
winter. It contains a
number of works by
Umbrian painters from the
14th to the 17th century,
including Puccio Capanna
and Andrea d'Assisi.

Rocca Maggiore €
Tel: 075 812033;
www.sistemamuseo.it.
Open daily Jul–Aug
0900–sunset, Sep–Jun
1000–sunset.

Look up on the way at the Renaissance façades above the shop windows, often framed by the Umbrian arch using a keystone shaped like an inverted teardrop. Nos 14–16, on the left, are the stumpy remains of a 13th-century defensive tower, and alongside is a 15th-century *palazzo* with Renaissance torch-holders and animal-head finials. Once the headquarters of the Guild of Masons, it still bears their insignia – a flower and pair of compasses – as well as the date, 1477. No 10 is the newly restored Palazzo Vallemani, and the site of the **Pinacoteca Comunale ❷**. Next door, No 12, is a fine 17th-century *palazzo* with an ornate balcony (it is now the Municipal Library). Opposite, at No 7, the Oratorio dei Pellegrini (Pilgrims' Chapel) was converted to a hostel for pilgrims in 1431. A 16th-century inscription on the fountain you pass to the right warns you not to use the water for laundry on pain of having your underwear confiscated. Via del Seminario, Via A Fortini and Via Portica link Via San Francesco to the **Piazza del Comune ❸**. Just before the piazza, at Via Portica 2, there is an entrance to the **Foro Romano ❹**.

The Temple of Minerva, or **SANTA MARIA SOPRA MINERVA ❺**, stands on the Piazza del Comune. The civic buildings of Assisi are diagonally opposite. The 13th-century Romanesque Torre del Comune (Municipal Tower) recalls the feuding Guelph and Ghibelline factions. Another reminder of those ancient conflicts is found in the battlements of the tower and the **Palazzo del Capitano del Popolo ❻** (Palace of the People's Captain) next door. The tower has fishtail Ghibelline crenellations, the palace has square Guelph ones (the latter added in 1927, long after the two sides had stopped murdering each other). Further up the square, on the opposite side, is the **PALAZZO DEI PRIORI ❼**.

The left-hand passageway that passes beneath the Palazzo descends to a small piazza dominated by the domed **Chiesa Nuova ❽**. This was built in 1615 on the supposed site of the birthplace of St Francis. Inside is the cell in which St Francis was imprisoned for stealing his father's cloth and selling it to pay for the rebuilding of San Damiano. The saint's birthplace is said to have been in the Via San Antonio, east of the church. Although St Francis was the son of a wealthy cloth merchant, a Latin inscription in the **Oratorio di San Francesco Piccolino ❾** informs us that 'the light of the world, St Francis, was born in the stable of an ox and an ass'.

From the Piazza del Comune, veer into the leftmost street out of the square, Via San Rufino. This steep and narrow lane climbs to the upper part of the town and levels out at the Piazza San Rufino, in front of **SAN RUFINO ❿**. Many visitors are not even aware that this cathedral exists at all, tucked away as it is some distance from the central square.

Detour: Walk up Via Porta Perlici and then climb the steep stone staircase called Vicolo San Lorenzo. It leads to the **Rocca Maggiore ⓫**,

Above
The Rocca Maggiore

'great rock' or 'fortress', which was once the mightiest castle in Umbria. The first castle was built in 1174 at the order of Frederick Hohestaufen, known to Italians as Barbarossa – Redbeard – who invaded Italy in 1155 to reassert the territorial claims of the Holy Roman Emperor against those of the Pope. Barbarossa's grandson, Frederick II, spent some time living in the castle under the care of Duke Conrad of Urslingen but, in 1198, the people of Assisi destroyed the castle in an uprising against the Duke's tyrannical rule. The present castle therefore dates to the rebuilding, this time under papal control, of 1367, with modifications carried out up to 1535. In later centuries, the people of Assisi used it as a source of building material. It was massively restored in the 19th century. The panoramic view from the central tower sweeps from the orange-brown rooftops of Assisi, the town's churches and campanile, down to the Vale of Spoleto.

Most of the narrow lanes that lead south from the Piazza San Rufino eventually descend to the Piazza and church of **SANTA CHIARA** ⑫, the burial place of St Clare, founder of the Poor Clares. In Assisi, the countryside that St Francis loved seems ever present. When you step out through the **Porta Nuova** ⑬, it is like stepping from a tame garden into a slightly wilder countryside (after you have crossed the busy road, Viale Vittorio Emanuele II, that encircles Assisi). The steep pedestrian road that leads to **SAN DAMIANO** ⑭, just over 1km in length, passes through tranquil olive groves where ancient and gnarled trees rise from a carpet of wildflowers and tall dark cypresses sign the direction to the little sanctuary.

St Francis (1181–1226)

It is not the least of St Francis's qualifications for sainthood that he appeared hopelessly mad to many of his contemporaries. The son of an Assisi cloth merchant took to kissing lepers and wearing hair shirts – nothing exceptional in the Middle Ages. But he went a step further and declared his love, with seeming promiscuity, to the sun, the moon, the elements and all God's creatures. He referred to his body as an 'ass', poverty as his 'bride' and death as his 'sister'. Francis has been seen as a medieval animal rights activist, social worker and Christianity's first environmentalist (Greenpeace International made him their patron saint). However, nothing that Francis did was more revolutionary than living in imitation of Christ, and it was by personal example as much as ideas that he influenced the Christian Church.

Also worth exploring

The **Eremo delle Carceri** is set in the woods halfway up Monte Subasio (4km east of Assisi). This is the site of several miracles attributed to St Francis. Despite the number of visitors, the hermitage does still have the feeling of remoteness, isolated as it is in a sea of evergreen holm oak. The cave, the Grotta di San Francesco, survives at the core of the modern complex, reached through a tiny narrow passageway and staircase off the diminutive chapel of Santa Maria. At the southern end of the hermitage, a path leads to a stone bridge, which crosses a precipitous ravine. By the side of the bridge, hanging over the brink of the ravine, is a broken and weathered oak – the one, so they say, where birds gathered to listen to St Francis preaching. From this spot, several pathways penetrate the dense woodland that surrounds the hermitage, skirting caves once occupied by St Francis and his followers.

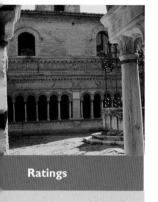

Assisi to Todi

Ratings

Scenery	●●●●●
Architecture	●●●●○
Art	●●●●○
History	●●●●○
Nature	●●●●○
Vineyards	●●●●○
Children	●●●○○
Shopping	●○○○○

The best way to commune with the spirit of nature-loving St Francis while driving a car is to leave Assisi through the back door of Porta Perlici, where few tourists ever venture, and drive to Spello on the ancient carriage road that curves around Monte Subasio. There are sweeping views across the Vale di Umbra, an ancient lake settled by Roman veterans who planted wheat, vines and olive trees – all still an important part of the local industry. This route then crosses the valley flats (skipping the *autostrada*) and the hills around Monte Martana. On the way, it links some of the most charming sights in Umbria: the Roman gates of Spello, the Romanesque square of Bevagna, the Renaissance frescos in Montefalco, and one of Umbria's oldest and most charismatic hill-towns, Todi.

BEVAGNA

ⓘ Pro Loco *Piazza Filippo Silvestri 1; tel and fax: 0742 361667; www.comune.bevagna.pg.it. Open 0930–1230 and 1530–1900, shorter hours in winter.*

Bevagna was much bigger in the 1st and 2nd centuries AD when it was Roman and called *Mevania*. Native son and poet Propertius called it 'cloudy Mevania, standing among rain-soaked fields'. The tree-lined **Piazza Garibaldi** lies just within the town walls. To the right, in the basement of Via Porta Guelfa 2, is a Roman bathhouse that still seems ready for business. Triton sports on its mosaic floor flanked by dolphins, octopuses, sea horses and lobsters. The scant remains of a Roman temple are still visible in Via Crescimbeni. The Romans used to breed sacred bulls in Bevagna, whose whiteness and deer-like expressions qualified them for sacrifice on an altar to Juno or Jupiter.

The sleepy main street of today's town, the Corso Matteotti, leads (right) into the Piazza F Silvestri with scarcely any buildings later than the 13th century. It shows the pride medieval citizens took in their status as an independent commune. The most elegant building, the Palazzo dei Consoli, was built in 1270 and now houses the Teatro

Above
Montefalco

Torti. The church of San Silvestro was built of Roman masonry. Almost windowless, the interior has a set of columns in the nave with mysterious motifs on them that might have been copied from an ancient Roman temple devoted to Isis. The church of San Michele also recycles material with Roman egg-and-dart mouldings. Strange beasts and angels adorn the portal.

MONTEFALCO

Montefalco produces a strong candidate for the 'best red' in Umbria – the full-bodied Sagrantino, as well as Sagrantino Passito, a heady dessert wine that tastes a little like port.

Because of its stupendous panoramic position, dominating the Topino and Clitunno plains, Montefalco likes to call itself the balcony (*ringhiera*) of Umbria. On a clear day, you can see almost everything – Perugia, Spello, Foligno, Bevagna and the Apennines. In the church of Sant'Agostino, on the main street, Corso G Mameli, there is a fresco which shows the view from Montefalco to Foligno as it was in the 15th century – much the same as today except for a lake (since drained). No less than eight saints were born here though it now prides itself on wine more than sanctity.

Museo Civico di San Francesco €
Ringhiera Umbra 6; tel: 0742 379598; www.comunemontefalco.it & www.sistemamuseo.it. Open daily Jun–Jul 1030–1300 and 1500–1900, Aug 1030–1300 and 1500–1930, Mar–May and Sep–Oct 1030–1300 and 1400–1800, Nov–Feb Tue–Sun 1030–1300 and 1430–1700.

The **Museo Civico** in the former church of San Francesco is one of the finest art museums in Umbria with a glorious fresco cycle in the apse (1450–52) by Florentine artist Benozzo Gozzoli. Twelve scenes from the life of St Francis reflect the formidable range of Renaissance painting technique and the influence of Fra Angelico. Montefalco itself features in the best scene of all, to the right of the window, in which St Francis preaches to the birds. In the nave of the former church is a potpourri of Umbrian painting that includes a very fine *Nativity* by Perugino and works by Mezzastris, Tiberio d'Assisi and Francesco Melanzio.

SPELLO

Pro Loco *Piazza Matteotti 2; tel: 0742 301009; www.comune.spello.pg.it*

An ancient Umbrian settlement chosen by Augustus as a place of retirement for veterans of his military campaigns, Roman *Hispellum* was demarcated by a wall some 2km around, and modern Spello, a town of just over 1,000 inhabitants, has scarcely grown beyond this boundary. The walls still stand to an impressive height, defining the shape of the town as it climbs up the narrow shoulder of a hill beneath Monte Subásio. Polygonal 12th-century towers flank the massive Roman Porta Venere.

Spello's artistic highlight is a lavish set of frescos by Pinturicchio in the Cappella Baglioni of Santa Maria Maggiore (Piazza Matteotti). He never created anything more sensual, exotic or colourful. Pinturicchio left a self-portrait hanging on the wall of the house in the scene where the Archangel Gabriel appears to the Virgin. The floor of the chapel also contributes to the rich effect. The 16th-century majolica tiles, made in Deruta (on the opposite side of the valley, *see page 208 and map on page 239*), are painted with dragons and griffins.

Below
Hilltop Spello

TODI

Informazioni turistiche *Piazza Umberto I, 6; tel: 075 8943395; fax: 075 8942406; e-mail: info@iat.todi.pg.it; www.comune.todi.pg.it & www.todi.net. Open 0900–1300 and 1500–1900, shorter hours in winter.*

Pro Loco *Via dei Condotti 9; tel: 075 8943933.*

San Fortunato €
Open daily 0930–1230 and 1500–1700.

Museo-Pinacoteca €
Palazzi Comunale, Piazza del Popolo; tel: 075 8943862; www.sistemamuseo.it. Open Tue–Sun Apr–Oct 1000–1330 and 1500–1800, Nov–Mar 1030–1300 and 1430–1700

Lo Studiolo *Corso Cavour 48; tel: 075 8944585. Charming collection of prints, books and antiques.*

The **Piazza del Popolo** has changed little in appearance since the end of the 14th century. The sense of being surrounded by medieval buildings, still used for their original purpose, is remarkable.

A town of great beauty, blessed with views over unspoiled countryside. Thanks to its strategic position on a hill between the valleys of the Tiber and the Naia, Todi was settled early by the Umbrians. Its original name, *Tuderte*, meant border, because the Etruscans were just next door. The town's coat of arms shows an eagle with a napkin in its talons. A legend says that Todi was founded on the spot where the eagle let the napkin drop, after seizing it from an Etruscan banqueting table. The people of the town – nicknamed Marzia after the Roman god of war – have a reputation for defending their liberty with great ferocity. They repulsed Hannibal and turned away Totila the Goth. Three sets of walls – Etruscan, Roman and medieval – still encircle the city. Inside, many medieval houses have been restored as weekend and holiday homes for Rome's jet set.

From the car park near the Piazza Oberdan (close to Santa Maria della Consolazione) it is a short climb to **San Fortunato**, the highest point in the town. The church has a magnificent Gothic portal, set into the half-finished façade that is bursting with biblical figures. The interior also feels buoyant thanks to the slender composite columns, encircled by clusters of shafts, rising up to massive Corinthian columns from which the roof vaults spring. The best fresco, in the fourth chapel on the right, is Masolino da Panicale's delicate and dreamy *Madonna and Child* (1432).

To the left of the church, a path leads down to Via San Fortunato and the Porta Marzia, the town's one surviving Etruscan gate. This straddles the Corso Cavour, the main street, which leads to the broad **Piazza del Popolo**. The Duomo, at the far end of the square, incorporates Romanesque, Gothic and Renaissance features. Inside, a dark crypt lurks beneath the cathedral – it was built on the site of an Etruscan temple. Upstairs, the entire west wall is painted with a familiar fresco, a 17th-century copy of Michelangelo's *Last Judgement* in the Sistine Chapel. From the cathedral steps, a left turn leads down the Via del Duomo for a look at the external detail of the Romanesque apse and for the views from the little belvedere. This stands on the site of one of four gates at the corners of the Piazza del Popolo that allowed the whole square to be sealed off and defended in the event of an attack.

Also on the square is the **Museo-Pinacoteca**, the town's picture gallery and archaeological museum, in the Palazzi Comunali. Aside from a modest collection of pictures, one of which is by Lo Spagna, there are historical odds and ends from Todi's long history – ceramics, coins and Etruscan and Roman finds. On the way back to the car park, look at the Renaissance church of Santa Maria della Consolazione. It has been attributed to Bramante, the architect of St Peter's, though it is more likely to have been built by a succession of wannabe Bramantes.

Accommodation and food

La Mulinella € *Ponte Naia 29, Todi; tel: 075 8944779. Closed Tue and Nov.* An earthy *trattoria* on the Tiber river just outside Todi. Everything on the menu is home-made and based on seasonal ingredients, from *tagliatelle al sugo d'oca* (in goose sauce) to the house speciality, a lamb dish called *agnello alla Mulinella*.

Perbacco € *Via Umberto I 16, Cannara; tel: 0742 720492. Evening only. Closed Mon and 20 Jul–20 Aug. No credit cards.* This is the onion capital of Umbria so you have to have onion soup, followed perhaps by *polenta con sputature di maiale* or *piccione in casseruola* (pigeon casserole) and the excellent local *pecorino* cheese.

Rifugio San Gaspare € *Strada Statale Flaminia, Monti Martani, Giano dell'Umbria; tel: 0742 90189. Closed Mon in winter and at end of Sep.* You can indulge a passion for grilled meat, watching it sizzle on a vast fire inside, or waiting on the terrace outside with mountain views.

Opposite
Todi in the early morning mist

Below
Fresco in Todi's San Fortunato church

La Cantina €€ *Via Cavour 2, Spello; tel: 0742 651775. Closed Wed.* A *trattoria* made in heaven (so come early) whose medieval dining room fills up with locals and visitors keen to devour hearty Umbrian dishes at low prices. Try the *coniglio in porchetta* (herb-stuffed rabbit), the grilled meats or *maccheroni dolci*, a pasta dessert.

Enoteca Antiche Sere €€ *Piazza Giuseppe Garibaldi 10, Bevagna; tel: 0742 361938. Closed Tue.* A renovated *palazzo* inn with a no-nonsense menu including simple pasta dishes, farro salad, lentils with arugula and pappardelle with hare.

Palazzo Bocci €€ *Via Cavour 17, Spello; tel: 0742 301021; fax: 0742 301021; fax: 0742 301464; www.palazzobocci.com.* Old *palazzo* near Santa Maria Maggiore.

Palazzo Brunamonti €€ *Corso Matteotti 79, Bevagna; tel: 0742 361932; fax: 0742 361948; www.brunamonti.it.* Sixteen elegant, fully furnished rooms in a restored palace full of *trompe-l'œil* fantasy.

Villa Pambuffetti €€€ *Via della Vittoria 20, Montefalco; tel: 0742 379417, fax: 0742 379245; www.villapambuffetti.com.* A 19th-century brick villa in its own park surrounded by cypresses.

Suggested tour

There are three roads to Spello – the one taken by this route and two others: the *autostrada*, obviously the fastest; and a dirt road that climbs right over Monte Subásio but is only recommended for four-wheel drive vehicles.

Total distance: 65km; detour adds 14km (return).

Time: Two to three days.

Links: The route begins in Assisi (*see page 228*), which marks the end of the tour of the Umbrian Apennines (*see page 225*). It crosses the Umbria valley, which leads to Spoleto (*see page 250*). There are two roads to Orvieto (*see page 276*) from Todi: the N79 over the hills, or the faster N448 along Lago di Corbara.

Route: Leave **Assisi ❶** through the northern gate of Porta Perlici and watch for a right turn after a few hundred metres. This leafy lane of a road takes you to the hamlet of Armenzano (759m) and then the village of Collepino (600m) snug within its medieval ring of walls. On the way, you will probably meet cyclists, walkers and people picnicking by the side of the road. You might be tempted to join them. **SPELLO ❷** is a pink and white city of travertine stone, of Roman gates and Renaissance frescos. It suffered in the earthquake but most of the damage has been repaired. A steep descent drops to the plain by the gates of the city (where there is a large dusty car park). To cross the valley, drive beneath the busy N75 (avoiding, at all costs, the maze of traffic around Foligno) and follow the signs for Cannara. You are now crossing an extinct lake. Drainage began under the Romans and, by 1600, it had virtually dried up. Crossing the Topino river, you'll find yourself in **Cannara ❸**, a city founded among the reeds in the Middle Ages. Today, it is the purple onion capital of Umbria and known for an unusual red wine called Vernaccia di Cannara. Take the first left after passing through town under the shadows of a magnificent walled cemetery. Continue south, cruising fields of tobacco, maize and sunflowers, to reach **BEVAGNA ❹**. A straight road leads out of town beneath an alley of plane trees and after just 6.5km climbs up to **MONTEFALCO ❺** (park outside the walls). A tranquil road leads from there through vineyards and olive groves to the evocatively named town of **Bastardo ❻**.

Detour: Follow the signs for **Giano dell'Umbria ❼**, founded by Norman invaders in the 11th century. It's a slow, twisty 7km up to the Rifugio San Gaspare and its panoramic viewpoint.

The road out of town skirts the Puglia river, then crosses it and climbs up to a broad ridge. There are no villages or towns, just green Umbrian hills and an occasional villa. In a strange outburst of road-building ambition, the road widens and resembles a traffic-free *autostrada* for a couple of kilometres before narrowing suddenly at a tiny place called Petroro. Carry on down to the River Tiber, cross under the Perugia *autostrada* and follow the curves up to **TODI** ❽.

Also worth exploring

At **Trevi**, the modern world is left behind as you step within the walls. Streets too narrow and steep for cars have been turned into minor works of art, paved with pebbles set in frames of stone or brick to divide the surfaces into patterns of squares, diamonds or herringbone. You never know what to expect around the next turning: ancient buildings pierced by medieval archways that offer glimpses of shady, flower-filled courtyards, oversailing buttresses and massive corbels holding up the jettied upper storeys of sombre *palazzi*.

Below
Trevi's narrow cobbled streets

Nera Valley and Spoleto

Ratings

Architecture	●●●●●
Monasteries	●●●●●
Nature	●●●●○
Scenery	●●●●●
Children	●●●●○
Food and drink	●●●●○
Walking	●●●●○
Museums	●●○○○

The upper valley of the River Nera – the Valnerina – is wild, dramatic and uncrowded, with the exception of the famous Marmore Falls. The heights of the surrounding hills are covered by beech forest and meadows that bloom in spring with violets, lilies and gentian. Willows, poplars and black alders line the riverbank, and trout and crayfish live in the streams. Crumbling fortresses and ancient towers are ubiquitous – a legacy of the time when papal and imperial forces fought each other for territorial power in Umbria. Just north of the valley, separated by a mountain and a tunnel, is Spoleto, a Romanesque hill-town with modern flair. Percy Bysshe Shelley was not the first or last traveller to call it 'the most romantic city I ever saw'.

ABBAZIA DI SAN PIETRO IN VALLE

ⓘ Abbazia di San Pietro in Valle €
Ferentillo; tel: 0744 780129; fax: 0744 380121; www.sanpietroinvalle.com. Open daily 1000–1200 and 1400–1700 (see page 252 for guesthouse contact information). If closed, stop at the friendly custodian's house on the left side of the road to the abbey.

It would be hard to exaggerate the beauty of this abbey, which is deeply secluded on a shelf of Monte Fionchi. It is the oldest monastery in Umbria and built, according to legend, on the site of the first Umbrian city. Its founder was the Lombard Duke of Spoleto, Faroaldo II. The Lombards invaded Italy in the wake of the Goths in the early 6th century AD and remained a powerful force in the region for several centuries. They arrived as Teutonic pagans but settled and adopted Christianity – inspired by the example of St Benedict, born a mere 24km from here in Norcia, and his Benedictine order of monks. When his son, Trasamondo II, deposed him in AD 720, Faroaldo II joined the Benedictines and founded this monastery.

Much of the abbey complex, including the noble campanile, dates from the 12th century, but there are some earlier remains. The peaceful small cloister, to the right of the abbey church, fuses sculptural fragments from Faroaldo's original building. The apse of the

8th-century church still stands and the extraordinary altar, carved with totemic figures and crude foliage, is inscribed with the names 'Ursus', the sculptor, and 'Iderico', who became Duke of Spoleto in AD 739. Several very fine 3rd-century Roman sarcophagi are displayed here; one of them, carved with Bacchic scenes, was supposedly used as Faroaldo II's tomb. Frescos of the nave, dating from the 1190s, illustrate the Creation, and Adam and Eve in the Garden of Eden (left), the Nativity and the Crucifixion (right). Few frescos of this date survive in such good condition. Art historians regard them as the first examples of an emerging Italian – as distinct from Byzantine – artistic style. Across the valley is the ruined hulk of the *castello* of Umbriano.

CARSULAE

Founded around 220 BC, and built on either side of the *Via Flaminia*, *Carsulae* blossomed briefly but was hit by an earthquake towards the end of the 1st century AD. Never rebuilt, the masonry was stolen and weeds gradually hid the remains. The ancient town was rediscovered again in the 16th century and excavations have continued sporadically ever since.

The only intact building is the 11th-century chapel of San Damiano, built of brick and stone taken from the Roman forum. Just in front of the church, the original *Via Flaminia* climbs up through the centre of the town, its stone-paved surface rutted with wheel grooves. Following the road northwards, you pass two ruined temples on the left. Their walls retain some original marble cladding. The forum comes next, then the law courts, followed by an expanse of unexcavated sheep pasture. To the right, in the distance, you can see the little village of Portaria clinging to a steep spur of the Naia valley. Finally you reach the northern gate of the town and the cemetery with two large intact funerary monuments, one a circular sepulchre.

On the left-hand side of the *Via Flaminia*, as you return, are the baths and cisterns. The amphitheatre, built into the sides of a large natural hollow, is the most complete structure on the site and stands side by side with the theatre. From here you can look back across a grassy plain littered with the fallen columns and marble fragments of this once impressive Roman town.

> Tacitus and Pliny visited *Carsulae* and described it as beautiful. The delicate pink colour of the stone remains hints at the lost splendour.

CASCATA DELLE MARMORE (THE MARMORE FALLS)

> **Cascata delle Marmore** € *Tel: 0744 62982; fax: 0744 362231; www.marmore.it. The park is open daily Jun–Sep 1000–2200, mid-Mar–May Mon–Fri 1000–1900, Sat–Sun 1000–2200; Oct–Mar Mon–Fri 1000–1800, Sat and Sun until 2000; Nov–mid-Mar 1100–1700. However, the waters are released according to a more complicated time schedule: Jun–Aug Mon–Fri 1100–1300, 1600–1800 and 2100–2200; Sat–Sun 1000–1300 and 1500–2200. At other times of year it ranges from once to three times a day.*

This stupendous waterfall – 162m in height – is actually man-made. The fall was engineered under the rule of the Roman consul Curius Denatatus in 271 BC. Surrounded by rivers, the plains around Terni were constantly subject to flooding, and always marshy. The Romans diverted the Velino river away from the plain in order to drain it and cut a channel to carry it northwards. The slight waterfall that already existed, where the Nera spills over the side of Monte Marmore, became a powerful cascade with the combined force of two rivers.

In 1938, the Velino was dammed at Lake Piediluco and the waters used to drive hydroelectric turbines. Consequently, the Marmore Falls flow at a trickle much of the time. At certain times, the sluice gates are opened and the pent-up torrent crashes thunderously down the rocks and creates a cloud of spray and multiple rainbows. If your first encounter with the falls whets your appetite to see them again, go at night when they are illuminated. You also have a choice of two viewpoints. The N209 out of Terni takes you to the base of the falls, whereas the N79 takes you to the top.

FERENTILLO

> **Museo delle Mummie** € *San Stefano crypt; tel: 0743 54395. Open Apr–Sep 0900–1230, 1430–1930; shorter hours in winter.*

Ferentillo lies at the foot of a wild and narrow valley. Its decaying walls climb both sides of the gorge, punctuated by ruined lookout towers. No army or lone traveller could pass this way without being funnelled through the village and challenged. It is not surprising that

The rugged Salto del Cieco valley, around Ferentillo, is home to peregrine and lanner falcons, porcupine, wild boar and lynxes.

this region remained a last stronghold of the emperor, so well was the gorge defended.

The village has a truly bizarre museum, the **Museo delle Mummie**. On display are bodies thrown into the crypt of San Stefano that were unintentionally desiccated and preserved by the biting winds that cut through the valley in winter. The cast of characters includes two soldiers from Napoleon's army who were lynched; an unwed mother who died in childbirth on a roadside along with her child; a farmer and lawyer – they killed each other in a quarrel over land – and a Chinese couple that succumbed to cholera on their honeymoon in the 1880s.

Below
Cascata delle Marmore

SPOLETO

ⓘ Informazioni turistiche *Piazza della Libertà 7; tel: 0743 238911; fax: 0743 46241; e-mail: info@iat.spoleto.pg.it; www.comune.spoleto.pg.it and www.prospoleto.it*

ⓝ Pinacoteca Comunale € *Palazzo Rosari Spada, Corso Mazzini; tel: 0743 45940; www.sistemamuseo.it. Closed indefinitely.* Most of the museum's collection dating up to the 15th century has been relocated to the recently renovated **Museo Nazionale del Ducato di Spoleto** in the Rocca Albornoziana (€ *Piazza Campello, tel: 0743 46434; www.sistemamuseo.it; open Wed–Mon 1030–1300 and 1530–1900)* and the **Palazzo Comunale** (open Mon–Fri 0730–1930. Free).

Galleria Civica d'Arte Moderna € *Palazzo Collicola, Via Loreto Vittori; tel: 0743 46434; www.visitspoleto.it. Open mid-Mar–mid-Oct 1030–1300, 1500–1830; shorter hours in winter.* A collection dating from the beginning of the 20th century that includes works from Italian artists Burri, Capograssi and Leonardi.

☾ Since the 1950s, Spoleto has become internationally famous for its Festival dei Due Mondi (Two Worlds Festival), founded by the Italian-American composer Giancarlo Menotti and held at the end of June and beginning of July.

Umbrian in the 7th–6th centuries BC, Spoleto became Roman in 241 BC. It played a major role in the Gothic wars and became the capital of the Lombard duchy of Spoleto in AD 570. The Umbrians, Romans and Lombards who built Spoleto appreciated its prime hill-top location and it showed its military value when the city successfully repulsed Hannibal in 217 BC, fresh from his victory at Lake Trasimeno. In the 9th century Spoleto was one of the most important cities in central Italy and at its apogee as an independent duchy ruled by the Lombards. Architecturally speaking, the Lombards picked up where the late Romans left off and its architectural development displays rare continuity from late antiquity to the beginning of the 13th century.

From the Piazza della Libertà you can see a Roman theatre (access through the Archaeological Museum) to the south. Next, the Corso Mazzini leads you past the Palazzo Rosari Spada, home to the **Museo del Tessile e del Costume** (€ *Via delle Terme; tel: 0743 46434; www.visitspoleto.it;* textiles and ancient costumes). The Via dello Sdrucciolo links the Palazzo to the perfect medieval Piazza del Mercato, with a splendid 18th-century fountain by Roman architect Costantino Fiaschetti. Veer into the Via di Visiale and look out for the **Palazzo Comunale** in the Piazza de Municipio; its ancient vaults contain the remains of a 1st-century AD Roman house, once claimed to be the home of Vespasia Polla, the mother of the Emperor Vespasian. Recently renovated, the Palazzo Comunale is graced by two frescos by Giovanni di Pietro, better known as Lo Spagna (because he was born in Spain); one shows the virtues (1512) and the other *Madonna and Child* (1516). This accomplished artist spent much of his life in Umbria where some of his works survive in churches dotting the region. The Palazzo is also hung with paintings from the city's former **Pinacoteca Comunale**.

The Piazza del Duomo (across the Via Fontesecca) is one of Umbria's most striking. To appreciate the full grace of the cathedral façade (1190), walk to the opposite end of the wide piazza and sit on the long stone bench at the foot of the wall. Of the exquisite rose windows, the central one is framed by two caryatids with symbols of the Evangelists carved in the corners. Inside, the best things are the floors of inlaid marble and the frescos by Filippo Lippi (in the sanctuary), the last he ever did. He was at the height of his powers and filled them with lyrical and tender figures, painted in vibrant colours. His tomb is in the right-hand transept.

The monumental fortress, the **Rocca Albornoziana**, towers above the town. Much of it was built with stone looted from the Roman amphitheatre. It was converted into a luxurious palace for Lucrezia and Cesare Borgia. More recently, the Rocca served as a maximum-security prison, holding the late Pope John Paul II's would-be assassin and Red Brigade terrorists. After several years of renovation it is now home to the **Museo Nazionale del Ducato di Spoleto** with objects and art dating from the 4th to the 15th centuries. Beyond the Rocca, another reason for climbing to the top of town is the **Ponte delle Torri**, the extraordinary aqueduct built in 1345 that spans the gorge between Monte Sant'Elia, on which the Rocca is built, and Monteluco, opposite. Water no longer flows along it (though it can be turned on if necessary) and it is possible to walk across the massive structure, 230m long and 80m high, to the wooded slopes of Monteluco, enjoying the views up and down the Tessino gorge.

Below
Spoleto's Duomo

TERNI

ℹ **APT office** *Via Cassian Bon 4; tel: 0744 423047; fax: 0744 427259; e-mail: info@iat.terni.it; www.comune.terni.it & www.umbria2000.it. Open Mon–Fri 0900–1300, Tue and Thu 1500–1800.*

🎨 **Pinacoteca Comunale O. Metelli** € *Palazzo Gazzoli, via del Teatro Romano 13; tel: 0744 59421. Open Tue–Sun 1000–1300 and 1600–1900.*

Terni claims to be the burial place of St Valentine (the Basilica of San Valentino is in the suburb of San Valentino, 2km south of the city centre). The head of the mummified saint was stolen in 1986 but his body remains and the town honours him with a festival on St Valentine's Day, 14 February.

The Industrial Revolution in peninsular Italy began in Terni – the 'Italian Manchester' – in the late 19th century. Terni built Italy's first steelworks, tapped the fast-flowing Velino river to generate hydroelectric power and began producing plastics as early as the 1920s. Unsurprisingly, the city was hit by Allied air raids during World War II. It is still the centre of the Italian armaments industry: the rifle used to assassinate President Kennedy was manufactured here; and rumours linked Terni to pieces of a supercannon bound for Iraq that were impounded in England before the Gulf War.

The part of the city that escaped destruction is concentrated around the cathedral (*park in the Corso del Popolo*), including a stretch of Roman wall. Close by is the Palazzo Gazzoli which houses the **Pinacoteca**, dedicated to both ancient and contemporary art. The collection includes Benozzo Gozzoli's *Marriage of St Catherine*; works by Miró, Kandinsky, Chagall and Léger; and industrial landscapes by naïf artist and shoemaker Orneore Metelli (1872–1938). The nearby church of San Salvatore, almost opposite the Palazzo Spada, is a circular sanctuary resembling a beehive from the inside. It might have been built as a temple to the sun, perhaps by the Umbrians as early as the 3rd century BC. The nave was added in the 12th century and the little Cappella Manessei in the 14th century.

Accommodation and food

If you want to stay in Spoleto during its famous summer event, the Festival of Two Worlds, book months, even a year, ahead. Hotel prices will be double.

Caffè da Vincenzo € *Via Cerquiglia 63/a, Spoleto; tel: 0743 47985. Closed Mon.* The number one address for the ritual consumption of Umbrian pastries and sweets, which are baked on the premises. It will also do for a light lunch, saving room for the home-made ice cream.

Pecchiarda € *Vicolo San Giovanni 1, Spoleto; tel: 0743 221009. Closed Thu except in summer.* Spoleto's best culinary bargain. The *gnocchi* filled with ricotta are perfect, and so is the house speciality, *pollo alla Pecchiarda*, a chicken de-boned and stuffed with ground meat and artichokes. The owner serves his own wine.

Abbazia di San Pietro in Valle €€ *SS 209 Valnerina, Macenano, Ferentillo; tel: 0744 780129; fax: 0744 435522; www.sanpietroinvalle.com.* This guesthouse has a dream setting in the green and mystic Nera valley, next to the secluded abbey of San Pietro.

Albergo-Trattoria del Ponte €€ *Via del Borgo 15, Scheggino; tel: 0743 61253.* Foodies will love this hotel because its restaurant is one of the

Above
Spoleto's Ponte delle Torri

best in the region and specialises in truffle-enhanced cooking. Speciality of the house is local crayfish with truffles.

Hotel Gattapone €€ *Via del Ponte 6, Spoleto; tel: 0743 223447; fax: 0743 223448.* Each of 15 comfortable rooms is decorated individually with antiques and Italian designer furniture. There are dramatic views of the Ponte delle Torri aqueduct and Tessino gorge. Reserve early.

Palazzo Dragoni €€ *Via del Duomo 13, Spoleto; tel: 0743 222220; fax: 0743 222225; www.palazzodragoni.it.* Its 15 bedrooms are divided between three floors in this *palazzo* filled with antiques, oriental carpets and Venetian glass chandeliers. Breakfast is served in a loggia with a view of the cathedral.

Sportellino €€ *Via Cerquiglia 4, Spoleto; tel: 0743 45230. Closed Thu and in Jul.* Come here for great starters such as *gnocchi*, the chewy pasta called *stringozzi* and, in season – of course – truffle dishes. If you don't like truffles, try the savoury *coniglio alla cacciatora* or *cacciagione*, or *ossobuco con i piselli* (oxtail with peas).

Suggested tour

Total distance: 87km; add 10km (return) for the detour by Lake Piediluco and another rugged 20km (return) to Monte Torre Maggiore.

Time: Two to three days.

Links: This route overlaps at *Carsulae* in the Middle Tiber and Nera Valley itinerary (*see page 274*). Spoleto is also the beginning of the Nera Valley and Monti Sibillini tour (*see page 264*).

Route: Drive north from **SPOLETO** ❶ and follow the signs for Norcia. After passing through a long tunnel, turn right (south). The first town is **Scheggino** ❷, rising on a slant around its triangular castle. Parts of the 12th-century walls are still standing. The town withstood a brutal siege by Picozzo Brancaleoni in 1522; part of it is built over an enchanting spring (to the left of the Nera). It is the home of the Urbani family and headquarters of their truffle empire. By some estimates, they control the collection and processing of 80 per cent of the truffles consumed in Italy and 40 per cent of the world market.

Below and opposite
Romanesque friezes from the façade of San Pietro Abbey showing (left) Jesus appearing to the Apostles by Lake Tiberias and (right) the Parable of the Sower

There are two roads up to **SAN PIETRO IN VALLE** ❸. Avoid the first one (with the rusty yellow signpost) and take the second that begins the climb up to the serene abbey on a cypress-lined avenue. A clearing below the church serves as the monastery car park. Back on the N209, it is just a couple of short kilometres to **FERENTILLO** ❹ , which straddles the road. The most interesting part of town (and the one with the mummies) is to the left (southeast).

Arrone ❺ is a couple of hundred metres off the N209. The town was founded by a family from Rome in the 9th century. The upper part of the village (called La Terra, The Land) is yet another fortified piece of the Valnerina's medieval war zone.

Detour: Take the road south from Arrone. It climbs then drops steeply and climbs again through endless olive groves on its way to **Lago di Piediluco** ❻ . As the road gets higher, fir trees take over and you enter a Parco Naturale Regionale, an area of protected highland that is still home to wild boar, not to mention a complex system of caves and potholes, mountain torrents, impenetrable forests of holm oak and flower-filled sheep pastures. After the Forca dell'Arrone pass, you have the first look at the lake. Steer northwest along the shore (on the N79). At a height of 365km, Lake Piediluco has a perimeter of about 17km and is the second largest lake in Umbria. It is irregular in shape with a depth of 19m. To rejoin the route, follow the signs for Cascata delle Marmore. The 'Belvedere Cascata' is in the village of Marmore. From here you can walk alongside the river channel and past the sluice that controls the water flow, down to the belvedere itself, a lookout point with a bird's-eye view of the falls.

Continue up the valley of Nera past the fortified town of Casteldilago and past the towns of Torreorsina and Collestatte (both were an ancient fief of the Orsini family), to the car park below the **CASCATA DELLE MARMORE** ❼. From there, several footpaths lead to the base of the falls. After the waterfall, drive on past Papigno, a medieval village with a moat that Lord Byron sketched while staying in the nearby Villa Graziani. The roofs are a strange shade of grey caused by an airborne residue from a carbide and calcium cyanide factory that is, mercifully, no longer in use. After the junction for Papigno is the sprawling Galleto power plant.

Driving through **TERNI** ❽, or getting out of it, poses a challenge. You can cross the town by following signs for Perugia but, later, you will want to take the road for San Gemini/Campitello (also signposted for Cesi and *Carsulae*). It rises above Terni through acres of olive groves before cresting at **Cesi** ❾, a town squeezed on to a narrow ledge of Monte Torre Maggiore. Its medieval builders nicked some of their stone from Roman *Carsulae*.

Detour: Brave the road that leads right (east) up to **Monte Torre Maggiore** ❿ and prepare for a vertical challenge. The 12th-century church of Sant'Erasmo is 790m up the mountainside, near an astronomical observatory and the fortified remains of an ancient Umbrian town. An unpaved dead end leads to a point near the summit (1,121m).

The road to *CARSULAE* ⓫ is unmissable thanks to a series of chocolate-brown signs with fallen Roman columns on them. Another 14km down into the valley floor, a pass under the *autostrada* and you arrive in **Acquasparta** ⓬. The thermal springs here were already in use in Roman times. Its most beautiful building is the 17th-century

Palazzo Cesi where Galileo was a guest in 1624. From the entrance to town, turn right (east) under the *autostrada* and prepare for a series of curves that become tighter as the road heads up to **Firenzuola** (480m) where the Lago di Arezzo reservoir comes into view cradled by the surrounding hills. A few more kilometres and you pass the *castello* of Baiano. Peaceful, wooded hills gradually give way to a wide valley on the way to Spoleto.

Also worth exploring

Most visitors to Umbria will, sooner or later, end up driving on the N3 between Spoleto and Perugia. They should all take a break from endemic road rage to honour the mythic **Fonti del Clitunno**. The sacred spring waters burst from the rock into a willow-fringed pool. Sadly, the nymphs have long since been driven away and the river god Clitunnus no longer issues oracles. Its fascination has survived though it doesn't attract the same class of visitor as in the days of Virgil and Lord Byron. Just a few metres up the road, the **Tempio del Clitunno** is one of Umbria's earliest churches, a mini Parthenon built in the 4th or 5th century for an early Christian martyr beside the crystal waters. Frescos inside (Christ with SS Peter and Paul), now indistinct, date from the 7th or 8th century and are among the earliest to have survived in Italy.

Nera Valley and Monti Sibillini

Ratings

Food	●●●●●
Mountains	●●●●●
Nature	●●●●●
Outdoor activities	●●●●●
Scenery	●●●●●
Walking	●●●●●
Wildlife	●●●●○
Architecture	●●●○○

This remote region offers some of the most scenic landscapes in central Italy. The national park of Monti Sibillini lies at the foot of the mountain range of the same name which rises above 2,400m. The park has pockets of true wilderness, alternating with solitary monasteries, churches, towers and castles. Wild orchids cover the vast highland plain of the Piano Grande in the spring. Norcia, the birthplace of St Benedict, lies at its edge. For all the saints that were born there, it was the sort of place you would go to talk to the Devil in the Middle Ages, a realm of necromancers, fairies and evil spirits. The local people had a reputation for the black arts – and a way with knives. They invented salami, sent a man to perform eye surgery on the Queen of England and castrated boys for the opera.

ABBAZIA DI SANT'EUTIZIO

ⓘ Abbazia di Sant'Eutizio € *Tel: 0743 99659. Open daily 0830–1145 and 1515–1800.*

The main attraction of this famous Benedictine abbey is its setting. It still seems as ideal for solitude and meditation as it must have been in the late 5th century when a Syrian monk laid the first stone. However, during much of the Middle Ages, the abbey was a point of power as well as light, ruling over the neighbouring region. Its wealth supported a major manuscript centre in the 10th–12th centuries (the library is now in the Vallicelliana in Rome). Its monks also played a role in medieval medicine, treating diseases with herbs from the Sibillini mountains.

The abbey has a façade with a rose window much like the one in Spoleto. It also has an 8th-century, sculpted fountain that belonged to an earlier church. The church's evocative interior has a single nave and a raised presbytery above a double-naved crypt. Frescos from the 15th and 17th centuries decorate the sepulchre of St Eutizio.

CASCIA

ℹ Informazioni turistiche *Piazza Garibaldi 1; tel: 074 71147; fax: 074 376630; e-mail: info@iat.cascia.pg.it.* This is a tourist office for all of eastern Umbria with information about the Valnerina, Norcia and Piano Grande.

Phenomenally popular in Italy, St Rita is the patron saint of impossibilities. The town where she was born is now completely monopolised by mass religious tourism focused on the Mussolini-era Basilica di Santa Rita, where the saint's mummified body is on display in a glass coffin. The vast neo-Romanesque and neo-Byzantine structure looks vaguely like a power plant. Local souvenirs include St Rita walking sticks topped by a bicycle bell and hung with a flask of potent green liqueur. The pilgrims, mainly women, are not architecture critics but would-be mothers and grandmothers, the elderly and infirm, and generally, people with a problem and faith in Rita. The rest of Cascia is interesting for its ensemble of medieval buildings and the Chiesa di San Francesco, adorned by wall frescos by Bartolomeo di Tommaso and paintings by Pomarancio and Cesarei.

MONTELEONE DI SPOLETO

🏛 Biga Museum € *Open daily 1000–1300 and 1400–1900. Ring at No 4 if it is closed.*

This prosperous high mountain village (978m) was the site of important Bronze and Iron Age settlements (with mines on Monte Birbone). Ancient stone fragments of its past are scattered across the green in front of the church of San Francesco. The church's Gothic portal is carved with lions, the symbol of the town, and the solitary figure of St Francis. The interior has pleasing 15th-century frescos.

A most extraordinary Etruscan chariot – the Biga – was found here in the 19th century. Made of hazelnut and covered in beaten bronze, it shows Thetis in the act of handing Achilles the armour that Hephaestus has made for him. The **Biga Museum** must make do with a copy: the original is in New York's Metropolitan Museum.

NORCIA

Castellina € *Piazza San Benedetto; tel: 0743 828044. Open irregular hours.*

Salumeria Fratelli Ansuini *Via Anicia 105; tel: 0743 816643; www.norcia.net/ansuini. The brothers are passionate hunters and make excellent salami of cinghiale (boar).*

Boutique del Pecoraro *Piazza San Benedetto 7; tel: 0743 816453. Specialists in pecorino (sheep's cheese).*

Truffles from Norcia are among the best in the world. The city holds a truffle festival in October.

St Benedict, the founder of Western monasticism, was born in Norcia (*Nursia* in Roman times) in AD 480. Benedict wrote the book on monastic life exercising a practical and spiritual influence for some 1,500-odd years. No wonder Pope Paul VI declared him 'patron saint of Europe' in 1964. Today, however, the little town of Norcia is far more preoccupied with pork than asceticism.

The Piazza San Benedetto is ringed by *norcineria*, butchers' shops selling locally produced *prosciutto* and endless varieties of salami ranging from tiny sausages to great meat-stuffed balloons. The Norcians claim to have invented salami and it may be true since sausage-makers in Italy are often called *norcini*. In the Middle Ages, they branched into other uses of knives – such as eye surgery and the castration of pubescent boys to qualify them for an operatic career.

The centre of Norcia has a certain rough charm. The best thing about the Basilica di San Benedetto is its elegant Gothic portal. The point of interest in the gloomy interior is the crypt, which was built against the foundations of the main temple of the Roman forum, supposedly on the spot where St Benedict was born. The altarpiece in the church (1621), painted by Filippo Napoletano, portrays St Benedict and Totila the Goth. They met in AD 542 towards the end of the lives of both men. Next to the church is the pinkish Palazzo Comunale, raised above a four-arched loggia. Opposite, the squat **Castellina**, built in 1554 as a papal stronghold, contains a small but intriguing museum with some rare 13th-century wooden figures of saints.

The Edicola (also known as the Tempietto, or little temple) is on the corner of Via Umberto in the north of the town. This low tower, built in the mid-14th century, is covered in inscriptions and tiny, detailed bas-reliefs of Masonic tools, the sun, Christ the Lamb, the instruments of the Passion, as well as very complex geometrical patterns and animal heads. No one quite knows what purpose this building served, but it may have been associated with a trade guild.

PARCO REGIONALE MONTI SIBILLINI

ℹ Casa del Parco *Via Solferino 22, Norcia; tel and fax: 0743 817090; www.sibillini.it. Open daily Jun–Sep 0930–1230, 1530–1830; Oct–May 0930–1230.*

Opposite
Monteleone di Spoleto

Below
The Monti Sibillini range, above Norcia

Located between Umbria and Le Marche, the park is a realm of woods, meadows, high-altitude lakes, perennial springs and glacial cirques. It is home to eagles and wolves, the rare marten and an almost extinct species of otter. There are a few ski lifts sharing the park with scattered traditional farms. The Sibillini mountains form the watershed between the Adriatic and Tyrrhenian seas. Among the ten peaks that are above 2,000m one can distinguish Monte Vettore (2,476m), Monte Sibilla (2,175m), Monte Redentore (2,448m), Monte Priora (2,332m) and Monte Argentella (2,201m). Eighteen hundred species of flowers bloom in the park such as edelweiss, Alpine anemone, moss campion and countless orchids.

Above
Statue of St Benedict in
Norcia's Piazza San Benedetto

Accommodation and food

Norcia is an excellent base from which to explore the surrounding region. Castelluccio, however, is best for hikers.

Sibilla € *Via della Fontana 69, Castelluccio; tel: 0743 870113.* A simple *pensione* with a restaurant specialising in dishes made from the sweet, locally grown lentils. Ask for a room with a view of the Piano Grande.

Taverna Castelluccio € *Via Dietro la Torre 8, Castelluccio; tel: 0743 821158. Closed Wed except in summer.* A brother-sister team runs this very rustic and *simpatica trattoria*. The best starters are home-made pasta such as *stringozzi* followed by anything with lentils.

Trattoria Pizzeria Da Franchina € *Via della Stazione 2, Sant'Anatolia di Narco; tel: 0743 61116.* A simple country *trattoria* serving home-made pasta and pizza.

Hotel Grotta Azzurra €€ *Via Alfieri 10, Norcia; tel: 0743 816513; fax: 0743 828076.* Just off the central square, this is a bustling place run by a friendly and attentive family. An open fireplace and rusty suit of armour decorate the dining room of its excellent restaurant, the Granaro del Monte – formerly the city's granary.

Below
The village of Castelluccio rises from the flat plain of the Piano Grande

Above
Monti Sibillini
National Park

Suggested tour

Total distance: 113km; detours add 60km (return to Castelluccio) and 11km (return to Roccaporena).

Time: The route involves strenuous mountain driving. Unless you are in a hurry, allow for two to three days.

Links: As in the previous chapter, this route begins and ends in Spoleto.

Route: Begin as in the previous chapter (*see page 254*), driving north on the N3 from **Spoleto** ❶. Follow the signs for Norcia. After you pass through the tunnel, turn left (north) on the N209. You soon pass the **Vallo di Nera** ❷ on the right. If it looks like a *castello* it is because it was one. You can still recognise some of the original fortified structure incorporated into village houses. The interior of the church of Santa Maria delle Grazie is covered in frescos with works by Lo Spagna in the apse; ask for the key at No 4 if it is closed. Thermal springs and a 19th-century bathhouse are the roadside attractions at **Borgo Cerreto** ❸.

Getting out of the car: A mountain railway once linked Spoleto to Norcia. Sadly, it was dismantled, beginning in 1968, but a few bits remain. From the centre of Borgo Cerreto, you can walk down a stretch of the track along the Nera river in the shade of alders and elms as far as a mineral water factory and, after crossing a bridge, the hamlet of Piedipaterno.

Further upstream, Triponzo (from *tre ponti* – three bridges) is where the Corno river meets the Nera. You have the option of heading straight for Norcia from here (and passing a string of ruined castles – Nortosce,

Argentigli and Biselli) but this route carries on further north to the town of **Preci** ❹, which dominates the Castoriana valley at the junction of the Norcia and Visso roads. In the Middle Ages, there was a school of surgeons in Preci with a hospital and medical library. Here, the skills acquired over the centuries in butchering pigs were refined and local surgeons performed eye operations and extracted gallstones. It still has a 13th-century castle. Carry on and watch for a yellow sign saying **ABBAZIA DI SANT'EUTIZIO** ❺ and turn left uphill a few hundred metres to reach the abbey.

Once you are back on the main road, drive through the hamlet of Piedivalle; Castoriana valley is a road where you will want to potter, downshift and daydream. The woods and pastures eventually give way to Forca d'Ancarano pass (1,008m). After cresting it, you have a first view of **NORCIA** ❻. The fertile plains south of Norcia are spread out to the right, irrigated by warm water springs that enable crops to be grown despite the cold. Next, down on the left, Norcia itself is revealed far away below, nestling into the side of a natural amphitheatre at the foot of the Sibillini mountain range. There is free parking outside the walls at the Porta Palatina.

Detour: Due south of Norcia, a dead straight road passes through the town's industrial zone and leads to the hamlet of Santa Scolastica, named after the twin sister of St Benedict. Take the left turn in the hamlet, signposted to Castelluccio. This is a wide and relatively straight road that climbs rapidly to a height of over 1,500m. Where the road divides at the summit of the pass, take another left turn. After a long haul of mountaineering with your car, you pass over the rim of Monte Ventosola and see the vast **Piano Grande** ❼ spread out before you. The landscape has changed completely: there are no more trees and nothing but bare, round hills and rocks. The empty plain, 8km in length, is as flat as a football pitch, and virtually empty except for the odd haystack and field hut. Much of Zeffirelli's film about the life of St Francis, *Brother Sun, Sister Moon*, was shot here. The lone hilltop hamlet just visible in the distance, **Castelluccio** ❽, is a scruffy working village that has few facilities for visiting tourists, hikers and skiers. It still lives by agriculture – Castelluccians crop hay from the plain to feed their cows and grow tiny sweet lentils for which the area is famous all over Italy.

Getting out of the car: Castelluccio is a perfect base for walking, surrounded as it is by a landscape of great natural beauty. Immediately to the east, Monte Vettore rises (2,476m), once believed to be the home of the prophetic Sibyl. The climb is not especially difficult in good weather if you are fit and well equipped, and will reward anyone interested in alpine flora. The trails are not always clearly marked so it is important to have a good map. However, in clear weather, the visibility is almost perfect since it is all grassland.

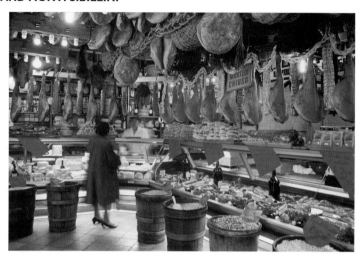

Right
Salumeria Fratelli Ansuini

Take the road that follows the pretty River Sordo to the junction of N320 and N396 at Serravalle.

Detour: Roccaporena ❾ is a pretty hamlet in a magnificent setting beneath limestone crags with extensive views. St Rita was born here and married (much to her disgust) in the 13th-century church of San Montano.

Getting out of the car: Nearby **Capanne di Collegiacone** is a good place to set out for mountain walks, following the footpaths through the pastures surrounding the village. More ambitious is the climb from Roccaporena to the narrow summit that overlooks it – named the Scoglio di Santa Rita.

There is never a lack of parking in **CASCIA ❿**. The town has huge car parks to accommodate the flow of visitors to the Sanctuary of the Saint of the Impossible. Beyond Cascia, the valley of the Corno river unfolds many kilometres of rocky and wooded scenery with the peak of Monte Coscerno on one side and Monte Birbone on the other. It is a majestic, rugged contrast to the civilised rural scenery in other parts of Umbria. **MONTELEONE DI SPOLETO ⓫** is an isolated mountain village in a broad valley surrounded by pastures. The road is particularly idyllic for the next few kilometres and you might well have to brake for flocks of sheep and shaggy mountain dogs. Occasionally, too, you may see small herds of Umbria's famed white cattle, still bred here as draught animals since the hillside fields are often too steep for tractors.

This spectacular mountain road descends steeply, twisting through stands of black pines and beech trees and swinging around dizzying bends. Rising out of the rock on the right (north) are the sheer flanks of Monte Coscerno and, opposite, the limestone mass of Monte di Civitella. **Gavelli ⓬** is the second highest village in Umbria (after Castelluccio) at 1,153m. The church of San Michele is the heart of the village; the frescos in the apse were painted by Lo Spagna in 1518 (*if it is locked, the guardian in the house across from it has the key; donations are always appreciated*). As you leave the village, there is an ideal picnic spot – a meadow with a small lake fed by natural springs.

The only other village on the way down is Caso, equally spectacular for its location. After countless bends in the road, you will be on level ground again in the Valnerina. Somnolent **Sant'Anatolia di Narco** ⓭ is not a bad place to chill out after hours behind the wheel. Nothing ever happens here but it has a good *trattoria* and a good story, too. It has been continuously inhabited since the 8th century BC, making it one of the oldest villages in Umbria. In 1883, the necropolis of Naharci was discovered and the findings packed off to the archaeological museum of Florence. Alternatively, return through the tunnel to Spoleto.

Also worth exploring

During the Middle Ages, **Cerreto di Spoleto** and its castle guarded the Vigi valley on one side and the Nera on the other. Behind the town is an arduous, scenic road that eventually arrives in Spoleto. The town has lots of elegant old *palazzi* to prove its former importance – one of them belonged to Umbria's famous medieval humanist, Giovanni Pontano. Cerreto fought with single-minded determination to avoid being swallowed by more powerful neighbours. Spoleto even kidnapped some of its families and forced them to live in a street that is still named Via dei Cerretani.

When troops from Norcia sacked it in the 15th century, the displaced Cerretani set off around Italy and Europe, selling herbs, spices and medicinal compounds. The exaggerated claims that they made for their products ensured that their name – corrupted to *ciarlatani* – became 'charlatan' in English.

Middle Tiber and Nera Valley

Ratings

Architecture	●●●●
Art	●●●●
History	●●●●
Scenery	●●●●
Children	●●●
Museums	●●●
Nature	●●●
Shopping	●

Curving around the base of Todi, an ancient Umbrian border town, the Tiber river flows towards Orvieto acquiring the nickname 'dead' in places and 'furious' in others before it enters Lago di Corbara. Swinging south, it dies again in the wide Alviano marsh before reviving and continuing towards Rome. The Nera river flows into it a few kilometres west of Narni. Even by Umbrian standards, this is varied landscape: sheer gorges interrupt gentle hills and misty hilltops drop into flat valleys. History, nature and industry all claim different pieces of it. The spectrum of architecture is broad – giant polygonal stones laid by mysterious Umbrians in Amelia, feats of Roman engineering along the ancient *Via Flaminia* from Narni to *Carsulae*, and an exquisite Lombard church that graces the hill-town of Lugnano in Teverina.

AMELIA

ⓘ Informazioni turistiche *Via Orvieto* 1; tel: 0744 981453; fax: 0744 981566; e-mail: info@iat.amelia.tr.it

The Roman historian Pliny made a point of claiming, improbably, that Amelia was founded in 1134 BC. The town's massive walls seem to belong to a world of myth rather than history. At the base, they are composed of oversize polygonal blocks, 2m or more across, interlocked with such skill that you can't slip a sheet of paper between them. They have survived Totila the Goth and countless earthquakes. Tiny gateways piercing the walls lead to a maze of steep cobbled streets and stone staircases.

The fire and earthquake-damaged churches do not, at first, look appealing, but the church of Santi Filippo e Giacomo, in Piazza Augustus Vera, has an elegant 15th-century cloister and a series of tombs (belonging to the local Geraldini family), dating to the same century, carved with bas-reliefs by Agostino di Duccio. The ugliness of the cathedral is mitigated by another tomb to Bishop Geraldini, also by Duccio, carved with a delicate Virgin and Child. The Turkish flags in the right-hand chapel were taken at the battle of Lepanto.

LAGO DI ALVIANO

Lago di Alviano
Reserve information office, Madonna del Porto, Guardea; tel: 0744 903715; www.comunedialviano.it. Open Sep–Apr Sat–Sun until sunset, Tue–Sun rest of year.

This is one of the most beautiful nature reserves in Umbria, although in summer the birds are conspicuous by their absence. Winter is really the time to appreciate its importance to migratory birds. The northern end has the best viewpoints.

Lugnano in Teverina

Come for the views: to the west are Monte Cimino (1,053m) in the province of Lazio and Monte Amiato (1,738m) in Tuscany. Looking east, you can see the castle of Alviano.

On a clear day, you can see much of central Italy from here, on top of one of the highest hills in the region. From this distance the Tiber valley looks idyllic as its railway and *autostrada* drift in and out of the haze. The hilltop location saved the town from the bloodthirsty Goths and the dreaded Saracens but not from Cesare Borgia, who sacked it in 1503.

At its core stands one of Umbria's finest Romanesque churches, **Santa Maria Assunta** (Our Lady of the Assumption). Its 13th-century loggia displays a wealth of mysterious sculpture carved along the capitals and eaves: symbols of the Evangelists, beasts, birds and human heads. The bearded, three-faced figure – one face-on and two in profile – carved on the left-hand wall represents the Trinity. The interior has a nearly complete set of 12th-century furnishings. The inlaid marble floor represents the three theological virtues: white for Faith, green for Hope and red for Charity. The column capitals are wonderfully carved – look for the man with a serpent dangling from his lips. Reliefs in the choir show Archangel Michael and the usual Dragon as well as two men who seem to be kissing. In an atmospheric crypt, among the slender columns and walls built of chunky travertine blocks, is an early 14th-century Crucifixion fresco and a triptych by Nicolò Alunno, representing the Assumption of the Virgin.

Opposite
Santa Maria Assunta
in Lugnano

Narni

ℹ **Pro Loco** *Piazza dei Priori 3; tel: 0744 715362; e-mail: iatnarni@narni.it*

☀ In May, on the feast of St Juvenalis, the town celebrates the *Festa dell'Anello*, the Festival of the Ring. Horsemen in knightly costume thrust lances through metal hoops, recalling the bravery of Narni's soldiers, notably the mercenary Erasmo di Narni (nicknamed *Gattamelata* – the honey cat), whose equestrian statue by Donatello can be seen in Padua.

Perhaps no Umbrian town has a more medieval atmosphere than Narni with so few tourists to appreciate it. Narni likes to call itself the 'centre of Italy' and it is, geographically. The southernmost of the Umbrian hill-towns, Narni stands high above the Nera river at a place where it has cut a gorge. Its cathedral stands broadside on to the wide Piazza Garibaldi and is dedicated to the town's first bishop and patron saint, Juvenalis. A 15th-century Renaissance portico fronts the church, but inside, most of it is Romanesque.

Narni's ancient heart, the Piazza dei Priori, lies to the left of the cathedral as you emerge. It is just wide enough to be a piazza. The 20-sided fountain in the centre bears a vague resemblance to Perugia's famous Fontana Maggiore. The Palazzo dei Podesta is clearly made up of three separate structures, including the stump of a 13th-century defensive tower. However, the six 15th-century mullioned windows give it a semblance of unity.

The narrow Via del Monte leads off the Piazza Garibaldi and climbs up through the medieval quarter. The **Rocca Albornoz** stands at the top of the hill – a papal castle built in the 1370s with astonishing views north and south. The adjacent park is a good spot for a picnic.

Accommodation and food

Fattoria Titignano € *Titignano, off the N79 between Orvieto and Todi; tel: 0763 308000; fax: 0763 308002; restaurant tel: 0763 308022; www.titignano.it.* Off-the-beaten-track *agriturismo*, with guest rooms for a two-night minimum stay. Stunning location in a natural park between Orvieto and Todi and overlooking Lake Corbara.

Pasticceria Persico € *Via della Doga 69/A; tel: 0744 750153.* Umbrian-style pastries and sweets of every description. Queue up with half of Narni!

Pomurlo Vecchio € *Located in Baschi, off the N448 between Orvieto and Todi (follow sign for Pomurlo); tel: 0744 950190; www.pomurlovecchio-lecasette.it.* Agriturismo in a rambling fortress/inn complex surrounded by a hilltop farm that supplies the *trattoria*. There are rooms for overnight guests, including a couple with views of Lake Corbara.

Bramante €€ *Via Orvietana 48, Todi; tel: 075 8948381; fax: 075 8948074; www.hotelbramante.it.* A former convent with its own park and garden, swimming pool, and panoramic views from the terrace.

Hotel dei Priori €€ *Vicolo del Comune 4, Narni; tel: 0744 726843; fax: 0744 726644; restaurant tel: 0744 722744.* Intimate medieval *palazzo* with stylish rooms on a quiet lane. Its **La Loggia** (€€) is the old town's best restaurant (*closed Mon and last two weeks of Jul*).

Suggested tour

Total distance: 134km; detour adds 2km (return).

Time: One day.

Links: Todi is the destination of the route on page 244. It intersects with the Nera Valley and Spoleto route at *Carsulae* (*see page 256*).

Route: Leaving **Orvieto ❶**, take the N79bis (follow the signs for Arezzo, do not take the N448). The old road to Todi is one of the most scenic in Umbria. In places, you could be in Ireland thanks to the many overgrown hedges along the road. But olive groves and vineyards will remind you that this is Italy. It climbs through a varied landscape of isolated farms, forest and bare hills, cut by deep ravines. There are ever-changing vistas and most of the journey you will be alone with nature. When you stop to take in the views the only sound you will hear is the hum of insects among the herbs and wildflowers. At **Prodo ❷** a castle looms out of nowhere and a jerky uphill turn reveals a wide stretch of Lake Corbara. The last view, as you approach the end of the journey, is the best. The steep tower of San Francesco rises up in the distance from **TODI ❸** in a landscape that would have

Opposite
Umbrian farmstead

looked almost the same to a medieval traveller. In Todi, the easiest thing to do with the car is to leave it near the church of Santa Maria della Consolazione and walk up into town. After retrieving it, drive south and get on the N3bis *autostrada* then exit at San Gemini.

Detour: The abandoned Roman town **Carsulae** ❹, on the *Via Flaminia* (*see page 247*), is just 1km east of the *autostrada*.

San Gemini ❺ is part modern spa, part fortified medieval village. You can, for example, play mini-golf. Its throbbing little heart is the Piazza Palazzo Vecchio where a medieval tower was recycled as an 18th-century campanile for the Palazzo Pubblico (town hall). The Chiesa di San Francesco, at the opposite end of town, has the oldest pair of wooden doors in Umbria.

Continue south through hilly vineyards to the valley of the Nera river and turn right. The first thing you see in **NARNI** ❻ is a chemical plant – but it gets better. Cross the bridge over the deep gorge of the river. Watch for the first left (just before a Co-op supermarket). Keep to the left down a dirt road that leads you directly under the only surviving arch (90m) of the astonishing **Ponte di Augusto**. The bridge was built in 27 BC. It was once 160m long and formed part of the ancient *Via Flaminia*. Even in ruins, it makes the adjacent modern bridge look like a school project. Return to the road and veer up its curves to Narni.

Slow down as you enter the impressive portal of Porta Ternana. For the adventurous driver, there is a road that threads all the way up to the **Rocca dell'Albornoz** with voyeurist peeks into the living rooms and dining rooms of Narni and alarming views down into the abyss where the Nera flows. The Rocca itself is a lovers' lane; don't be surprised if couples sitting in their cars occasionally disappear from view.

Upon leaving Narni, retrace the curves back down to the N3, and take the N205 (Amelia is signposted) up a road that unleashes glimpses of the Nera valley and surrounding hills at every other bend. It surmounts a series of ridges to reach **AMELIA** ❼, where there is free parking outside the Etruscan walls. Drive around the city and north over a narrow bridge above a nameless gorge through which flows a tributary of the Tiber. From here on, the road bores through an oak forest so dense you will see little else until **LUGNANO IN TEVERINA** ❽ comes into sight.

The drive up to the central piazza is steep. From there the church of **Santa Maria Assunta** is just a few metres further on. Get back on the road. Cruise towards another hill-town on the horizon, **Alviano** ❾, with yet another wide vista and a view of the Tiber valley from a slightly lower elevation. The road drops down abruptly into the Tiber valley and follows the railway track along the humid **LAGO DI ALVIANO** ❿.

Carry on along the overgrown bank of the swampy Tiber until the road mounts higher and **Baschi ⓫** comes into sight perched above the Tiber valley. Erosion is a severe threat to this peaceful town graced by the 11th-century church of San Nicolò with a glowing buff-coloured baroque façade. Turn left on the N448, which crosses the Tiber going west and return to Orvieto (*see page 276*).

Also worth exploring

Petrified tree trunks similar to sequoias were discovered in 1987 near the village of **Dunarobba**. The forest grew over a million years ago on the banks of the ancient lake *Tiberino*, which occupied the whole of the valley between Spoleto, Perugia and Todi. A mud slide caused by an earthquake submerged 40 trees with a girth of 3–4m. Group visits are possible. (*For information, contact the Centro di Paleontologia Vegetale Foresta Fossile in Avigliano Umbro, tel: 0744 940348; www.forestafossile.it. Open Apr–Jun, Sep–Nov Fri–Sun 1000–1300, 1530–1830; Jul–Aug Tue–Sun 1000–1300, 1600–1900. Call ahead to confirm.*)

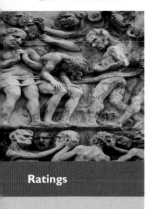

Orvieto

Ratings

Architecture	●●●●●
Art	●●●●●
History	●●●●●
Scenery	●●●●●
Children	●●●●○
Vineyards	●●●●○
Nature	●●○○○
Shopping	●○○○○

A medieval Pope predicted that Orvieto would float up to heaven on Judgement Day. It seems to already be on its way – thrust up into the Umbrian sky by a plateau of extinct volcanoes. Vineyards grow at the foot of its sheer cliffs in eroded volcanic soil that gives its famous white wine a distinct crispness. Of all the Etruscan cities that belonged to the League of 12 cities, Orvieto is the biggest puzzle. Despite overwhelming archaeological evidence of its importance, scholars still don't agree on its Etruscan name or history. The maze of tunnels beneath the city only adds to the mystery. Orvieto's cathedral is a stunning example of its unique cultural heritage. Related in style to the cathedral of Siena, it nevertheless surpasses it. Art historian Jacob Burchhardt called it 'the greatest and richest polychrome monument in the world'.

Below
Orvieto's cathedral

ℹ **Informazioni turistiche** *Piazza Duomo 24; tel: 0763 341772; fax: 0763 344433; www.comune.orvieto.tr.it and www.orvietoonline.it.* Open Mon–Fri 0800–1400 and 1600–1900, Sat–Sun 1000–1300 and 1500–1800. The Tourist Office sells a *Carta Orvieto Unica,* a city card that covers admission to several museums and monuments, use of the town's electric minibuses and parking for five hours in the funicular car park.

Sights

Duomo

Orvieto's cathedral is, without a doubt, the finest of its period in Italy. From the foundations to the gables, white travertine and dove-grey tufa alternate in horizontal bands. Such refinement is not Umbrian in character. For parallels you have to look west, to Siena in Tuscany. The sumptuous mosaic of the façade is a rarity among Italian churches. By

Duomo *Piazza Duomo; tel: 0763 342477; fax: 0763 340336. Open daily Nov–Feb 0730–1245, 1430–1715; Mar and Oct 0730–1245, 1430–1815; Apr–Sep 0730–1245, 1430–1915. Free.*

Cappella di San Brizio € *Tel: 0763 342477. Open Mon–Sat Nov–Feb 1000–1245, 1430–1715; Mar and Oct until 1815; Apr–Sep until 1915; Sun Oct–Jun 1430–1745; Sun Jul–Sep 1430–1845. Only 25 people in the chapel at a time. Tickets can be purchased from the Tourist Office.*

contrast, the interior is calm and uncluttered, illuminated by alabaster-paned windows. Pews, monuments and baroque edifices have been swept away, leaving us with an uninterrupted view across the sun-dappled floor of ox-blood coloured marble. The sublime nave, Romanesque in conception and Gothic in details such as pointed arch windows, is remarkably unified.

There is scarcely anything else in art like the world-famous frescos (1499–1504) by Signorelli in the **Cappella di San Brizio**, restored in 1996 to their glory after seven painstaking years. They depict the Apocalypse, the torments of hell and the Resurrection. Charon ferries the dead across the infernal waters of the Styx while metal-winged monsters and green-faced demons rush the legions of the damned into the underworld. The scene brilliantly expresses a sense of the world ending in chaos with twisted bodies flying everywhere as if, suddenly, there were no force of gravity. Skeletons then drag themselves out of the ground, acquire flesh and once again become youthful, innocent-looking men and women. Michelangelo was deeply influenced by Signorelli in his painting of the ceiling of the Sistine Chapel.

Musei Archeologici Claudio Faina €€
Piazza Duomo 29; tel: 0763 341511; fax: 0763 341250; www.museofaina.it. Open Apr–Sep daily 0930–1800, Oct–Mar Tue–Sun 1000–1700.

Palazzo Papale (Museo Archeologico Nazionale) € Piazza Duomo; tel: 0763 341039; www.archeopg.arti.beniculturali.it. Open daily 0830–1930 (Jun–mid-Sep Sat until 2300).

Palazzo Soliano/Museo Greco/Museo dell'Opera del Duomo
€ Piazza Duomo 24; tel: 0763 344605; fax: 0763 344664; www.sistemamuseo.it. Open Oct–Mar daily 1030–1300 and 1400–1730, Apr–Sep Mon–Fri 1030–1300 and 1430–1830, Sat–Sun until 1900.

Pozzo di San Patrizio €
Viale Sangallo; tel: 0763 343768; fax: 0763 344664; www.sistemamuseo.it. Open daily May–Aug 0900–2000, Mar–Apr and Sep–Oct 0900–1900. Shorter hours in winter.

Palazzo Faina (Musei Archeologici Claudio Faina)

This is one of the most important archaeological collections in Umbria and stunning testimony to what a well-heeled private collector could get his or her hands on in the 19th century. In addition to Etruscan sculpture and pottery, there are three vases (found in the necropolis of the Crocefisso del Tufo) by Exekias, the most important Greek Attic vase painter in the 6th century BC. They were imported by Etruscans from Greece.

Palazzo Papale (Museo Archeologico Nazionale)

Built for a bishop in the 12th century, the palace was redecorated a hundred years later by two different popes. It is easy to overlook, squeezed between the cathedral and the Palazzo Soliana. The palace contains the Museo Archeologico Nazionale. Its pride and joy is a badly damaged but fascinating tomb painting (ask to have the lights turned on) that depicts banqueting in the afterlife. There are also many other objects found in the Etruscan tombs of the burial ground at Settecamini, from a complete set of armour to polished mirrors.

Palazzo Soliano

This palace of tufa stone was built for Pope Boniface VIII in 1297 and contains two museums. The ground-floor **Museo Greco** is filled with works by the sculptor Emilio Greco (1915–95), the artist responsible for the modern bronze doors of the Duomo. His athletic nude beauties take full control of the space, thrusting bronze legs and perky breasts in all directions. Upstairs, the **Museo dell'Opera del Duomo** has a self-portrait by Luca Signorelli and a collection of sculpture that includes work by Andrea Pisano and the early baroque genius Francesco Mochi.

Pozzo di San Patrizio

Alongside the public gardens that surround the remains of the 14th-century Fortezza and the ruins of an Etruscan temple, is a highly unusual artesian well. The 63m well was dug in 1527 on the orders of Pope Clement VII, preparing for a siege that never came. It took ten years to sink.

An ingenious double helix staircase, lit by openings in the well shaft, was constructed to allow packhorses to descend to collect water and ascend via a separate set of steps, thus avoiding collisions. The design might have been influenced by Leonardo da Vinci who designed a similar staircase for a brothel and, later, for Château Chambord in France.

Halfway down the shaft, you will pass an Etruscan tomb that was discovered during the excavation. The descent into the dark and chilly depths is steep, and the ascent even more so, but it is well worth it for the ever-changing vistas through the shaft openings and the strange subterranean lighting effects.

Accommodation and food

Orvieto wines: *secco* and *Abbocato*

Winemaking in Orvieto dates back to the Etruscans. Today, it produces one of the best-known Italian white wines. The *secco* (dry) wines represent the lion's share of its production. But one of Orvieto's best wines is its opposite: Orvieto *Abbocato* is a traditionally made, naturally sweet wine. Pope Gregory XVI commanded in his will that his body be washed in it.

Bar-Pasticceria Gastronomia Montanucci Nazzareno € *Corso Cavour 21–23; tel: 0763 394707.* The oldest café in the city and the perfect place for some home-made *baci* – chocolate 'kisses'. You are not supposed to lunch on kisses, so have a *panino* (sandwich) first.

La Vulpe e L'Uva € *Via Ripa Corsica 1; tel: 0763 341612. Closed Mon and Jan; also Tue during Oct–Mar.* Probably the best traditional *trattoria* in town. Mostly locals eat here. Home-made pasta filled with duck is a speciality.

Hotel Palazzo Piccolomini €€ *Piazza Ranieri 36; tel: 0763 341743; fax: 0763 391046; www.hotelpiccolomini.it.* A former nobleman's palace near the historic heart of the city. The easiest way to reach it is to drive through the Porta Maggiore.

I Sette Consoli €€ *Piazza Sant'Angelo 1a; tel: 0763 343911. Closed Wed.* This tiny restaurant does daring things with Umbrian standards. It has a most rewarding *menu degustazione* (tasting menu) – five courses, with three kinds of wine. The à la carte menu includes (in season) artichoke casserole, stuffed pumpkin flowers, terrine of pheasant and truffles, and stuffed gooseneck.

La Badia €€€ *La Badia 8, 5km south of Orvieto; tel: 0763 301876; fax: 0763 305396; e-mail: labadia.hotel@tiscalinet.it. Closed Jan–Feb.* This medieval abbey, partly in ruins, was founded by Benedictine monks. The 13th-century church has noted frescos, cloisters, a refectory and a 12-sided bell tower. The abbey was already in use as a holiday resort by 15th-century cardinals. Today, Count Diumi di Sterpeto has converted the former abbot's palace to a many-starred hotel.

Hotel Maitani €€€ *Via Lorenzo Maitani 5; tel: 0763 342011; fax: 0763 342012; www.hotelmaitani.com.* The hotel terrace has a panoramic view of the Orvieto cathedral. Fortunately, it has parking, too.

Suggested tour

Visitors are encouraged to park in Orvieto Scalo, the modern lower town. From there a funicular railway whisks you up to the Piazza Cahen, the western end of the city and the beginning of this route. There is another car park below the walls on the west side at Campo della Fiera (equipped with a lift and wheelchair access). In the city itself, a large, free car park is just off Via Roma (a sharp right turn on entering Piazza Cahen).

Total distance: 2km.

Time: If you don't visit more than one museum, it is possible to do this route in a day trip and perhaps squeeze in a visit to the Orvieto

Underground and still see the sun set over the Etruscan city of the dead, **Crocefisso del Tufo**. By then, you will wish for a second day.

Links: Orvieto is an exit on the *autostrada* to Rome and easy to reach from Tuscany. The Crete and Val d'Orcia route passes within a few kilometres (*see page 105*).

Route: Take the 19th-century funicular up to the square of **Piazza Cahen ❶** and enjoy the view of the Paglia valley on the way. On the right, as you exit, is the medieval **POZZO DI SAN PATRIZIO ❷**, the extraordinary Renaissance well that was never put to use. Next to it is the stone foundation of an Etruscan temple, built almost 2,000 years earlier, at the end of the 5th century BC. The **Rocca Albornoz ❸** is to the left – a fortress erected in 1364 to show that the Pope was boss in political as well as spiritual matters but demolished a generation later in disgust by the people of Orvieto. Today, it makes a spectacular public garden. Looking further left (north) you also see the much older medieval gate of Postierla. Cross the Piazza and stroll down Corso Cavour. Turn left at Via Duomo, which narrows and curves past shops selling ceramics into Piazza Duomo. The stone benches on the wall opposite the cathedral are an ideal place to rest while contemplating one of the glories of Umbria, Orvieto's **DUOMO ❹**. It is bounded by the **PALAZZO FAINA ❺** to the west, the **PALAZZO PAPALE ❻** to the east and the **PALAZZO SOLIANO ❼** to the south.

Detour: Beneath Orvieto is an underground labyrinth, created over 3,000 years of history as inhabitants dug an infinite number of caves in the plateau of tufa stone that the city rests on. The caves intersect and branch out in all directions beneath the modern city. It is a barely tapped reservoir of historical and archaeological information. Guided tours of the **Orvieto Underground** leave from the Tourist Office (**€€€** *Piazza Duomo 24; tel: 0763 344891. Start 1100 and 1600*).

Retrace your steps down the Via Duomo and take a left turn at the Corso Cavour. **Piazza della Repubblica ❽** is on the site of the Etruscan and Roman forums and remained the centre of commercial life through the Middle Ages.

Cross the Piazza and take the right-hand Via Fillippeschi, keeping to the left to find your way down the narrow Via della Cava. The street is named after the **Pozzo della Cava ❾**, a well that might have been used in Etruscan times which was expanded by Clement VII in 1527 (*open daily except Tue 0800–2000*). The street ends in the Porta Maggiore. Turn left – just before the gate – up Vicolo Malcorini and climb up to the city wall. The lane widens a bit (becoming Ripa Serancia) and leads to **Piazza San Giovanni ❿** and a dizzying view right over a cliff of golden brown rock. Carry on along the ancient rampart and duck left into the next lane, the Via Ripa Medici. It crosses the Piazza de'Ranieri and leads into Via Garibaldi, which funnels you back into Piazza della Repubblica. Return to Piazza Cahen along Corso Cavour.

Also worth exploring

The most accessible of Orvieto's cities of the dead – the **Necropoli Etrusca del Crocefisso del Tufo** – is just below the walls to the northwest on the road that leads to Piazza Cahen. The dank tombs are empty. Their contents are in museums, in Orvieto, across Europe and in North America. This particular city reveals a remarkably egalitarian sense of town planning. Constructed of huge blocks of travertine, each tomb is almost the same with the name of the deceased scratched into the architrave above the entrance such as *Mi spuries achilenas* (I am Spurie Achilena). Orvieto was a multicultural city in the 6th and 5th centuries BC, with a politically correct cemetery policy. In addition to Etruscans, there are Umbrians, Oscans and Latins buried here.

Language

'It is truly a pleasure to hear the Tuscans speak. Their expressions, full of imagination and elegance, give an idea of the pleasure one must have felt in ancient Athens when people spoke the melodious Greek that resembled a constant stream of music.' *Madame de Staël*

Basics

yes/no	si/no
thank you	grazie
please	per favore
you are welcome	prego
excuse me	scusi
I'm sorry	mi dispiace
I would like	vorrei
I don't understand	non capisco
I don't like that	non mi piace
I would prefer	preferisco
okay	va bene
big/little	grande/piccolo
hot/cold	caldo/freddo
open/closed	aperto/chiuso
right/left	destra/sinistra
good/bad	buono/cattivo
fast/slow	presto/lento
much/little	molto/poco
expensive/cheap	caro/economico

Driving

car	la macchina
petrol station	il distributore
full	pieno
petrol/diesel	la benzina/il gasolio
unleaded	senza piombo
check out	controllare
air pressure	la pressione
oil	l'olio
water	l'acqua
breakdown	il guasto
accident	l'incidente
it doesn't work	non funziona
motor	il motore
ignition	l'accensione

Signs

attenzione	watch out
deviazione	detour
divieto di accesso/senso vietato	no entry
divieto di sosta/sosta vietata	no parking
incrocio	crossroads
limite di velocità	speed limit
parcheggio	parking
pericolo	danger
pronto soccorso	first aid
rallentare	slow down
senso unico	one-way street
strada chiusa	road closed
strada senza uscita	dead-end
tenere la destra	keep right
traffico limitato	restricted access
uscita veicoli	exit
vietato fumare	no smoking
vietato il sorpasso	no overtaking
vietato il transito	no through traffic
zona rimorchio	tow away zone

Numbers

1	uno
2	due
3	tre
4	quattro
5	cinque
6	sei
7	sette
8	otto
9	nove
10	dieci
11	undici
12	dodici
13	tredici
14	quattordici
15	quindici
16	sedici
17	diciassette
18	diciotto
19	diciannove
20	venti
21	ventuno
22	ventidue
30	trenta
40	quaranta
50	cinquanta
60	sessanta
70	settanta
80	ottanta
90	novanta
100	cento
101	centuno
110	centodieci
200	duecento
500	cinquecento
1,000	mille
5,000	cinquemila
10,000	diecimila
50,000	cinquanta mila
1,000,000	un milione
2,000,000	due milione

$1/2$	un mezzo	1kg	un chilo
$1/4$	un quarto	1 pound	mezzo chilo
$1/3$	un terzo	1 litre	un litro
100gm	un etto		

Index

Acknowledgements

Project management: Cambridge Publishing Management Limited
Project editor: Karen Beaulah
Series design: Fox Design
Cover design: Liz Lyons Design
Layout: PDQ Digital Media Solutions Ltd/Cambridge Publishing Management Limited
Map work: Polly Senior Cartography/Cambridge Publishing Management Limited
Repro and image setting: PDQ Digital Media Solutions Ltd/Cambridge Publishing Management Limited
We would like to thank John Heseltine for the photographs used in this book, to whom the copyright belongs, with the exception of the following:

Christopher Catling (pages 14, 15, 37, 76, 202B, 206, 224, 230, 231, 234, 236, 238, 242, 245, 246, 251, 254, 255 and 256); **Fototeca ENIT/Vito Arcomano** (page 18); **Pictures Colour Library** (page 258); **Spectrum Colour Library** (page 115); **Travel Ink** (page 92); **World Pictures** (pages 16, 52, 114 and 264); **Wikimedia Commons** (pages 249 Gunnar Bach Pedersen, 260 Zyance and 271 Mattana).

Feedback form

We're committed to providing the very best up-to-date information in our travel guides and constantly strive to make them as useful as they can be. You can help us to improve future editions by letting us have your feedback. Just take a few minutes to complete and return this form to us.

When did you buy this book? ....
....

Where did you buy it? (Please give town/city and, if possible, name of retailer)
....
....

When did you/do you intend to travel in Tuscany and Umbria?...
....

For how long (approx)? ....

How many people in your party? ....

Which cities, national parks and other locations did you/do you intend mainly to visit?
....
....
....
....

Did you/will you:
❏ Make all your travel arrangements independently?
❏ Travel on a fly-drive package?
Please give brief details: ....
....

Did you/do you intend to use this book:
❏ For planning your trip?   ❏ Both?
❏ During the trip itself?

Did you/do you intend also to purchase any of the following travel publications for your trip?
Thomas Cook Travellers: Florence and Tuscany...
A road map/atlas (please specify) ....
Other guidebooks (please specify) ....

Have you used any other Thomas Cook guidebooks in the past? If so, which?

....

....

Please rate the following features of *Drive Around Tuscany & Umbria* for their value to you (circle VU for 'very useful', U for 'useful', NU for 'little or no use'):

The *Travel facts* section on pages 14–23	VU	U	NU
The *Driver's guide* section on pages 24–9	VU	U	NU
The *Highlights* on pages 40–41	VU	U	NU
The recommended driving routes throughout the book	VU	U	NU
Information on towns and cities, National Parks, etc	VU	U	NU
The maps of towns and cities, parks, etc	VU	U	NU

Please use this space to tell us about any features that in your opinion could be changed, improved, or added in future editions of the book, or any other comments you would like to make concerning the book:

....

....

....

....

....

....

....

....

Your age category: ❑ 21–30   ❑ 31–40   ❑ 41–50   ❑ over 50

Your name: Mr/Mrs/Miss/Ms ....

(First name or initials) ....

(Last name) ....

Your full address (please include postal or zip code):

....

....

....

....

Your daytime telephone number: ....

Please detach this page and send it to: Drive Around Series Editor, Thomas Cook Publishing, PO Box 227, The Thomas Cook Business Park, 9 Coningsby Road, Peterborough PE3 8SB.

Alternatively, you can e-mail us at: *books@thomascook.com*